T0330176

Modelling the Composition of Government Expenditure

Modelling the Composition of Government Expenditure

John Creedy

Victoria University of Wellington and New Zealand Treasury

Solmaz Moslehi

Monash University, Australia

Edward Elgar

Cheltenham, UK • Northampton, MA, USA

Published by
Edward Elgar Publishing Limited
The Lypiatts
15 Lansdown Road
Cheltenham
Glos GL50 2JA
UK

Edward Elgar Publishing, Inc.
William Pratt House
9 Dewey Court
Northampton
Massachusetts 01060
USA

A catalogue record for this book
is available from the British Library

Library of Congress Control Number: 2011925766

ISBN 978 0 85793 673 8

Printed and bound by MPG Books Group, UK

Contents

I Introduction

II Voting Models

List of Tables

List of Figures

Acknowledgements

This book makes substantial use of a number of journal articles, though they have been considerably revised and rearranged. These are Creedy and Moslehi (2009, 2010a, 2010b, 2011) and Creedy et al. (2010a, 2010b). We are grateful for permission to use these papers here and we should again like to thank the referees for their constructive comments. Parts of the book have been presented at the following conferences and workshops: these include the PhD Conference at the Australian National University (2008); the Macroeconomic Workshop at the University of Auckland (2008); the Macroeconomic Workshop at the University of Melbourne (2008); the PhD Workshop in Economics at Monash University (2008); the Australian Public Choice Conference at Deakin University (2009); the PGPPE Workshop at the University of Graz (2009); the 13th ZEI International Summer School at Bonn (2009); and the 14th Australasian Macroeconomics Workshop at Deakin University (2009).

Part I

Introduction

Chapter 1

Introduction

The composition of government expenditure varies considerably across countries. For instance, on average the share of expenditure on transfer payments in democratic countries is higher than in non-democratic countries, although non-democratic countries have higher income inequality than democratic countries. In contrast, the share of expenditure on public goods in democratic countries is lower than in non-democratic countries. The average share of total expenditure on education and health in these two groups of countries is similar. However, the variation across non-democratic countries is considerably higher than among democratic countries.

There are substantial variations even among developed democratic countries in their tax and expenditure policies, although these countries share similar economic and political regimes. For example, the US has relatively high income inequality and combines a low overall tax rate with a low ratio of expenditure on transfer payments to that on public goods. Scandinavian countries typically combine low inequality with high tax rates and substantially higher expenditure on transfer payments relative to public goods. British Commonwealth countries (Australia, Canada, UK and New Zealand) have higher income inequality than Scandinavian countries (Denmark, Finland, Norway and Sweden) and yet devote much less to transfer payments compared with public goods.

3

These variations naturally raise the question of what determines the composition of government expenditure. The aim of the present book is to explore this question using a range of modelling approaches. It investigates the extent to which the composition is influenced by, for example, the nature of individuals' preferences for private and public goods and the degree of heterogeneity in the population. The modelling approaches allow for different economic environments, involving the types of expenditure considered, the time period of analysis (whether single or multi-period) and the behaviour of individuals.

In addition, different decision mechanisms are investigated. Broadly, the composition of expenditure is examined using political economy and public finance frameworks. The former 'positive' approach examines government expenditure under voting. The main emphasis is on majority voting by selfish individuals, though alternatives are briefly examined (for example, where voters have some regard for inequality, or where 'probabilistic voting' applies and voting behaviour reflects a political bias). The second 'normative' approach examines the composition of government expenditure if the choice is made by a single disinterested individual (one who is not a member of the population concerned) whose value judgements are summarised by an evaluation, or social welfare function expressed in terms of individuals' utilities. Hence the judge or decision maker is considered to be a utilitarian, with an individualistic 'welfarist' evaluation function involving a trade-off between equity and efficiency.

Attention is necessarily restricted to quite small, and even simple, models in terms of the heterogeneity and the kind of economic structure imposed. Even with such models, it is seen that the analysis rapidly involves complexities which would otherwise become intractable. This kind of problem is of course familiar from well-known models which concentrate on the determinants of the size, rather than the composition, of government expenditure. Similarly, much of the focus is on the allocation of tax revenue between just two components of government expenditure: these are referred to in terms of a transfer payment and a public good. In the majority voting framework this avoids severe problems of multidimensional voting. However, in some cases, expenditure on public education is also examined: this has interesting implications in view of the effects on each individual's productivity.

The emphasis here is thus on attempting to understand possible explanations of differences in expenditure patterns by exploring alternative modelling approaches. However, empirical analyses are also carried out whereby potential orders of magnitude of various components of the models are obtained. The empirical analyses may therefore be described as illustrative of the models and approaches. Thus, no claim is made that the models are properly subject to empirical econometric tests, and of course the models are in many ways too simple to capture all the complexities of reality: nevertheless it is argued here that they can help in considering important factors and inter-relationships involved.

The models can also help to shed some light on earlier empirical results which have been obtained using reduced-form specifications which have not considered the structure of models in any detail. Indeed, in the case of the normative approaches any kind of empirical testing would not be meaningful. But it is possible to consider what kind of value judgements appear to be consistent with observed expenditure patterns. Ideally, it would be useful to have time series data about a range of countries, but such data are simply not available. Furthermore, it is likely that there would be insufficient variation over time in important variables. Attention is therefore restricted to cross-country comparisons, though here there are important data limitations associated with the measurement of expenditure components and wage rates, which are discussed in detail.

Within both the political economy and public finance approaches, relatively few studies have concentrated on the composition of expenditure. The vast majority of the literature has instead given more attention to the total government size or the tax rate. Typically in the models a single type of government expenditure, usually a transfer payment, is financed by income taxation. The choice of government expenditure level in these models is determined, via the government budget constraint, by the tax rate. It is well known that explicit solutions (both for voting and optimal tax models) can be obtained only if strong assumptions are made, for example about individuals' preferences and the extent of population heterogeneity. However, a major result which arises from the majority voting models in this literature is that a lower median income relative to mean income increases the demand for redistributive expenditure. Similarly, in the optimal tax literature, a higher degree of basic inequality (of individuals' ability levels and hence wage rates) gives rise to a higher tax rate and thus more redistribution.

However, empirical cross-sectional studies have not unambiguously confirmed this result. Lind (2005) summarises empirical studies concerning this relationship, based on cross-sectional data for a range of countries, and finds mixed results. There are of course many complicating factors and differences among countries which are not included in the simple models. These complications include the existence of multiple social contracts, the prospects of relative income mobility, multidimensional policies, race and the question of redistribution versus social insurance: they are surveyed by Harms and Zink (2003) and Borck (2007). Furthermore, Tridimas and Winer (2005) emphasise the role of political influence and thus the 'supply side' of government.

There are, in addition, dynamic issues and adjustment lags which are not modelled in cross-sectional analyses. For example, changes in policy may respond to changes in inequality with a significant lag. According to Persson and Tabellini (2000, p. 123), in most countries 'transfers rose most quickly during the 1960s and 1970s, when income inequality was generally on the decline; during the 1980s and 1990s, in contrast, inequality instead turned upward, whereas redistributive transfers rose less quickly'. Such dynamic aspects are not modelled here.

Since the emphasis of the present study is on the composition of expenditure, rather than its total, the income tax rate is instead assumed to be exogenously fixed: it is not a decision variable. The tax rate is assumed to be determined by a separate process. It may be thought of as determined by some conventional view regarding taxable capacity, or other constraints are imposed on governments regarding the rate. Bearse *et al.* (2001) also assume that the tax rate is given exogenously, when examining majority voting over a uniform transfer and public education. A similar assumption is also made by Tridimas (2001, p. 308) and Tridimas and Winer (2005), who consider voting over tax-financed public goods. Tridimas (2001, p. 308) suggested that this assumption 'is less restrictive than it first appears, since in practice governments are often constrained in the policy instruments that they may vary at any one time'. In practice, tax and expenditure policies are usually debated separately and stronger constraints are usually imposed on changes in income tax rates. Allowing the tax rate to be endogenous would raise considerable difficulties both with multidimensional voting, as discussed by, for example, Mueller (2003, pp. 87-92), and maximisation of social welfare functions. It is also possible to envisage the decision problem considered here as a second stage in a two-stage process, where the first stage concerns only the tax rate, and the second stage concerns the composition of expenditure conditional on a given tax rate.[1]

A strong result of the present study is that the various models examined here, using different structures and different decision mechanisms, give rise to a general result regarding basic inequality and redistribution, which may be compared with the result of the earlier literature concerned with the choice of government size. It is found that a more redistributive structure – in terms of a higher proportion of expenditure being devoted to transfer payments – is associated with a higher degree of wage rate inequality. Importantly,

---

[1] On such two-stage voting in a public choice context, see McCaleb (1985), who emphasises uncertainties involved during the first stage.

inequality can in all cases be defined in terms of the proportional difference between a particular measure of location of the wage rate distribution, and the arithmetic mean wage. In positive majority voting models the measure of location is the median wage. In normative optimal expenditure models, where a social welfare function is maximised, the location measure turns out to be a type of welfare-weighted mean wage. The welfare weights depend on the degree of inequality aversion of the judge or decision maker. In general the optimal expenditure allocation, expressed in terms of such an inequality measure, does not provide a closed-form solution. However, an approximation is proposed which allows the general property to be transparent.

However, numerical illustrations show that the relationship between (appropriately defined) inequality and the ratio of transfer payments to public goods expenditure is relatively flat over the relevant range of inequality. This may shed some light on why empirical studies have found mixed results concerning inequality and redistribution.

1.1   Outline of the Book

The remaining chapter in Part I of this book is also introductory in nature. Chapter 2 provides an initial exploration of the basic issues which arise when attempting to model the composition of government expenditure in a simple static model, where there are just two components of expenditure. First, it considers the division between a transfer payment and a pure public good. Second, the division between a transfer payment and tax-financed education is examined. The choice of the composition of government expenditure is modelled for three decision mechanisms. These mechanisms are majority voting, stochastic voting and a decision maker who maximises a social welfare function. In order to focus attention on alternative choice mechanisms, incomes are assumed to be fixed. Individuals differ only in their ability, and hence wage, levels. There is no heterogeneity in tastes.

Special attention is given to the relationship between the composition of expenditure and inequality. It is shown that inequality can be regarded as the proportional difference between the arithmetic mean income and another 'measure of location' of incomes: the precise location measure depends on the particular choice mechanism investigated. Using the majority voting result, the weight attached to the public good in utility functions is calculated for a sample of democratic countries, suggesting that different preferences for public goods resulting from cultural differences may be an important determinant in shaping the composition of government expenditure.

Part II of this book is devoted to analyses of voting models of government expenditure. Incentive effects are the key aspects when looking at transfer payments and the composition of government expenditure given the tax rate. Chapter 3 extends the fixed income analysis of Chapter 2 and studies majority voting over the division between expenditure on public goods and on transfer payments. A static model is constructed in which individuals have different abilities but similar preferences for consumption, leisure and public goods. Majority voting is made conditional on the tax rate in a proportional income tax structure. The voting equilibrium is studied within three environments. First, a baseline approach is considered where self-interested individuals vote on public goods. Individuals derive utility from private consumption, public goods and leisure. Then, in order to study the effect of altruism on majority choice, the baseline model is extended by allowing voters to care not only about their own consumption but also about inequality.

The model is then extended in Chapter 4 to consider how home production affects voting outcomes regarding the composition of government expenditure. Despite the importance of home production in some contexts, it is found that within the models examined, it has relatively little effect on the choice of the expenditure composition. For this reason, home production is neglected in the remainder of this book.

Chapter 5 turns to a dynamic model, in an attempt to deal with some of the limitations of a static environment. For instance, a static model does not allow forward-looking decisions, such as investment, and the way they interact with policy choices to be examined. For example, increasing the level of expenditure on redistribution, for a given tax rate, affects investment in physical or human capital. In addition, if capital accumulation is added to the model, increasing the transfer payment reduces the incentive for saving and raises the interest rate and decreases the real wage. These effects cannot be studied in a static environment.[2]

Chapter 5 examines the majority voting result for the division of government expenditure between public goods and redistribution in a partial equilibrium dynamic environment. This choice is considered in the context of an overlapping generations model in which a pure public good and a transfer payment, in the form of a pension, are tax-financed on a pay-as-you-go (PAYG) basis. The decision clearly involves much more than simply the redistribution of income among members of the same cohort. The unconditional pension requires a decision regarding income shifting between periods within the life cycle as well as intra- and inter-generational redistribution. Young individuals in the first period of their life pay tax to finance expenditure on public goods and pensions. Therefore there is 'social contract' across generation. The PAYG scheme must make the majority of each cohort better off than the private saving alone. Individuals support a public saving or a PAYG scheme as long as they receive higher welfare. The condition for support of social contract is obtained and it is shown to be an extension to the famous Aaron (1966) and Samuelson (1958) result. The decision mechanism involves majority voting by members of each cohort regarding desired pension and public goods expenditure during the retirement period, on the understanding that during the working period each cohort finances the expenditure previously agreed by the preceding cohort and voters are

---

[2]The focus clearly differs from the large literature concerned with the effects on growth of different types of government expenditure; see the survey by Irmen and Kuehnel (2009).

aware of the nature of the government budget constraint. In order to attempt to understand the way in which preferences and economic conditions may combine to influence the composition of expenditure, this chapter uses analytical results to produce an implied weight attached to public goods for each country.

Part III turns to the consideration of government expenditure in an optimal choice context. Chapter 6 uses the same framework as Chapter 3, but instead of examining the majority voting outcome, the choice of a social planner who maximises a social welfare function is considered. The social welfare function represents the value judgement of the social planner, and reflects an explicit trade-off between equity and efficiency.

In Chapter 7, the approach is extended to the more complex case of three components of government expenditure, by adding public education expenditure to the model. This is not considered in a voting framework because of the familiar problems with multidimensional voting. Despite the extra complexity arising from education expenditure by the government, where wage rates as well as labour supplies are endogenous, explicit solutions are obtained for expenditure shares.

Chapter 8 returns to the basic dynamic overlapping generations model of Chapter 5, to consider the maximisation of a welfare function defined over multiple generations.

Part IV turns to general equilibrium modelling. Chapter 9 examines the division of government expenditure between a pension and public goods in the context of a dynamic general equilibrium model with overlapping generation of heterogeneous individuals. In this chapter, a majority voting mechanism is considered in which individuals vote on the share of redistributive expenditure in the next period, for a given tax rate. The basic context is thus similar to that considered in Chapters 5 and 8. However, the rate of interest and wage rates are endogenous, as a result of the explicit modelling of the production function. The general equilibrium environment allows consideration of the relationship between endogenous policy variables and capital accumulation and total output.

Chapter 2

Alternative Choice Mechanisms

The previous chapter began by recognising that there are substantial variations in the composition of government expenditure across countries. The aim of this chapter is to investigate the choice of the composition of government expenditure in very simple contexts. This is useful in order to obtain an initial understanding of the structure of alternative models and the way in which different choice processes can be examined. The present analysis looks at two basic allocation frameworks. First, the division between a transfer payment and a pure public good is considered. Second, the choice is modelled of the division between a transfer payment and tax-financed education, considered as a publicly provided private good. Complexities arising from the potential interaction with a privately financed education sector are not examined here.[1] In addition, concentration is on the case where there is heterogeneity only with respect to abilities. Individuals are therefore assumed to have similar tastes.

For comparison purposes, three decision mechanisms are examined. The first involves the widely used simple majority voting method, where only a selfish median voter is decisive. The second mechanism examined is sto-

---

[1] Expenditure on education is classified as a publicly provided private good in Bearse *et al.* (2001), Borck (2008) and Soares (2006). In these studies education is provided publicly, financed by a proportional income tax, but individuals can choose to use this or pay for private education at the market price.

chastic voting, involving the maximisation of a political support function; in this case the mean, variance and skewness are relevant in determining voting outcomes. Stochastic voting allows voting over multidimensional issues to be considered, unlike majority voting where severe problems arise with more than one dimension. Examples of the use of this voting model in the context of public expenditure include Tridimas and Winer (2005), where individuals vote on tax rates and public goods, and Tridimas (2001), who considered different categories of expenditure. In addition, Hassler *et al.* (2005) applied probabilistic voting in the context of overlapping generations with transfer payments and found that the voting outcome implied more redistribution than the social planner's choice. Dolmas (2008) applied probabilistic voting in a simple growth model with tax on consumption, labour and capital income, as well as a lump-sum transfer and exogenous government expenditure.[2] The third choice mechanism examined is that of maximisation of a social welfare function by a disinterested decision maker.

Special attention is given to the relationship between the composition of expenditure and inequality. This allows consideration of the question of the extent to which higher inequality produces a choice in favour of a higher proportion of expenditure being devoted to equalising transfer payments. Despite the apparent substantial differences between the approaches, it is shown that a synthesis is available which allows easy comparisons between the alternative methods. The chapter shows that, in each model, the expenditure composition is found to depend on income inequality, where inequality is defined in terms of the proportional difference between arithmetic mean income and another measure of location of the income distribution. The precise location measure depends on the particular choice mechanism investigated.

In view of the emphasis on comparing alternative choice mechanisms, for simplicity incomes are assumed to be fixed. This does not affect the main

---

[2]Probabilistic voting models are also examined by, for example, Bernasconi and Profeta (2007), Coughlin (1982), Coughlin and Nitzan (1981) and Lindbeck and Weibull (1987).

comparisons of interest here. However, when looking at the relationship between the transfer payment and the given tax rate, it is simply necessary to keep in mind that incentive effects are likely to produce a concave schedule. Incentive effects are modelled in subsequent chapters, and it is found that many of the basic comparisons between expenditure shares and inequality, and among choice mechanisms, are not significantly affected.

Relatively few studies have concentrated on the composition of expenditure. The political economy literature has instead given more attention to the total government size or tax rate. Most studies focus on one type of government expenditure, either public goods expenditure or redistributive transfer payments, and consider voting on the tax rate. For example, Meltzer and Richard (1981), Krusell and Rios-Rull (1999) and Borck (2007) consider redistributive expenditure and Tridimas (2001) and Tridimas and Winer (2005) look at expenditure on public goods. However, Bearse *et al.* (2001) examined majority voting over a transfer payment and public education, conditional on the tax rate, in a static framework. As explained in the previous chapter, the present book follows the second line of approach and concentrates on the composition of government expenditure for a given tax rate.

Section 2.1 considers the allocation of expenditure between transfer payments and a public good, using the three decision mechanisms mentioned above. A majority voting equilibrium is shown to exist and the ratio of expenditure levels is found to depend on the median voter's income as a ratio of arithmetic mean income. Using this result, the weight attached to the public good in utility functions is calculated for a sample of democratic countries, suggesting that different preferences for public goods resulting from cultural differences may be an important determinant in shaping the composition of government expenditure. Using a general form of welfare function, the composition of government expenditure is examined. These results are then compared with stochastic voting outcomes.

Section 2.2 combines a transfer payment with tax-financed public education expenditure instead of a public good.[3] This clearly involves a different kind of trade-off. A higher transfer payment involves less education spending and reduces incomes, thereby affecting individuals' budget constraints (in addition to the change in the transfer); in the previous case lower public good expenditure feeds into individuals' utility functions directly.

2.1 Choice of Public Goods and Transfer Payment

This section examines choices regarding a transfer payment, b, and consumption of a public good, Q, under three decision mechanisms. In the first approach, self-interested and selfish individuals vote over the choices in a majority voting context. In the second approach the composition of expenditure is obtained by maximising a social welfare function which summarises the value judgements of an individual decision maker. Third, stochastic voting, allowing for biases of voters concerning political parties, is examined.

First, the specification of individuals' preferences, and the government budget constraint, which apply to all choice mechanisms, are examined. Consider person i's preferences for private consumption, c_i, where the consumer price index is normalised to unity, and consumption of a public good, Q, which is non-rival and non-excludable. Suppose i's preferences are described by the general direct utility function:

$$U_i = U\left(c_i, Q\right) \tag{2.1}$$

All individuals pay a proportional income tax, at the rate τ. As the pure public good is non-excludable, the individual's budget constraint is:

$$c_i = y_i\left(1 - \tau\right) + b \tag{2.2}$$

---

[3]However, the present analysis does not consider the kind of public versus private education issues examined by, for example, Epple and Romano (1996), Fernandez and Rogerson (1995), Glomm and Ravikumar (1992), Haupt (2005) and Haupt and Uebelmesser (2009).

In this framework, where incomes are fixed, consumption is given simply by (2.2).

The public good is produced with a constant unit production cost of P. The total cost is recovered through the tax system, in view of its non-excludable nature, with a 'tax price' per person of PQ/N, where N is the population size. The latter thus may be thought to affect outcomes, as a higher population means that the cost is shared among more people. It seems useful to restrict attention to utility functions which avoid expenditure shares, rather than total amounts, depending on N. Hindriks and Myles (2006) examine a number of models involving the choice of a non-rival public good, in each of which population size appears as a determinant. However, they do not discuss the implications of large N. Some authors have argued that population heterogeneity is increased as population size increases, which has quite different effects: see Shelton (2007, pp. 2234-2235) for more discussion and a review of the literature.

In the present context it is desirable to avoid outcomes involving a movement entirely to public good expenditure as N increases. It can be shown that the use of homothetic utility functions where, in addition, the marginal rate of substitution is a linear function of the ratio of quantities consumed, satisfies this requirement. The following analysis thus uses the form:

$$U_i = c_i Q^\gamma \tag{2.3}$$

which clearly has the required properties mentioned above. This is of course a simple monotonic transformation of the standard Cobb–Douglas form. For example if $U = x^\alpha y^{1-\alpha}$, taking the αth root gives $xy^{(1-\alpha)/\alpha}$. The need for the ratio of marginal utilities of private to public goods to depend linearly on Q/c_i restricts attention to a special case of the more general 'linear preference system' of Allen and Bowley (1935).

The government budget constraint requires the revenue from income taxation to be equal to the sum of expenditure on transfer payments and the public good. Thus:

$$\tau\bar{y} = b + \frac{PQ}{N} \qquad (2.4)$$

2.1.1   Majority Voting

This subsection examines the majority choice of expenditure on the public good and the transfer payment. The general approach involves obtaining individuals' indirect utility functions in terms of one policy variable, using the government budget constraint to eliminate the other. Then a check can be made for single-peakedness, which guarantees a voting equilibrium. If this exists, the solution for the majority voting outcome is found by maximising the median voter's indirect utility with respect to the policy variable.

Although there are two variables, the universal transfer payment and expenditure on the public good, to be determined by voting, one degree of freedom is lost because of the existence of the government budget constraint. Voting is therefore one dimensional, where voters are assumed to understand the nature of the constraint and have sufficient information about it.

The Solution

Substituting c_i from (2.2) and b from (2.4) into the direct utility function gives indirect utility, V_i, in terms of Q:

$$V_i = \left\{ y_i (1-\tau) + \tau\bar{y} - \frac{PQ}{N} \right\} Q^\gamma \qquad (2.5)$$

Since $\partial^2 V_i / \partial Q^2 < 0$, preferences regarding Q, for given τ, are single-peaked. Hence the median-voter theorem can be applied, whereby majority voting is determined by the choice, Q_m, of the median voter, who has $y_i = y_m$. Both b_m and Q_m must be positive, so that $0 < Q_m < \tau\bar{y}$. Maximising V_m with respect to Q_m and some rearrangement gives:

$$\frac{PQ_m}{N} = \frac{\gamma}{(1+\gamma)} \bar{y} \left\{ \tau + \frac{y_m}{\bar{y}} (1-\tau) \right\} \qquad (2.6)$$

Clearly a relatively low value of γ, the weight attached to consumption of the private good in utility functions, implies a relatively low choice of public goods. In the trivial case where $\gamma = 0$, and voters obtain no utility from the public good, this reduces to the simple form $b_m = \tau \bar{y}$. As income distributions are positively skewed, $y_m/\bar{y}$ is less than one. Also, with higher equality, or higher $y_m/\bar{y}$, majority voting results in higher expenditure on public goods. The majority choice of expenditure on transfer payments, using the government budget constraint, becomes:

$$b_m = \frac{1}{(1+\gamma)}\bar{y}\left\{\tau - \gamma(1-\tau)\frac{y_m}{\bar{y}}\right\} \tag{2.7}$$

Higher basic inequality leads to a more redistributive expenditure policy, for given τ. Indeed the ratio $b_m/\bar{y}$ falls linearly as $y_m/\bar{y}$ increases, from $\tau/(1+\gamma)$ when $y_m/\bar{y} = 0$ to $(\tau - \gamma(1-\tau))/(1+\gamma)$ when $y_m/\bar{y} = 1$. Furthermore, $b_m/\bar{y}$ increases linearly as τ increases, from $b_m/\bar{y} = 0$ when $\tau = \{1 + (1/(\gamma y_m/\bar{y}))\}^{-1}$ to $(1 - (\gamma y_m/\bar{y}))/(1+\gamma)$ when $\tau = 1$. The ratio, $R_m = b_m/(PQ_m/N)$, is given by:

$$R_m = \frac{\frac{1}{\gamma}\tau - \frac{y_m}{\bar{y}}(1-\tau)}{\tau + \frac{y_m}{\bar{y}}(1-\tau)} \tag{2.8}$$

The majority choice of the composition of expenditure, for given τ, thus depends on the taste parameter γ and the median income relative to the arithmetic mean. The ratio is independent of the units of measurement of incomes and of the population size. Differentiation of R_m with respect to $y_m/\bar{y}$ gives $(\partial R_m/\partial(y_m/\bar{y})) < 0$. Hence a reduction in $y_m/\bar{y}$, that is an increase in inequality, produces a higher proportion of expenditure devoted to the redistributive transfer payment. Also, $\partial^2 R_m/\partial(y_m/\bar{y})^2 > 0$, which implies that the ratio of transfer payment expenditure to public goods increases at an increasing rate as inequality rises. Furthermore, it can be shown that R_m increases with τ at a decreasing rate but, because incentive effects are neglected here, it does not turn downwards. Thus $\partial^2 R_m/\partial\tau^2 < 0$ and when

$\tau = 1$, $\partial R_m / \partial \tau = y_m / \gamma \bar{y}$. Also, there is a negative relationship between the weight attached to public goods, γ, and the ratio of expenditure on transfer payment to public goods.

It is possible to define a set of income inequality measures, $I_L = 1 - y_L / \bar{y}$, where y_L is some measure of location. Hence the majority voting outcome is a function of inequality, $I_m = 1 - y_m / \bar{y}$, although the median voter, acting entirely selfishly, has no desire to reduce inequality except insofar as the median gains from redistribution.

Some idea of the sensitivity of expenditure shares to parameter variations is shown in Figure 2.1, which displays the relationship between R_m and $y_m / \bar{y}$ for alternative tax rates and the weight attached to public goods. The majority choice of R_m increases as the tax rate is increased, and decreases as the weight attached to public goods increases. The parameter variations considered are 10 and 20 per cent changes around the baseline values. The baseline parameters are set at $\tau = 0.41$ and $\gamma = 0.2$, which give a ratio of transfer payments to public goods of 1.9 when $y_m / \bar{y} = 0.85$: these correspond to averages for a sample of democratic countries (discussed below). Figure 2.1 shows that the ratio of expenditures is more sensitive to changes in the preferences parameter than changes in the tax rate or inequality.

As expected from the analytical result, increasing $y_m / \bar{y}$ reduces R_m at a decreasing rate for all tax rates and preference parameters. However, the numerical examples show that, over the most relevant range of $y_m / \bar{y}$, which is around 0.85, the response of the expenditure ratio to a change in inequality is expected to be relatively small. A negative relationship between inequality and government size, or the tax rate, is a core result in the theoretical literature inspired by Romer (1975) and Meltzer and Richard (1981). Given the flatness of the profiles in Figure 2.1, it is perhaps not surprising that cross-sectional empirical studies do not produce clear results, as mentioned in Chapter 1.

Alesina and Glaeser (2004) suggested that differences in the composi-

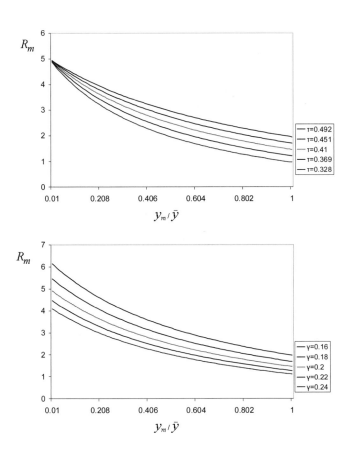

Figure 2.1: Variation in Expenditure Ratio for Alternative Tax Rate and Weight Attached to Public Goods

tion of government expenditure cannot be explained by economic theories
in which higher inequality leads to higher redistribution. Instead, they suggested (2004, p. 220) that there are different attitudes towards redistribution,
based partly on views regarding income mobility. In the present context such
differences in expenditure patterns can in fact be consistent with inequality
differences, if there are different preferences for public and private goods
across countries. This is considered in the following subsubsection.

Cross-country Comparisons

An indication of the variation in expenditure shares, along with aggregate
tax rates and the ratio of the median income, y_m, to arithmetic mean income, $\bar{y}$, for several groups of countries is given in Table 2.1. This gives
average shares for several expenditure groups, with the coefficient of variation in parentheses. For each country, the average value over the period
2000–2006 was obtained. Further details regarding data sources and trans-
formations are provided in Chapter 3, where more extensive use is made of
the data. A major division is between democratic and non-democratic countries. The *Polity IV* (2007) dataset provides an index of democracy for all
countries, which varies between 0 and 10, with 10 representing the highest
level of democracy. For present purposes, the group of democracies includes
countries with an index of democracy of 9 and 10 since the year 2000. Total
expenditure is obtained as the sum of expenditure by general government
on defence, public order and safety, environmental protection, health, education and social protection. Transfer payments contain expenditure on
sickness and disability, old age, survivors, family and children, unemployment and housing. Public goods are measured as the sum of expenditure on
defence, public order and safety and environmental protection. Compared
with democracies, non-democratic countries on average have higher income
inequality, a lower tax rate, a higher share of expenditure on public goods,
and a lower share of expenditure on transfer payments and health and edu-

cation. The variation among non-democratic countries is also substantially larger than among democratic countries.

Table 2.1: Expenditure Shares for Different Country Groups

Group	Expenditure Shares			Aggregate Tax Rate	Ratio $y_m/\bar{y}$
	Transfer Payments	Education and Health	Public Goods		
All Democracies	0.43	0.33	0.24	0.41	0.85
	(0.18)	(0.16)	(0.23)	(0.16)	(0.05)
Scandinavian	0.49	0.32	0.19	0.50	0.90
	(0.06)	(0.08)	(0.12)	(0.08)	(0.01)
Commonwealth	0.39	0.38	0.23	0.38	0.84
	(0.10)	(0.09)	(0.12)	(0.09)	(0.01)
Continental Europe	0.45	0.31	0.24	0.41	0.84
	(0.15)	(0.17)	(0.22)	(0.14)	(0.04)
Developing	0.39	0.32	0.29	0.38	0.87
	(0.09)	(0.13)	(0.11)	(0.20)	(0.05)
United States	0.23	0.45	0.32	0.30	0.75
Non–democratic	0.33	0.31	0.37	0.32	0.78
	(0.33)	(0.24)	(0.30)	(0.40)	(0.15)

It was suggested above that variations in preferences for public goods relative to private goods may, in the context of the model, explain the equivocal results reported in the literature concerning the effect on redistributive policies of inequality. Hence, it is of interest to consider, using equation (2.8), the implied value of γ for each country, given data on tax rates, the ratio of median to mean income and the ratio of expenditure on transfer payments to public goods. The resulting average and coefficient of variation of γ for various groups and countries are reported in Table 2.2. Scandinavian countries have the lowest weight attached to public goods, 0.17. The average value of γ for Commonwealth countries and continental European countries is close to the average of all democratic countries. However, the coefficient of variation for Commonwealth counties is less than the other group of countries. This indicates a similar preference for public goods relative to private consumption among Commonwealth countries. The average value of γ for the sample of developing democratic countries is 0.22, which is higher than the average of all democratic countries. The US and Israel have the highest γ among the democratic countries. The implied γ for Scandinavian countries is greater than Commonwealth countries by just 0.02, yet the sensitivity results reported above suggest that even such a small difference noticeably affects the ratio of expenditure on transfer payments to public goods.

Table 2.2: Weight on Public Goods for Different Country Groups

Group	Mean Value of γ	Coefficient of Variation
All	0.20	0.22
Scandinavian	0.17	0.12
Commonwealth	0.19	0.03
Europe	0.19	0.22
Developing	0.22	0.16
US	0.27	
Israel	0.31	

2.1.2 A Social Welfare Function

This subsection examines the policy decision regarding the composition of expenditure where choices are made by an independent judge, whose value judgements are summarised by a social welfare function, W, defined as a general function of indirect utilities. Hence:

$$W = W\left(V_1, ..., V_N\right) \tag{2.9}$$

which is assumed to be concave with respect to b and Q. This implies that the associated social indifference curves, giving combinations of Q and b which leave W unchanged, are convex. An optimal allocation of expenditure is obtained as a point of tangency of the highest social indifference curve which can be reached subject to the government's budget constraint relating Q and *b.* The optimal policy is thus given from the condition:

$$\left.\frac{db}{dQ}\right|_{\tau} = \left.\frac{db}{dQ}\right|_{W} \tag{2.10}$$

Differentiating W totally with respect to public good expenditure and the transfer payment gives:

$$dW = \left(\sum_{i=1}^{N} \frac{\partial W}{\partial V_i} \frac{\partial V_i}{\partial b}\right) db + \left(\sum_{i=1}^{N} \frac{\partial W}{\partial V_i} \frac{\partial V_i}{\partial Q}\right) dQ \tag{2.11}$$

Consider social indifference curves relating combinations of Q and b for which W is constant. Setting $dW = 0$ gives the slope of indifference curves, $\left.\frac{db}{dQ}\right|_{W}$, as:

$$\left.\frac{db}{dQ}\right|_{W} = -\frac{\sum_{i=1}^{N} \frac{\partial W}{\partial V_i} \frac{\partial V_i}{\partial Q_G}}{\sum_{i=1}^{N} \frac{\partial W}{\partial V_i} \frac{\partial V_i}{\partial b}} \tag{2.12}$$

This slope can be expressed more conveniently by defining v_i as the welfare weight attached to an increase in i's income; that is:

$$v_i = \frac{\partial W}{\partial V_i} \frac{\partial V_i}{\partial b} \tag{2.13}$$

and:

$$\sum_{i=1}^{N} \frac{\partial W}{\partial V_i} \frac{\partial V_i}{\partial Q} = \sum_{i=1}^{N} v_i \left(\frac{\partial V_i/\partial Q}{\partial V_i/\partial b}\right) \tag{2.14}$$

Substituting (6.5) and (8.9) into (6.4) gives:

$$\left.\frac{db}{dQ}\right|_{W} = -\sum_{i=1}^{N} v_i' \left(\frac{\partial V_i/\partial Q}{\partial V_i/\partial b}\right) \tag{2.15}$$

with $v_i' = v_i/\sum_{i=1}^{N} v_i$. The slope of social indifference curves is therefore a weighted sum of the ratio of $\partial V_i/\partial Q$ to $\partial V_i/\partial b$.

Hence differentiating $V_i = \{y_i (1 - \tau) + b\} Q^\gamma$ gives terms $\partial V_i/\partial Q = \gamma V_i/Q$ and $\partial V_i/\partial b = Q^\gamma$. Appropriate substitution, and writing $\tilde{y} = \sum_{i}^{N} v_i' y_i$, gives:

$$\left.\frac{db}{dQ}\right|_{W} = -\frac{\gamma}{Q} \{\tilde{y} (1 - \tau) + b\} \tag{2.16}$$

The government budget constraint in this model takes the simple linear form in (2.4). Hence:

$$\left. \frac{db}{dQ} \right|_{\tau} = -\frac{P}{N} \qquad (2.17)$$

Equating slopes, and using $PQ/N = \tau \bar{y} - b$, gives the optimal transfer, b_W, as the solution to:

$$b_W = \frac{\bar{y}}{(1+\gamma)} \left\{ \tau - \gamma(1-\tau)\frac{\tilde{y}}{\bar{y}} \right\} \qquad (2.18)$$

This takes exactly the same form as equation (2.7), except that b_m is replaced by b_W and the median income, y_m, is replaced by the welfare-weighted average, $\tilde{y}$: the corresponding inequality measure is thus $I_W = 1 - \tilde{y}/\bar{y}$. Hence the optimal transfer takes the same form as the solution given in (2.6) above and the expression for the expenditure ratio takes the same basic form as in equation (2.8).

However, this result is actually far from straightforward in view of the complexity of the welfare weights, v_i', even for simple forms of the social welfare function. Equation (2.18) does not in fact provide a closed-form solution for b_W. As in standard optimal tax analyses, the solution to the nonlinear equation (2.18) can be obtained numerically using a simulated distribution of incomes and searching for the value of b which gives the highest W, while making use of the government budget constraint.

It would clearly be convenient if $\tilde{y}$ could be replaced by a term that did not itself depend on the optimal value of b, thereby providing an approximation to the optimal value which could easily be expressed (and, if desired, calculated) using (2.18). This would facilitate analysis of the comparative static properties of the model. Consider an approximation for $\tilde{y}$ in the case, ubiquitous in the literature, where the social welfare function takes the iso-elastic form:

$$W = \frac{1}{1-\varepsilon} \sum_{i=1}^{N} V_i^{1-\varepsilon} \qquad \varepsilon \neq 1, \varepsilon > 0 \qquad (2.19)$$

The aim is to obtain an approximation which allows the earlier results to be treated as closed-form solutions and thus to consider more easily their comparative static properties. The individual utility functions take the form:

$$V_i = \{y_i (1 - \tau) + b\} Q^\gamma \tag{2.20}$$

Hence $\partial V_i / \partial b = Q^\gamma$ and $\partial W / \partial V_i = V_i^{-\varepsilon}$, and:

$$v_i = \frac{\partial W}{\partial V_i} \frac{\partial V_i}{\partial b} = \{y_i (1 - \tau) + b\}^{-\varepsilon} Q^{\gamma(1-\varepsilon)} \tag{2.21}$$

Suppose b is small relative to y_i: this is clearly not a good approximation where y_i is small, but is discussed further below. In this case an approximation for $\tilde{y} = \sum y_i (v_i / \sum v_i)$, denoted $\tilde{y}_A$, is obtained as:

$$\tilde{y}_A = \frac{\frac{1}{N} \sum y_i^{1-\varepsilon}}{\frac{1}{N} \sum y_i^{-\varepsilon}} \tag{2.22}$$

This can be further simplified using the assumption that income is lognormally distributed as $\Lambda(y| \mu, \sigma^2)$, with mean and variance of logarithms of μ and σ^2 respectively. Using the properties of the lognormal, and on shifting to a continuous distribution the summation signs in the previous expression are replaced by integrals:

$$\tilde{y}_A = \exp\left[\mu + \frac{\sigma^2}{2}(1 - 2\varepsilon)\right] = \exp\left[\mu + \frac{\sigma^2}{2}(1 - \varepsilon)\right] \exp\left[\frac{-\varepsilon\sigma^2}{2}\right] \tag{2.23}$$

When the final term in this expression is close to, but less than, unity we can exclude the last part. However, the use of the assumption that b can be neglected in (2.21) actually attaches too much weight to the lower incomes, and thus imparts a downward bias to the approximation. One approach is thus to 'correct' for this downward bias by excluding the last term in (6.28). This gives:

$$\tilde{y}_A = \exp\left[\mu + \frac{\sigma^2}{2}(1 - \varepsilon)\right] \tag{2.24}$$

Thus $\tilde{y}_A$ is closely related to Atkinson's measure of the inequality of income. Following Atkinson (1970), let y_{ede} denote the 'equally distributed equivalent' income, representing the equal income which gives the same welfare as the actual distribution, using $W = \frac{1}{1-\varepsilon}\sum_{i=1}^{N} y_i^{1-\varepsilon}$. This is the same as the above but with V replaced by y. Thus:

$$y_{ede} = \left(\frac{1}{N}\sum_{i=1}^{N} y_i^{1-\varepsilon}\right)^{\frac{1}{1-\varepsilon}} \tag{2.25}$$

Again using the lognormal properties, the median and mean income are $y_m = e^{\mu}$ and $\bar{y} = e^{\mu_t + \sigma^2/2}$. The term $y^{1-\varepsilon}$ has mean and variance of logarithms of $(1-\varepsilon)\mu$ and $(1-\varepsilon)^2\sigma^2$, so that:

$$y_{ede} = \exp\left((1-\varepsilon)\mu + (1-\varepsilon)^2\frac{\sigma^2}{2}\right)^{\frac{1}{1-\varepsilon}} = \exp\left(\mu + (1-\varepsilon)\frac{\sigma^2}{2}\right) \tag{2.26}$$

Hence:

$$\tilde{y}_A = y_{ede} \tag{2.27}$$

Furthermore:

$$\frac{y_{ede}}{\bar{y}} = \frac{\exp\left(\mu + (1-\varepsilon)\frac{\sigma^2}{2}\right)}{\exp\left(\mu + \frac{\sigma_t^2}{2}\right)} = \left(\exp\left(-\frac{\sigma^2}{2}\right)\right)^{\varepsilon} \tag{2.28}$$

and using the fact that $y_m = \exp\mu$:

$$\frac{y_{ede}}{\bar{y}} = \left(\frac{y_m}{\bar{y}}\right)^{\varepsilon} \tag{2.29}$$

If $\tilde{y}_A$ is approximated by y_{ede}, (2.29) gives the required relationship between income ratios.

It is important to test the value of the above approximation. Hence values of the expenditure components using the approximation $\tilde{y}_A = y_{ede}$ were compared with those obtained using a simulated population of size 15000 drawn at random from a lognormal distribution with $\mu = 9.0$ and $\sigma^2 = 0.5$, which imply that $\bar{y} = 10405$ and $y_m/\bar{y} = 0.78$. Using the simulated distribution, a range of values of b were investigated (the value of b was increased by 10 each time). For each b the government budget constraint was used to obtain Q and the resulting values were used to calculate each individual's level of utility. These were then used to obtain social welfare for a specified inequality aversion parameter, ε. Finally, given a large number of W measures, the maximum gives the optimal composition. Table 2.3 gives the results for a range of parameter values for γ and inequality aversion, ε, with $\tau = 0.35$.

Table 2.3: Optimal Composition of Expenditure: Alternative Solutions

ε	Approximation			Simulation			
	b	PQ/N	R	b	PQ/N	R	$\%\Delta W$
$\gamma = 0.2$							
0.8	2111.82	1529.77	1.38	2180.1	1461.5	1.49	−0.0049
0.5	2039.95	1601.65	1.27	2090.1	1551.5	1.35	−0.0067
0.2	1962.47	1679.12	1.17	1990.1	1651.5	1.20	−0.0024
$\gamma = 0.5$							
0.8	582.05	3059.53	0.19	810.1	2831.49	0.29	−0.0546
0.5	438.30	3203.29	0.14	620.1	3021.49	0.21	−0.0710
0.2	283.35	3358.24	0.09	380.1	3261.49	0.12	−0.0243

These results show that the approximation does indeed give values of expenditure levels and ratios which are close to those obtained using a large simulated population.[4] The percentage difference of the social welfare function using the approximation from that obtained by simulation, shown in the final column of the table, is in each case found to be extremely small. This reflects the relative flatness of the profile relating W to b (for given parameter values) as well as the closeness of the approximation.

The optimal expenditure levels and their ratio can thus be expressed in terms of $y_m/\bar{y}$, just as in the majority voting framework, except that there is an additional degree of nonlinearity in the expressions, involving the term ε. The majority voting outcome and the social welfare maximising outcome are approximately the same in the special case where $\varepsilon = 1$. These results

---

[4]Furthermore, comparisons showed that the use of the equally distributed equivalent income was superior to that of (6.28).

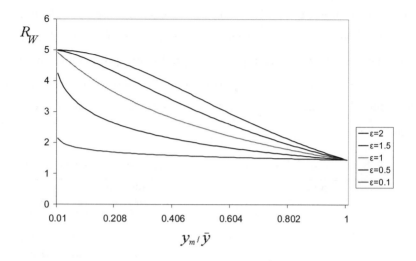

Figure 2.2: Variation in R_W with $y_m/\bar{y}$ for Different ε

suggest that it may be difficult empirically to discriminate between majority voting and optimal allocation frameworks. In this case it is not possible to obtain implicit values of inequality aversion, since both γ and ε cannot be observed directly.

Figure 2.2 shows profiles of the variation in R_W with $y_m/\bar{y}$ for different ε and benchmark variables and parameters, with $\tau = 0.4$ and $\gamma = 0.2$. It shows that the social planner's choice of $b_W/(PQ_W/N)$ falls as inequality falls, or $y_m/\bar{y}$ increases towards unity. For ε less than one, the optimal proportion of expenditure devoted to transfer payments is substantially less than the majority voting outcome. Also, R_W is much less sensitive to changes in inequality for ε less than one.

One property of the model is that the chosen value of the transfer payment increases with the given tax rate. As a result, the ratio, R, increases continually with τ. However, this clearly arises because labour supply incentive effects are not modelled. This is the major result that is likely to be modified when allowance is made for incentive effects of taxation. An increase in τ has, in addition to a 'tax rate effect' which causes revenue to increase, a 'tax base effect' whereby total income falls. At some point the second effect dominates and total revenue falls as τ increases at higher levels. The profiles of b and of R against τ are thus likely eventually to turn downwards at some stage.

2.1.3   Stochastic Voting

This section considers stochastic voting instead of the simple majority voting mechanism discussed above. Suppose the population consists of K groups of individuals, where group k has population proportion n_k, for $k = 1, ..., K$, so that $\sum_{k=1}^{K} n_k = 1$. Within each group individuals have the same income, so that if there are two political parties, A and B, with associated policies, individuals within each group have the same indirect utility except for a stochastic element. Voter i in group k prefers party A if:

$$V_{k,A} > V_{k,B} + s_{i,k} + g \qquad (2.30)$$

The term $s_{i,k}$ represents member i of group k's additive bias towards party B, and for the kth group $s_{i,k}$ lies between $-s_k^*$ and $+s_k^*$.[5] This bias is considered to arise from factors which are not related to the policies of the parties. In addition g represents a population-wide additive bias towards party B. The $s_{i,k}$ are random variables, along with g. The introduction of random components involves a substantial change to the voting framework, compared with the deterministic model in which the probability of an individual voting

---

[5] An alternative specification of bias in which the additive form in (2.30) is replaced by a multiplicative form, whereby what matters are the relative sizes of $V_{k,A}$ and $V_{k,B}$ rather than the absolute sizes, leads to a formulation which is additive in the logarithms. The objective function is thus expressed as a weighted geometric mean of indirect utilities, rather than a weighted arithmetic mean, such that $S = \sum_i \eta_i \log V_i$. The voting outcome is considerably sensitive to the specification of bias. Dolmas (2008) looks at the voting equilibrium for taxes in a probabilistic voting model, and finds that it is affected by assumptions about the form, additive or multiplicative, of random non-policy elements. Here, only the additive form of bias is examined.

for party A switches from 0 to 1, as $V_{k,A}$ switches from being less than, to greater than, $V_{k,B}$.

As the $s_{i,k}$ represent additive biases, they are centred around zero – a negative value indicates a bias towards party A. For the kth group, suppose the values of $s_{i,k}$ lie between $-s_k^*$ and $+s_k^*$. The population bias takes values between $-g^*$ and $+g^*$. Hence groups are distinguished by the range of values which the bias towards party B can take, for people within the group. Members of the group have different views – these may for example be thought of in terms of strength of ideological bias or bias depending on personal characteristics of party members (unrelated to their policies).

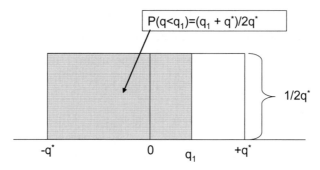

Figure 2.3: A Rectangular Distribution

Further progress is helped by giving more structure to the distributional framework. Suppose the distribution of biases within each group is assumed to be uniform within the relevant range; that is, the density functions of the variables follow rectangular distributions. Figure 2.3 illustrates a uniform or rectangular distribution of a variable, q, taking values between $-q^*$ and $+q^*$. Since the area underneath the uniform density function must be 1, the uniform density, the height of the rectangle, must equal $1/2q^*$. Furthermore, the probability of observing a value less than or equal to, say, q_1 is the shaded area to the left of q_1, so that $P(q \leq q_1) = (q_1 + q^*)/2q^*$. This property is used in what follows.

From (2.30) there is, within each group, a threshold value of $s_{i,k}$, say s'_k, such that all individuals with $s_{i,k} < s'_k$ vote for party A. This is given by:

$$s'_k = V_{k,A} - V_{k,B} - g \qquad (2.31)$$

Using the above general result for rectangular distributions, the proportion of each group voting for party A, $p_{k,A}$, is equal to the proportion with $s_{i,k}$ below s'_k, and is given by:

$$
\begin{aligned}
p_{k,A} &= \frac{s'_k + s^*_k}{2s^*_k} \\
&= \frac{1}{2} + \frac{V_{k,A} - V_{k,B} - g}{2s^*_k} \qquad (2.32)
\end{aligned}
$$

The proportion of individuals, over all groups, who vote for party A is the weighted sum:

$$p_A = \sum_{k=1}^{K} n_k p_{k,A} \qquad (2.33)$$

Here p_A is a random variable because it is a function of the random variable g. The probability of party A winning the election, $P(A)$, is equal to the probability that $p_A \geq \frac{1}{2}$. This requires the probability that $\sum_{k=1}^{K} n_k p_{k,A} \geq \frac{1}{2}$, or:

$$P(A) = P\left[\sum_{k=1}^{K} n_k \left(\frac{1}{2} + \frac{V_{k,A} - V_{k,B} - g}{2s^*_k}\right) \geq \frac{1}{2}\right] \qquad (2.34)$$

This can be rewritten as:

$$P(A) = P\left[\sum_{k=1}^{K} \frac{n_k}{s^*_k}(V_{k,A} - V_{k,B}) + \frac{1}{2}\sum_{k=1}^{K} n_k - g \sum_{k=1}^{K} \frac{n_k}{s^*_k} \geq \frac{1}{2}\right] \qquad (2.35)$$

and since $\sum_{k=1}^{K} n_k = 1$, this becomes:

$$P(A) = P[g \leq g_A] \qquad (2.36)$$

where:

$$g_A = \left(\frac{1}{\sum_{k=1}^{K} \frac{n_k}{s^*_k}}\right) \sum_{k=1}^{K} \frac{n_k}{s^*_k}(V_{k,A} - V_{k,B}) \qquad (2.37)$$

This probability is the area of the rectangle with height $1/2g^*$ and base $g^* + g_A$, so that the probability of party A winning is:

$$P(A) = \frac{1}{2} + \frac{1}{2g^*} \left(\frac{1}{\sum_{k=1}^{K} \frac{n_k}{s_k^*}} \right) \sum_{k=1}^{K} \frac{n_k}{s_k^*} (V_{k,A} - V_{k,B}) \qquad (2.38)$$

Suppose party A wishes to maximise this probability by selecting a policy, conditional on party B having selected its policy. Since $V_{k,B}$, g^*, the s_k^* and n_k are constant, the first-order condition for a maximum is the same as that required to maximise:

$$\sum_{k=1}^{K} \left(\frac{1}{2s_k^*} \right) n_k V_{k,A} \qquad (2.39)$$

This is a weighted sum of the indirect utilities, and since the densities are $1/2s_k^*$, the weights can be interpreted as the probabilities, within each group, of having a bias towards party B within the relevant range (from $-s_k^*$ to $+s_k^*$). The indirect utilities obviously depend on the policy choices, so that (in addition to the sizes of the groups) the values of $1/2s_k^*$ play an important role in the determination of party A's optimal policy. A small change in policy has a larger effect on its support by voters in group k, the larger is the density, $1/2s_k^*$ (that is, the smaller is the range of biases of members of the group). This contrasts significantly with the deterministic majority voting framework, where only the preferences of the median voter count, provided conditions required for the existence of an equilibrium are satisfied. For example, if higher-income groups have a more concentrated bias, compared with lower-income groups, they have a relatively larger importance in determining the policy decision of party A, despite the fact that lower-income groups may form a majority of the population (with a positively skewed income distribution). An implication is therefore that voting over a tax and transfer system may well result in less redistribution than under the basic deterministic majority voting model.

Several further important implications follow from this. The situation facing party B is symmetric with that of A, which implies that – as each

party is assumed to be trying to maximise its chances of winning the election
– the policies of the two parties converge. Hence both parties can be regarded
as having the same objective function:

$$S = \sum_{k=1}^{K} \left(\frac{1}{s_k^*}\right) n_k V_k \tag{2.40}$$

where of course V_k is regarded as a function of policy variables and the 2 in
the denominator can obviously be ignored. This can be written as:

$$S = \sum_{k=1}^{K} \eta_k V_k \tag{2.41}$$

with $\eta_k = n_k/s_k^*$. This common objective therefore looks very much like a
social welfare function expressed as a weighted sum (or weighted arithmetic
mean) of indirect utilities. This is a form of utilitarian welfare function,
except that the weights do not depend on value judgements of the decision
maker or judge whose views are represented by the social welfare function.
The weights are determined by the bias characteristics of the different income
groups. A special case of (2.41) arises if all $s_k^* = s^*$ for all k, in which case
the objective function to be maximised is exactly the same as the 'classical
utilitarian' social welfare function.[6]

This framework does not place any restriction on the number of policy instruments under consideration. Hence there are no problems of the existence
of a voting equilibrium, such as those which can arise with deterministic voting. However, two conditions need to hold in the stochastic voting model.
First, voters' utilities should be concave functions of political platforms. Second, the density of ideologies should not be a sharply increasing function: in
the present model the distribution of $s_{i,k}$ is uniform, which satisfies this con-

---

[6]The utilitarian form has also been rationalised in terms of a social contract among
individuals making a type of 'constitutional choice' behind a veil of ignorance, in which
all outcomes are treated as being equally likely. This argument was first stated by Edge-
worth. A social contract arising from extreme risk aversion leads to the Rawlsian maxi–min
evaluation function.

dition. See Acemoglu and Robinson (2007, p. 365) for more details about the conditions required for probabilistic voting.

Consider the division of expenditure between transfers and a public good. Each party maximises the support function, the expected vote in (2.41), subject to the government budget constraint. Indirect utility for an individual in the k takes the form $\{y_k(1-\tau)+b\}Q^{\gamma}$. The first-order conditions with respect to transfer payments and public goods are as follows:

$$\sum_{k=1}^{K} \eta_k Q_S^{\gamma} = \lambda \tag{2.42}$$

$$\sum_{k=1}^{K} \eta_k \gamma \{y_k(1-\tau)+b_S\}Q_S^{\gamma} = \lambda \frac{pQ_S}{N} \tag{2.43}$$

where λ is the Lagrangian multiplier associated with the government budget constraint. Also, pQ_S/N and b_S are the per capita expenditure on public goods and transfer payments under stochastic voting. The above first-order conditions with the government budget constraint give:

$$\frac{pQ_S}{N} = \frac{\gamma\bar{y}}{(1+\gamma)}\left\{\tau+(1-\tau)\frac{\tilde{\bar{y}}}{\bar{y}}\right\} \tag{2.44}$$

$$b_S = \frac{\bar{y}}{(1+\gamma)}\left\{\tau-\gamma(1-\tau)\frac{\tilde{\bar{y}}}{\bar{y}}\right\} \tag{2.45}$$

Where $\tilde{\bar{y}} = \sum_{k=1}^{K} y_k\left(\eta_k/\sum_{k=1}^{K}\eta_k\right)$ and is a weighted average income. The weights, $\eta_k/\sum_{k=1}^{K}\eta_k$, are a function of political influence, η_k. Recall that $\eta_k = n_k/s_k^*$, which shows that the group size, n_k, as well as the group density, s_k^*, affect the weighted average income under stochastic voting. The latter shows the sensitivity of the voters in each group to the economic policies.

The ratio of expenditure on transfer payments to public goods with stochastic voting, R_S, therefore becomes:

$$R_S = \frac{\frac{1}{\gamma}\tau-(1-\tau)\frac{\tilde{\bar{y}}}{\bar{y}}}{\tau+(1-\tau)\frac{\tilde{\bar{y}}}{\bar{y}}} \tag{2.46}$$

The stochastic voting results for the expenditure on public goods and transfer payments and their ratio take similar forms to the utilitarian choices, except that $\tilde{y}$ is replaced by $\tilde{\tilde{y}}$. Basically, $\tilde{y}$ and $\tilde{\tilde{y}}$ are just different weighted average incomes. The weight in the stochastic voting objective depends on the group size and the group densities whereas the weight in the benevolent government case depends on the value judgement of the decision maker.

Comparing the stochastic voting results with the median voter's choice of public goods and transfer payment indicates that the two expressions are identical except for the fact that the majority choice depends on $y_m/\bar{y}$ whereas stochastic voting depends on $\tilde{\tilde{y}}/\bar{y}$. In the median-voter framework only the median individual is the decisive voter and the relative position of the median to the arithmetic mean plays the crucial role. In probabilistic voting, not only does the group size play an important role but also the responsiveness of voters in each group affects the outcome.

In the case of no bias, where $\eta_k = 1$, comparison with the social welfare function considered earlier shows that the voting equilibrium coincides with $\varepsilon = 0$; that is, it is the same as the optimal allocation resulting from a 'classical utilitarian' welfare function where only the sum of utilities matters. More generally, covariances are required, which means that further structure needs to be added to the model regarding the joint distribution of η and y.

Comparative statics results with respect to τ and γ are similar to the majority voting case. In addition, b_S and pQ_S/N are linearly decreasing and increasing in $\tilde{\tilde{y}}/\bar{y}$ respectively. Moreover, as with the other mechanisms there is a negative relationship between $\tilde{\tilde{y}}/\bar{y}$ and the ratio of expenditure on transfer payments to public goods in stochastic voting. The weight of different groups in the political support function, η_k, is one of the main determinants of the composition of government expenditure in the stochastic model. The derivatives of per capita expenditure on transfer payments and public goods with respect to η_k are given by:

$$\frac{\partial \left(pQ_S/N \right)}{\partial \eta_k} = \frac{\gamma \left(1 - \tau \right) \left(y_k - \tilde{y} \right)}{\left(1 + \gamma \right) \sum_{k=1}^{K} \eta_k} \tag{2.47}$$

$$\frac{\partial b}{\partial \eta_k} = -\frac{\gamma \left(1 - \tau \right) \left(y_k - \tilde{y} \right)}{\left(1 + \gamma \right) \sum_{k=1}^{K} \eta_k} \tag{2.48}$$

Suppose income in group k is lower than the weighted average income, $\tilde{y}$. Consequently, voters in this group support less expenditure on public goods and more expenditure on transfer payments. For instance, suppose there are three groups of individuals: poor, middle-income and rich. If the political influence of the group of poor falls, the expenditure on transfer payments decreases relative to public goods. The political influence of the poor can fall by reducing the share of poor in the whole population or increasing the responsiveness of voters in the group of poor to changes in the economic policy.

2.2   Choice of Education and Transfer Payment

Instead of the choice of allocation of tax revenue between a transfer payment and a tax-financed non-rival public good, suppose it is required to choose the combination of a redistributive transfer payment, b, and a quantity of tax-financed public education per person, E. The same amount of education is received by each individual, considered to be a private rather than a public good. This involves total spending on education of NpE, where p is the cost per unit of education. The role of education is to increase human capital, reflected in a higher pre-tax income of each individual. The following subsections consider alternative choice mechanisms in turn.

The present approach contrasts with Bearse *et al.* (2001), who examine transfers and public education, both of which are financed by a proportional income tax, and voting is on the composition of government expenditure for a given tax rate. However, individuals decide whether to use the publicly provided education or buy private education, which leads to double-peaked preferences where the single crossing condition can be violated.[7]

For simplicity, suppose there is no externality of the kind where the education of one person enhances the productivity of other individuals (for example, where teamwork is involved). Nevertheless there is an important spillover effect arising via the tax structure because the education of other individuals raises the tax base. The assumption used in previous sections regarding incentives is retained, namely that labour supplies and hence pre-tax incomes are not influenced by the tax and transfer system. Nevertheless y_i is endogenous as it is influenced by the choice of E. It is determined via the following Cobb–Douglas human capital production function:

$$y_i = \delta y_{0,i}^\theta E^{1-\theta} \qquad (2.49)$$

where $y_{0,i}$ is i's 'base' value of income. Rearrangement of (2.49) gives:

$$\frac{y_i}{y_{0,i}} - 1 = \delta \left(\frac{E}{y_{0,i}}\right)^{1-\theta} - 1 \qquad (2.50)$$

which implies that equal education spending per person produces a proportional increase in income above the base value that is higher for lower-income individuals. In this simple model, education is therefore equalising, though in a different manner from that of the transfer payment. Furthermore, the transfer payment has no effect on the tax base, unlike education expenditure.

Consider first the government's budget constraint, which is:

$$b + pE = \tau \bar{y} \qquad (2.51)$$

where $\bar{y}$ is, as before, arithmetic mean income given by:

$$\bar{y} = \frac{1}{N} \sum y_i = \delta E^{1-\theta} \left(\frac{1}{N} \sum y_{0,i}^\theta\right) \qquad (2.52)$$

---

[7]Borck (2008) uses a similar framework to study voters' preferences for centralised versus local public education. Numerical simulations show that the group of rich and poor voters prefer centralisation and the middle classes prefer local education. Soares (2006) extends the political economy model of public-funded education by using a general equilibrium overlapping generations model with altruism.

It is convenient to write $\bar{y}_{0,\theta} = \left(\frac{1}{N}\sum y_{0,i}^{\theta}\right)^{1/\theta}$. Although this notation involves the use of a bar above the variable, y, the θ subscript in $\bar{y}_{0,\theta}$ indicates that it is a generalised mean rather than an arithmetic mean. The generalised mean also contrasts with the 'moment of order θ about the origin' which is $\frac{1}{N}\sum y_{0,i}^{\theta}$. Hence the units of the generalised mean correspond to those of the original variable, $y_{0,i}$.

Hence:

$$\bar{y} = \delta E^{1-\theta}\bar{y}_{0,\theta}^{\theta} \qquad (2.53)$$

Substituting into the budget constraint (2.51) gives:

$$b = \tau\delta E^{1-\theta}\bar{y}_{0,\theta}^{\theta} - pE \qquad (2.54)$$

Assume that individuals obtain no direct consumption benefits from education. Hence, it is appropriate simply to consider their net income, or consumption, as the maximand. Hence individuals are concerned with:

$$c_i = y_i(1-\tau) + b \qquad (2.55)$$

2.2.1 Majority Voting

Consider first the choice of expenditure policy by majority voting. Substituting for b from (6.18) into (2.55), consumption can be expressed in terms of E, whereby:

$$c_i = \delta E^{1-\theta}\left\{y_{0,i}^{\theta}(1-\tau) + \tau\bar{y}_{0,\theta}^{\theta}\right\} - pE \qquad (2.56)$$

It can be seen that $\partial^2 c_i/\partial E^2 < 0$, confirming that preferences regarding E are single peaked. Therefore the median-voter theorem can be applied, whereby the per capita majority choice of expenditure on education, pE_m, is determined by the preferences of the median voter, with $y_{0,m}$. Setting

$\partial c_m / \partial E_m = 0$ and solving for E_m gives:[8]

$$pE_m = (P_E)^{1-\frac{1}{\theta}} \, \bar{y}_{0,\theta} \, \{\delta (1-\theta)\}^{\frac{1}{\theta}} \left\{ \tau + (1-\tau) \left(\frac{y_{0,m}}{\bar{y}_{0,\theta}} \right)^{\theta} \right\}^{\frac{1}{\theta}} \qquad (2.57)$$

Thus, using government budget constraint:

$$b_m = \left(\tau \delta \bar{y}_{0,\theta}^{\theta} E_m^{-\theta} - p \right) E_m \qquad (2.58)$$

The majority choice of the ratio of the transfer payment to education expenditure, R_m, is:

$$R_m = \frac{1}{1-\theta} \left\{ 1 + \left(\frac{1}{\tau} - 1 \right) \left(\frac{y_{0,m}}{\bar{y}_{0,\theta}} \right)^{\theta} \right\}^{-1} - 1 \qquad (2.59)$$

and is independent of δ and p. It can be shown that $\partial R_m / \partial \tau > 0$, implying that expenditure on transfers increases relative to education, though this result is likely to be different when incentive effects are modelled.

Differentiation of R_m with respect to θ gives $\frac{\partial R_m}{\partial \theta} > 0$. Hence a raise in θ produces a higher proportion of expenditure devoted to the redistributive transfer payment. Higher θ implies that education is less effective in increasing the average level of productivity, so voters vote on lower education and higher transfer payment.

Figure 2.4 shows the variation in R_m with $\frac{y_{0,m}}{\bar{y}_{0,\theta}}$ for different values of θ, for a benchmark tax rate of $\tau = 0.35$. Also, it is necessary to consider values of θ which, along with other parameters and variables, give positive values of the transfer payment and reasonable absolute and relative values of expenditure. In the following numerical example, θ is allowed to vary between 0.65 and 0.85. As expected, the ratio of expenditure on transfer payments to education increases as θ is increased.

---

[8] If the monotonic transformation $U_i = c_i^{\alpha}$ is considered instead of simply maximising c_i, indirect utility, V_i, can be written in terms of Q using (2.55) and the first-order condition for i's most preferred value of Q is $\frac{\partial V_i}{\partial Q} = \frac{\alpha V_i}{c_i} \frac{\partial c_i}{\partial Q} = 0$. The trivial solution where $V_i = 0$ can be ignored, and the condition for a maximum is, as above, $\frac{\partial c_i}{\partial Q} = 0$.

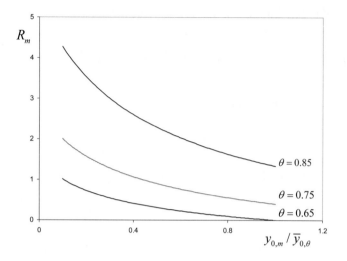

Figure 2.4: Variation in R_m with $y_m/\bar{y}$ for Different θ

2.2.2   A Social Welfare Function

Consider the maximisation of a social welfare function expressed in terms of the net income of each individual, so that:

$$W = W\left(c_1, ..., c_N\right) \tag{2.60}$$

Hence c_i replaces V_i in the previous expression for W. The use of, say, $V_i = c_i^{\alpha}$ makes no difference to the result.

Following the same procedure as discussed in section 7.2, but with E replacing Q, the optimal value corresponds to a tangency solution where the highest social indifference curve touches the government budget constraint. The slope of social indifference curves is given by:

$$\left.\frac{db}{dE}\right|_W = -\sum_{i=1}^{N} v_i' \left(\frac{\partial c_i/\partial E}{\partial c_i/\partial b}\right) \tag{2.61}$$

with $v_i' = v_i / \sum_{i=1}^{N} v_i$ and $v_i = \frac{\partial W}{\partial c_i}\frac{\partial c_i}{\partial b}$. The slope of the budget constraint is:

$$\left.\frac{db}{dE}\right|_{\tau} = (1-\theta)\tau\delta E^{-\theta}\bar{y}_{0,\theta}^{\theta} - p \tag{2.62}$$

It can be shown that substitution for $\partial c_i/\partial E$ and $\partial c_i/\partial b$, and solving for E_W gives the same result as in equation (2.57), but with $y_{0,m}$ replaced by $\tilde{y}_{0,\theta}$, defined as the weighted generalised mean:

$$\tilde{y}_{0,\theta} = \left(\sum_{i=1}^{N} v_i' y_{0,i}^{\theta} \right)^{1/\theta} \tag{2.63}$$

This is indeed a general property of these types of model. The expression giving the solution for optimal values takes the same form as that for majority voting outcomes, with the difference that the median income is replaced by a welfare-weighted mean income.

Again, the complexities associated with the welfare-weighted term, $\tilde{y}_{0,\theta}$, may be overcome by approximating it using the equally distributed equivalent value of basic income, $y_{0,i}$, and assuming lognormality of the distribution of $y_{0,i}$: this follows the same approach as set out for the previous model. In this case, lognormality also implies that in general the equally distributed equivalent, raised to the power, say η, of a variable x is the same as the equally distributed equivalent of x^{η}. Also, the equally distributed equivalent for aversion of ε is just the generalised mean for a power of $1 - \varepsilon$. Thus:

$$\frac{\tilde{y}_{0,\theta}}{\bar{y}_{0,\theta}} = \left(\frac{y_{0,m}}{\bar{y}_{0,\theta}} \right)^{\varepsilon} \tag{2.64}$$

where ε is the degree of relative inequality aversion. Furthermore, if the mean and variance of logarithms of the distribution of y_0 are μ_0 and σ_0^2, then $\bar{y}_{0,\theta} = \exp\left(\mu_0 + \frac{\theta\sigma_0^2}{2}\right)$. Comparison with (2.59) shows that θ and ε have a similar effect on the variation in R with $y_{0,m}/\bar{y}_{0,\theta}$, as the exponent on the latter is the product, $\theta\varepsilon$.

2.2.3 Stochastic Voting

As in Subsection 2.1.3, suppose the population is divided to K groups, with the proportion in each group of n_k, so that $\sum_{k=1}^{K} n_k = 1$. Each party maximises the number of votes and the policies of the two parties converge. The

support function is given by (2.41), where η_k is n_k/s_k^* and V_k is the indirect
utility of group k, regarded as a function of policy variables, and is:

$$V_k = \delta y_{0,k}^\theta E^{1-\theta}(1 - \tau) + b \tag{2.65}$$

The probabilistic voting outcomes are obtained by maximising the support
function subject to the government budget constraint. Therefore:

$$pE_S = (p)^{1-\frac{1}{\theta}}\, \bar{y}_{0,\theta} \left\{\delta \left(1 - \theta\right)\right\}^{\frac{1}{\theta}} \left\{\tau + (1-\tau)\frac{\sum_{k=1}^{K} \eta_k y_{0,k}^\theta}{\bar{y}_{0,\theta}^\theta \sum_{k=1}^{K} \eta_k}\right\}^{\frac{1}{\theta}} \tag{2.66}$$

$$b_S = \left(\tau \delta \bar{y}_{0,\theta}^\theta E_S^{-\theta} - p\right) E_S \tag{2.67}$$

where pE_S and b_S are per capita expenditure education and transfer payments with stochastic voting. In this case $y_{0,m}^\theta$ is replaced by a term given by
$\sum_{k=1}^{K} \eta_k y_{0,k}^\theta / \sum_{k=1}^{K} \eta_k$, defined as the weighted generalised mean, where each
weight is a function of the political influence. As before, the general proper-
ties of the alternative mechanisms are similar, but further progress requires
assumptions about the joint distribution of η_k and $y_{0,k}$, about which *a priori*
information is difficult to specify.

2.3   Conclusions

This chapter has investigated the choice of the composition of government
expenditure in simple static models, in terms of the outcome of majority
voting, the maximisation of a social welfare function which makes the value
judgements of a disinterested judge explicit, and stochastic voting in which
voters' biases play an important role. Choices were considered to be conditional on an exogenously fixed tax rate. The structures examined include a
transfer payment combined with a pure public good, and a transfer payment
with tax-financed education.

It was shown that, in each case, explicit solutions can be obtained for the
majority choice of expenditure components, and these were shown to depend

on a measure of inequality defined in terms of the ratio of the median to the arithmetic mean pre-tax income. A higher degree of skewness was found to be associated with a more redistributive expenditure structure (that is, relatively more revenue being devoted to a universal transfer payment or basic income). This corresponds to the property of existing models which focus on the determination of the tax rate, rather than the composition of expenditure, in models having only a redistributive transfer payment.

In the case of maximisation of a social welfare function, the median income is replaced by a welfare-weighted mean income, with weights depending on the degree of inequality aversion of the judge, though this does not provide a closed-form solution. However, it was shown that explicit solutions for the expenditure share can be approximated using an equally distributed income measure in place of the welfare-weighted mean income. The majority choice was consequently found to be approximately the same as the optimal choice in the case where the social welfare function displays constant relative inequality aversion of unity. The welfare-weighted mean income can, furthermore, be adapted to deal with cases of stochastic voting where maximisation of a support function has technical similarities with maximisation of a welfare function, though the interpretation is very different. The stochastic voting framework has the advantage, unlike simple majority voting, that it does not rely on single-peaked preferences. The outcome depends on other moments of the income distribution rather than simply the median.

When the allocation is between a transfer payment and expenditure on education, similar results were found to apply when comparing alternative choice mechanisms, except that instead of the distribution of income, the relevant distribution was of initial ability.

Despite the simplicity of the models, for example in terms of the specification of the degree of population heterogeneity and tax structure, they can nevertheless provide useful insights into the nature of the basic relationships involved. In particular, the relationship between expenditure shares and inequality, and the comparisons between alternative choice mechanisms, are seen to hinge on different measures of inequality, all based on the relative difference between arithmetic mean income and a measure of location. The following Parts of this book add further structure to these models.

Part II

Voting Models

Chapter 3

Transfer Payments and Public Goods

The previous chapter examined, as one of the frameworks considered, majority voting over the division between expenditure on public goods and on transfer payments. The analysis used the assumption that incomes are fixed and thus independent of the tax and expenditure policy. The present chapter extends that analysis by allowing the labour supply of each individual to be endogenous. In order to guide the specification of a relationship that can be estimated using information on a cross section of democratic countries, a simple model is constructed in which individuals with similar preferences, but differing abilities and thus wage rates, vote for government expenditure on a public good. As in the previous chapter, and discussed in Chapter 1, the choice is made conditional on the tax rate in a proportional income tax. Hence voting is over only one dimension. A sufficient condition for a majority voting equilibrium to exist is that preferences are single peaked, and this condition is satisfied in the present model.[1]

The resulting level of a transfer payment, in the form of a basic income, is given by the government's budget constraint. The framework of analysis

---

[1] In voting over the tax rate in models with a basic income and flat tax, it is known that preferences are not single-peaked. But a voting equilibrium exists if agent monotonicity holds, whereby the rankings of individuals are not affected by the tax structure; see Roberts (1977).

is entirely static, so that current government expenditure is financed only by current tax revenue. Despite the simplicity of the model, it is seen to provide useful insights into the various relationships involved in voting over the composition of expenditure.

The analysis contrasts with earlier studies which have tended to concentrate on the majority choice of transfer payments, and thus on the relationship between fundamental inequality in the wage rate distribution and desired redistribution of net income achieved through a tax and transfer system. Those studies are associated with the Romer (1975), Roberts (1977) and Meltzer–Richard (1981) framework involving majority voting over a linear tax.[2] Redistribution usually arises entirely from the self-interest of voters who balance the desire for a higher transfer payment against the limits on the government's ability to redistribute income, which are imposed by labour supply incentive effects.[3]

In the present model, the existence of expenditure on public goods, which affects individuals' utility directly, creates a further trade-off. The benefits of higher transfer payments, which (via individuals' budget constraints) allow the consumption of more goods and leisure, are balanced against the desire for public goods which enter utility functions but are subject to a tax price rather than a consumer price. The emphasis on choice of the composition of expenditure therefore differs from those studies which have introduced more sophistication into the Romer–Roberts–Meltzer–Richard framework in order to demonstrate that a higher degree of wage inequality need not necessarily be associated with a majority choice in favour of more redistribution. It is

---

[2]On voting over redistributive taxation see also Krusell and Rios-Rull (1999) and Azzimonti *et al.* (2006). See also the survey by Borck (2007), who gives special attention to models which modify the extent to which inequality may lead to a majority equilibrium involving higher taxation, and thus redistribution via a transfer payment.

[3]In the standard linear tax model, the majority voting equilibrium is characterised by equality between the elasticity of average gross earnings with respect to the tax rate and a measure of inequality of earnings, equal to 1 minus the ratio of median earnings to average earnings. This may be compared with the optimal tax result obtained by Tuomala (1985), where the median wage is replaced by a welfare-weighted wage.

found here that a preference for more redistribution – in terms of a greater share of public expenditure being devoted to transfer payments – does result from more inequality, though to a relatively small extent over the relevant range.[4] This relationship is illustrated using cross-sectional data on a group of democratic countries.

The basic model and framework of analysis are described in Section 6.2, which derives the indirect utility function of each individual, expressed in terms of expenditure on the public good and the given tax rate. Section 3.2 shows that the conditions for a majority voting equilibrium are satisfied, and generates closed-form solutions for public good expenditure and the implied transfer payment. The solutions depend on the ratio of median to arithmetic mean wage rates. The relevant relationships are investigated using numerical examples, in view of the high degree of nonlinearity involved in the analytical expressions, so that the relationships are not transparent. Section 3.3 extends the model by considering the potential effects of an altruistic desire for redistribution on the part of voters. An aversion on the part of voters for inequality in the distribution of net income is specified. A closed-form solution for the majority voting equilibrium is not available, but numerical results demonstrate relatively little sensitivity of the composition of expenditure to the degree of inequality aversion on the part of voters. In Section 3.4, the construction of a special cross-sectional dataset for democratic countries, along with estimation of the ratio of median to arithmetic mean wage rates, is described. The resulting data are then used in regression analyses using a specification based on the model.

---

[4] A modification to the Romer *et al.* framework, involving the composition of expenditure, was made by Moene and Wallerstein (2001). They considered separate redistributive and insurance motives for transfer payments, some of which are received only by those who do not work. They found that higher skewness of the wage distribution is associated with lower spending on insurance against income loss.

3.1   The Basic Model

This section derives individuals' preferences for public good expenditure, given the income tax rate. The direct utility function and optimal consumption and labour supply, for an individual who faces a given wage rate and tax rate and receives a non means-tested transfer payment, or basic income, are examined in Subsection 3.1.1. The government budget constraint, derived in Subsection 6.2.2, means that a degree of freedom in policy choices is lost and the value of the unconditional transfer payment is determined for a given tax rate and level of public good provision. Hence, as shown in Subsection 3.1.3, the indirect utility function can be expressed in terms of public good expenditure and the tax rate in this static model.[5] Earnings are the only source of income and tax revenue is devoted only to the provision of the pure public good and the transfer payment.

3.1.1   Individual Consumption and Labour Supply

Each individual is assumed to derive utility from consumption, c, leisure, h, and the public good.[6] A judgement must be made regarding the way this is modelled. Since a pure public good is by definition non-excludable, all individuals are assumed to consume the same amount, Q_G. In view of its non-rival nature a standard consumer price cannot be modelled. However, the cost of the public good enters each individual's budget constraint through the fact that it must be tax-financed, so that individuals contribute in proportion to their earnings. In addition, a higher level of the public good involves a

---

[5]The model therefore ignores the effect of government policies on saving. In a dynamic context, complexities can arise from changes in the identity of the median voter and inter-generational conflict, commitment and time consistency. On dynamic voting models, see Krusell and Rios-Rull (1999), Tabellini and Alesina (1990), Hassler *et al.* (2005), Azzimonti *et al.* (2006) and Hassler *et al.* (2007).

[6]Alternative approaches are clearly possible. For example, Tridimas (2001) constructed a probabilistic voting model (individuals vote for parties, where the probability function is based on preferences). This involved demand functions for a range of private and public goods, where the unit cost of each public good was treated as its price.

trade-off, through the government's budget constraint whereby expenditures are financed on a pay-as-you-go basis and the tax rate is fixed, in that it requires a reduction in the size of the transfer payment. The effective 'price' of the public good is reflected in the associated partial loss of transfers and, since this affects labour supply, it also influences the amount of tax paid.

The direct utility function is assumed to be Cobb–Douglas, so that (omitting individual subscripts):

$$U = c^\alpha h^\beta Q_G^{1-\alpha-\beta} \tag{3.1}$$

Suppose that individuals have similar preferences but different productivity levels and therefore wage rates, w. Although all individuals consume the same amount of the public good and have similar preferences, higher-wage individuals experience higher marginal utility in view of the multiplicative nature of utility functions. The public good is assumed only to enter individuals' utility functions; that is, it does not affect their productivity. The model has the property of 'hierarchical adherence' (or 'agent monotonicity'), so that the tax rate does not affect the ranking of individuals by income. High-wage individuals are consistently better off in terms of utility, so there is incentive compatibility.

The choice of Q_G is not determined at the individual level, since individuals cannot be excluded, but is determined along with the tax system via a democratic process. The price of private goods is normalised to unity, so that consumption and net earnings are equal. Let p denote the cost per unit of the public good which, in this partial equilibrium framework, is considered to be fixed. Suppose there is an unconditional and untaxed transfer payment of b per individual. There is a simple proportional income tax, with the rate, t, so that the price of leisure is $w(1-t)$. Therefore the form of each individual's budget constraint is:

$$c = w(1-h)(1-t) + b \tag{3.2}$$

The transfer payment per person is restricted to be positive, so that, for example, public goods expenditure cannot be financed from a poll tax. Borge and Rattsø (2004), in contrast, examine the finance of public services using a combination of a progressive property tax and a regressive poll tax. However, they do not consider income taxes and thus do not allow for labour supply variations.

Define full income, M, as the net income obtained if all the individual's endowment of one unit of time is devoted to work, so that:

$$M = w(1-t) + b \tag{3.3}$$

The budget constraint can thus be expressed as:

$$c + hw(1-t) = M \tag{3.4}$$

Using the standard properties of the Cobb–Douglas utility function, the demand for private goods and leisure can be written as:

$$c = \left(\frac{\alpha}{\alpha+\beta}\right) M = \alpha' M \tag{3.5}$$

$$h = \left(\frac{\beta}{\alpha+\beta}\right) \frac{M}{w(1-t)} = \beta' \frac{M}{w(1-t)} \tag{3.6}$$

where $h < 1$, that is the individual works, if the wage rate exceeds a wage threshold, $w_{\min}$, such that:

$$w_{\min} = \frac{\beta'}{1-\beta'} \frac{b}{1-t} \tag{3.7}$$

Consequently, gross earnings, y, of workers are given by:

$$
\begin{aligned}
y &= w(1-h) \\
  &= w(1-\beta') - \frac{b\beta'}{(1-t)}
\end{aligned} \tag{3.8}
$$

and are a linear function of the wage rate.

3.1.2 The Government Budget Constraint

The government budget constraint requires that total revenue from the proportional income tax, equal to $t \sum_{i=1}^{n} y_i$ for a population of n individuals, is sufficient to finance the transfer payment and the public good, $nb + pQ_G$. Hence:

$$b + \frac{pQ_G}{n} = t\bar{y} \tag{3.9}$$

where $\bar{y}$ denotes arithmetic mean earnings. Consider average earnings in the case where not all individuals have a wage level above $w_{\min} = \frac{\beta'}{1-\beta'} \frac{b}{1-t}$, so that some individuals do not work. Using $y_i = w_i(1 - \beta') - \frac{b\beta'}{(1-t)}$, average earnings are:

$$\bar{y} = \frac{1}{n} \sum_{w > w_{\min}} \left\{ w_i (1 - \beta') - \frac{b\beta'}{(1 - t)} \right\} \tag{3.10}$$

Let $F_1 (w_{\min})$ and $F (w_{\min})$ denote respectively the proportion of total wage (rates) and the proportion of people with $w < w_{\min}$. These correspond to the ordinate and abscissa of the Lorenz curve of wage rates at the point where $w = w_{\min}$. Then:

$$\bar{y} = \bar{w} (1 - \beta') \{1 - F_1 (w_{\min})\} - \frac{b\beta'}{(1 - t)} \{1 - F (w_{\min})\} \tag{3.11}$$

where $\bar{w}$ denotes the arithmetic mean wage rate. This expression gives rise to considerable complexities. The analysis is simplified by the assumption that $w_i > w_{\min}$ for all individuals, implying that everyone works. Hence setting F_1 and F equal to zero gives average income of:

$$\bar{y} = \bar{w}(1 - \beta') - \frac{b\beta'}{(1 - t)} \tag{3.12}$$

The effect of having some non-workers would be to reduce the median voter's preferred ratio of the social transfer to the public good per person, in view of the greater incentive effects of higher transfer payments. However, the basic form of relationships would be unchanged.

By substituting (6.17) in (3.9), it is possible to express b in terms of average earnings, the tax rate and G, as:

$$b = \frac{t\bar{w}(1-\beta') - \frac{pQ_G}{n}}{1 + \beta'\frac{t}{(1-t)}}$$

(3.13)

This constraint involves the loss of a degree of freedom in policy choices, so that voting is effectively over just one dimension.

3.1.3   Indirect Utility

The indirect utility function, V, is obtained by substituting the solutions for c and h given above into the direct utility function, so that:

$$V = \left(\alpha'^\alpha\beta'^\beta\right)(w(1-t))^\alpha\left(\frac{M}{w(1-t)}\right)^{\alpha+\beta}Q_G^{1-\alpha-\beta}$$

(3.14)

Furthermore, writing:

$$k = \alpha'^\alpha\beta'^\beta\left(w(1-t)\right)^\alpha$$

(3.15)

V becomes:

$$V = k\left(\frac{M}{w(1-t)}\right)^{\alpha+\beta}Q_G^{1-\alpha-\beta}$$

(3.16)

Indirect utility is therefore a function of, among other things, b and Q_G. The government's budget constraint implies, as shown above, that these cannot be chosen independently. In the present approach, individuals are assumed to be fully aware of this constraint, so that voting is over only one of the two expenditure levels, with the other being clearly implied. In examining the properties of the model, emphasis is placed below on the ratio of expenditure levels $R = b/(pQ_G/n)$.[7] Thus substituting (6.18) into (3.3) gives full income in terms of Q_G as:

$$M = w(1-t)\left\{1 + \left(\frac{\bar{w}}{w}\right)\left(\frac{1-t}{t} + \beta'\right)^{-1}\left(1 - \beta' - \frac{pQ_G}{nt\bar{w}}\right)\right\}$$

(3.17)

---

[7]It is not possible to express indirect utility in terms either of R or expenditure proportions. If $\xi = b/t\bar{y}$, then $(G/n)/t\bar{y} = 1 - \xi$; these are easily obtained from R, since $\xi = 1/(1+R)$.

and substituting this expression into (7.7), V can be expressed in terms of the two policy variables t and Q_G, the arithmetic mean wage rate in relation to the individual's wage rate, and preference parameters.

3.2 Collective Choice

This section examines policy decision regarding the composition of expenditure – the transfer payment relative to public good expenditure per person – in the case where choices are based on the majority voting outcome. Individuals are thus assumed to have sufficient information about the government's budget constraint so that the full implications for b of any policy choice of t and Q_G are known.

3.2.1 Majority Voting

Voting is assumed to concern the level of Q_G for a given tax rate t, so that one dimension only is involved.[8] It is well known that a majority voting equilibrium exists, in which the median voter dominates, if all individuals have single-peaked preferences. In the present context this is guaranteed if the relationship between V and Q_G is concave for all individuals, so that:

$$\frac{\partial^2 V}{\partial Q_G^2} < 0 \tag{3.18}$$

By differentiating (7.7) twice with respect to Q_G, it is possible to show that this requirement is satisfied for all individuals. Hence the choice of Q_G, for given t, is based on the preferences of the median voter who, in the present model, is the individual with the median wage. Letting an m subscript refer to the median voter, V_m is obtained by substitution into (7.7) and (6.13), with (3.17), and majority choice satisfies the first-order condition:

$$\frac{\partial V_m}{\partial Q_{G,m}} = 0 \tag{3.19}$$

---

[8]It would be possible to use the present framework to examine the case where a two-stage voting procedure is used, in which individuals vote over the tax rate, knowing the outcome of a conditional vote over government expenditure on public goods.

It can be shown that:

$$\frac{\partial V_m}{\partial Q_{G,m}} = k_m \left(\frac{M_m}{w_m(1-t)}\right)^{\alpha+\beta} Q_{G,m}^{-(\alpha+\beta)}$$

$$\times \left((1-\alpha-\beta) - \frac{pQ_{G,m}}{n}\frac{(\alpha+\beta)M_m^{-1}}{(1+\beta'\frac{t}{1-t})}\right)$$

$$= 0 \qquad\qquad (3.20)$$

Hence the term in curly brackets in (3.20) must be zero and, substituting for M_m, this gives:

$$\frac{pQ_{G,m}}{n}\frac{(\alpha+\beta)}{(1+\beta'\frac{t}{1-t})}\left(w_m(1-t) + \frac{t\bar{w}(1-\beta') - \frac{pQ_{G,m}}{n}}{(1+\beta'\frac{t}{1-t})}\right)^{-1} = (1-\alpha-\beta)$$

$$(3.21)$$

which, after some manipulation, can be solved to give $pQ_{G,m}/n$ as:

$$\frac{pQ_{G,m}}{n} = (1-\alpha-\beta)\{w_m + t(1-\beta')(\bar{w} - w_m)\} \qquad (3.22)$$

The left hand side of this expression represents the expenditure on the public good per capita. This shows that it increases linearly with t.

The resulting value of b_m is given by appropriate substitution into (6.18). For positive values of the social transfer, the given tax rate must exceed the value, $t_{\min}$, where:

$$t_{\min} = \left(\frac{1}{1-\beta'}\right)\left[1 + \left(\frac{\bar{w}}{w_m}\right)\left(\frac{\alpha+\beta}{1-(\alpha+\beta)}\right)\right]^{-1} \qquad (3.23)$$

In addition, the tax rate is also subject to an upper limit, given the assumption that all individuals work, so that for sensible values the social transfer must remain sufficiently below the minimum wage. Even for a symmetric distribution of wage rates, it can be shown that $b_m > 0$ if $t > (1-\alpha-\beta)(\alpha+\beta)/\alpha$. Hence, with sufficient revenue the median voter would prefer some redistributive transfer payments in addition to the tax-financed public good.

The focus here is on the ratio of the transfer payment to the expenditure on the public good per person, rather than absolute values. It can be shown that this ratio, $R_m = b_m / (pQ_{G,m}/n)$, is given by:

$$R_m = \frac{1-t}{1-t(1-\beta')} \times$$

$$\left[\left(\frac{1}{1-\alpha-\beta} \right) \left\{ \frac{w_m}{\bar{w}} \left(\frac{1}{t(1-\beta')} - 1 \right) + 1 \right\}^{-1} - 1 \right] \quad (3.24)$$

This result shows that the ratio of the transfer payment to public goods expenditure per person depends, among other things, on the ratio of median wage rate to average wage rate. In a positively skewed distribution this latter ratio is of course less than unity. In other words the composition of government expenditure is determined by the skewness of the distribution of wage rates. For example, any growth in productivity, with no change in skewness, has no direct effect on the majority choice of the composition of expenditure.

An increase in the ratio of the median wage to the average wage (where the former is less than the latter) implies that the positive skewness, and hence degree of inequality of the distribution, decreases. Strictly, inequality and skewness refer to different concepts. However, in the context of positively skewed distributions, they are closely related: for example in lognormal distributions, both depend only on the variance of logarithms. It is standard in the literature on voting models to refer to the ratio of median to mean income in terms of inequality. It can be shown that for all values, $\partial R_m / \partial (w_m/\bar{w}) < 0$, and the second derivative, $\partial^2 R_m / \partial (w_m/\bar{w})^2 > 0$. Hence, more equality reduces R_m at a decreasing rate, while higher inequality causes government expenditure to move towards a more redistributive policy with relatively larger transfer payments, compared with expenditure on public goods.

An increase in the average wage rate, with an unchanged median, clearly reduces $w_m/\bar{w}$ and therefore increases inequality, leading to an increase in relative and absolute expenditure on the transfer payment, while also increasing expenditure on the public good. An increase in the median wage rate, with an unchanged arithmetic mean wage, has a positive effect on public goods and total expenditure but, because it involves a reduction in inequality, reduces the absolute social transfer and the ratio of the transfer to public good expenditure.

It can be shown that $\partial^2 R_m/\partial t^2 < 0$, so that there is a concave relationship between R_m and t. The first derivative $\partial R_m/\partial t$ is positive for low values of t and negative for relatively higher values. This is dominated by a concave relationship between b_m and t, given the linear relationship between pQ_G and t mentioned above. The concavity of R_m with respect to t is therefore strongly affected by the labour supply effects of taxes and transfers.

A property of the expression for R_m in (6.24) is that the cost per unit of the public good per person does not appear on the right hand side. Thus in determining expenditure shares, neither n nor p appears. Indeed, the elasticity of R_m with respect to p is -1. For this reason it is often convenient below to discuss results in terms of the majority choice of expenditure, $G_m = pQ_{G,m}$, rather than in terms of $Q_{G,m}$. This property of the model arises from the use of the homothetic Cobb–Douglas utility function, which in the standard demand context is known to imply constant expenditure shares, independent of prices. Here it ensures that the expenditure share does not depend on the scale of the economy, either in terms of the absolute income levels or population size and, importantly, the economy does not move into a situation in which only one good (either the private or the public good) is consumed. The choice of utility function in models of this kind was discussed in Chapter 2 above.

3.2.2 Numerical Examples

This subsection provides numerical examples of the sensitivity of majority voting outcomes to variations in selected parameters of the model, in particular the tax rate, t, and the ratio of the median wage to the arithmetic mean wage, $w_m/\bar{w}$. In addition to illustrating characteristics of the framework which are not immediately obvious, it helps to motivate the specification used for empirical work in Section 3.4 below. A set of benchmark parameters are shown in Table 3.1. The preference parameters of $\alpha = 0.48$ and $\beta = 0.4$ are chosen so that, with $t = 0.35$, the proportion of time devoted to labour supply is sensible. Also, these preference parameters and tax rate give $R_m = 0.64$, which is close to the average value of 0.63 for the sample of 24 democratic countries. See Table 3.2 in Subsection 3.4.1 for data on the average value of R for a sample of democratic countries. The arithmetic mean and median wage rate, expressed in annual terms, are \$70000 and \$60000 respectively. These are consistent with a lognormal distribution with mean and standard deviation of logarithms of hourly wage rates of 2.87 and 0.56: these are similar to those for Australia. Using the properties of the lognormal distribution, the arithmetic mean and the median hourly wage rate are $20.64 = \exp(2.87 + 0.56/2)$ and $17.64 = \exp(2.87)$: see Aitchison and Brown (1957). Furthermore, the maximum hours per day are set at 13 to obtain annual equivalents.

Table 3.1: Benchmark Parameter Values

Parameter	Value
α	0.48
β	0.40
t	0.35
$\bar{w}$	70000
w_l	7350
n	20×10^6

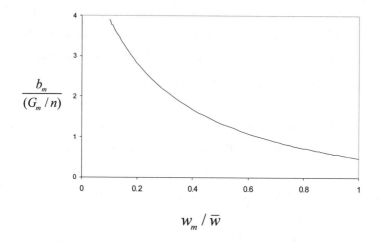

Figure 3.1: Variation in $b_m/(G_m/n)$ with $w_m/\bar{w}$

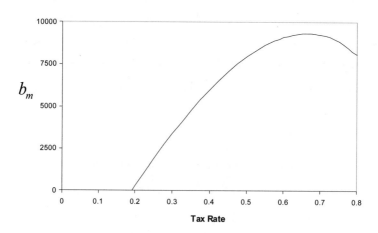

Figure 3.2: Variation in Basic Income with Tax Rate

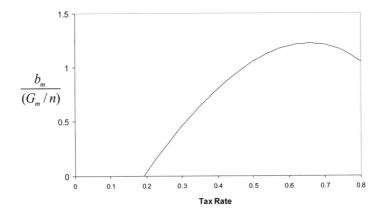

Figure 3.3: Variation in Expenditure Share with Tax Rate

Figure 3.1 shows the relationship between $b_m/(G_m/n)$ and $w_m/\bar{w}$, given the other benchmark values. It illustrates the fact that the majority choice of $b_m/(G_m/n)$ falls at a decreasing rate as inequality falls, that is, as $w_m/\bar{w}$ increases. The diagram suggests that in empirical work a specification involving the reciprocal of $w_m/\bar{w}$ would be useful. Importantly, it shows that the extent to which R_m falls as equality increases is expected to be small in the relevant range of values: as shown below, empirical orders of magnitude for $w_m/\bar{w}$ are around 0.8, where the profile is relatively flat.

Figure 3.2 shows the variation in the majority choice of the basic income as the tax rate (considered here to be exogenous) increases. In contrast with the linear variation in G_m, b_m shows the familiar inverted U shape. Figure 3.3, showing the choice of R_m as t varies, displays a similar pattern, clearly dominated by that of b_m.

3.3 Voters Care About Inequality

This section considers how majority voting outcomes may change when individuals care about the inequality of net income. It is assumed that individual labour supply and consumption decisions continue to be made selfishly according to the maximisation of $U = c^\alpha h^\beta Q_G^{1-\alpha-\beta}$ as above, so that the expressions for optimal values of c and h, along with the form of the government budget constraint, are unchanged. However, equality matters when individuals vote over the level of the public good.[9] This implies, for example, that high-wage individuals do not moderate their labour supply in order to reduce earnings inequality, but vote for some redistribution through the tax system.

Suppose the indirect utility function is augmented by an additive term containing the coefficient of variation of net income, η_z, as follows:

$$V_i = k_i \left(\frac{M_i}{w_i(1-t)} \right)^{\alpha+\beta} Q_G^{1-\alpha-\beta} - \lambda \left(1+\eta_z\right)^\xi \qquad (3.25)$$

Here, λ and ξ reflect the aversion to inequality. When λ is zero, individuals do not care about inequality of net income when they vote.

Net income of individual type i is $(1-t)y_i + b$ and substituting for y_i from (7.6) gives:

$$z_i = (1-\beta')\left(w_i(1-t) + b\right) \qquad (3.26)$$

Arithmetic mean net income is therefore $\bar{z} = (1-\beta')\left(\bar{w}(1-t) + b\right)$. The variance of net income, σ_z^2, is:

$$\begin{aligned} \sigma_z^2 &= E(z_i - \bar{z})^2 \\ &= (1-\beta')^2(1-t)^2\sigma_w^2 \end{aligned} \qquad (3.27)$$

where σ_w^2 is the variance of the wage rate distribution. The coefficient of variation of net income is therefore expressed as:

$$\eta_z = \frac{\sigma_z}{\bar{z}} = \eta_w \left\{ 1 + \frac{b}{\bar{w}(1-t)} \right\}^{-1} \qquad (3.28)$$

---

[9] This type of assumption is also made by Galasso (2003), although in his approach individuals have a self-centred inequality aversion in that they are concerned with their own position relative to some reference group. A self-centred approach is also explored by Tyran and Sausgruber (2006).

where $\eta_w = \sigma_w/\bar{w}$ is the coefficient of variation of wages.

As in the case where $\lambda = 0$, individuals are assumed to vote on the level of public good expenditure, with a fixed tax rate, where the transfer payment is determined by the government's budget constraint. Therefore, the policy space is unidimensional. Concavity of the indirect utility function again guarantees the single-peakedness of preferences over Q_G. It can be shown that the second derivative, $\frac{d^2 V_i}{dQ_G^2}$, is unequivocally negative so that the relationship between V and Q_G is concave. Consequently, the median voter is decisive. Setting $dV_m/dQ_G = 0$, it is found that the majority voting equilibrium is the root of:

$$\Phi = (1 - \alpha - \beta) - \Psi \tag{3.29}$$

where:

$$\Phi = \frac{pQ_{G,m}}{n} \frac{(\alpha + \beta)}{(1 + \beta' \frac{t}{1-t})} \left(w_m(1-t) + \frac{t\bar{w}(1-\beta') - \frac{pQ_{G,m}}{n}}{(1 + \beta' \frac{t}{1-t})} \right)^{-1} \tag{3.30}$$

$$\Psi = \frac{\lambda \xi \eta_w \left(1 + \eta_w \left(1 + \frac{b}{\bar{w}(1-t)}\right)^{-1}\right)^{\xi - 1} \left(1 + \frac{b}{\bar{w}(1-t)}\right)^{-2} pQ_{G,m}^{(\alpha+\beta)}}{\bar{w}(1-t)n \left(1 + \beta'(\frac{t}{1-t})\right) k_m \left(\frac{M_m}{w_m(1-t)}\right)^{\alpha+\beta}} \tag{3.31}$$

Equation (3.29) cannot be solved explicitly for $Q_{G,m}$. However, some insight into this can be obtained by recognising that Φ is the same as the left hand side of equation (3.21) above, when $\lambda = 0$, and is an increasing convex function of $Q_{G,m}$. In addition, $(1 - \alpha - \beta) - \Psi$ is decreasing in $Q_{G,m}$. The profiles of Φ and $(1 - \alpha - \beta) - \Psi$ are shown in Figure 3.4, where it is convenient to work in terms of $G_m = pQ_{G,m}$ rather than $Q_{G,m}$. The voting equilibrium for $\lambda = 0$ is at point A in the figure, and for $\lambda \neq 0$ it is at point B. Clearly a concern for inequality reduces the majority choice of G and increases the transfer payment, b, for a fixed t.

As G_m/n increases, the amount available for the transfer payment falls so that the tax and transfer system is less redistributive. However, it is found that over a wide range of G_m/n, there is relatively little variation in η_z.

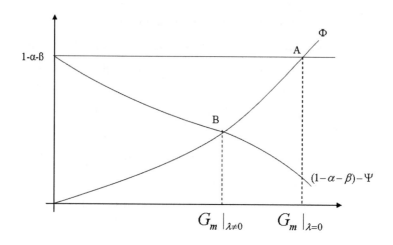

Figure 3.4: Equilibrium With and Without Inequality Aversion

3.3.1   Numerical Examples

Although an analytical result is not available for (3.29), numerical methods can be used to solve the nonlinear equation for the majority voting outcome. Again, given the emphasis here on expenditure shares, Figures 3.5 and 3.6 show the median voter's choice of expenditure on public goods, G_m, and the transfer payment, b_m, for alternative values of η and ξ.

From these two diagrams it is clear that, as expected, raising the degree of inequality aversion reduces the majority choice of the share of public good expenditure. However, the reduction is quite small over a wide range of ξ, except for the highest values of λ. In the model, labour supply incentive effects impose a strong constraint on the ability to redistribute income (that is, to raise b for a given tax rate, by reducing G). Furthermore, the public good enters the utility function directly, so for the median voter there is a clear cost of reducing inequality which cannot be shifted to higher-income earners (and hence higher taxpayers).

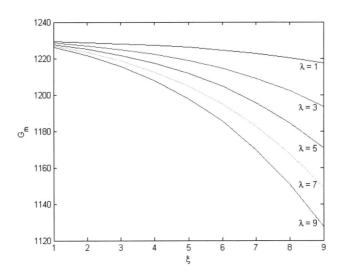

Figure 3.5: Inequality Aversion and Choice of G_m

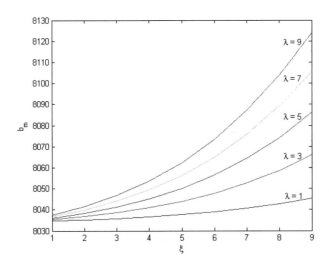

Figure 3.6: Inequality Aversion and Choice of Basic Income

3.4   Data and Empirical Results

This section uses cross-sectional data for a sample of democracies to investigate the variation in the ratio of transfer payments to public good expenditure per capita. Such an exercise must inevitably be highly tentative. Clearly, voting in practice does not correspond to the simple model examined above, voting arrangements vary across different democracies, and public expenditure and reported data are not neatly divided into public good and transfer components. A major problem is clearly raised by the data requirements as it is possible only to obtain approximations to the variables needed. While it may be thought that time series data for particular countries would be more appropriate, there would be insufficient variation in $w_m/\bar{w}$, a point also stressed by Moene and Wallerstein (2001, p. 872). The construction of the sample is described in Subsection 3.4.1 and the regression results are reported in Subsection 3.4.2.

3.4.1   The Data

The first question regarding the data concerns the countries to be included in the analysis. For example, a simple selection of OECD countries would not be appropriate as it is important to include similar levels of democracy. The Polity IV (2007) dataset provides, for each country, an index of democracy. This index varies between 0 and 10, the latter representing the highest level of democracy. It was decided to include those countries with an index from 9 to 10 since the year 2000. These include parliamentary, presidential and semi-presidential countries. The resulting 24 democratic countries included in the sample are: Australia, Austria, Belgium, Canada, Cyprus, Denmark, Finland, France, Germany, Greece, Hungary, Ireland, Italy, Lithuania, Mauritius, Netherlands, Norway, Portugal, Slovenia, Spain, Sweden, United Kingdom, United States and Uruguay. This sample does not contain all countries with an index of 9 and 10. Some countries, such as Japan, New Zealand,

Papua New Guinea and Trinidad and Tobago, are excluded because the data are not available. Furthermore, Costa Rica, the Czech Republic, Israel, Jamaica and Switzerland had to be excluded because the data were incomplete.

In practice there is not always a clear distinction between pure public and private goods. Using the *Government Finance Statistics Yearbook* (2000–2006), public good expenditure was obtained as the sum of expenditure by governments on the following categories: defence, public order and safety, economic affairs, environmental protection, health, education and social protection. However, part of expenditure on education and health clearly consists of publicly provided private goods rather than pure public goods. The results reported below are for the case where one third of expenditure on education and health is considered to be expenditure on public goods. Experiments were carried out using different proportions but these had little effect on the results. Although it is not possible to obtain an independent measure of the cost per unit of pure public goods, this is not necessary since the analysis is carried out using the ratio of expenditure shares, R, as dependent variable.

A difficulty also arises with the measurement of transfer payments. These are modelled above as a basic income, but in practice countries vary in the type of transfer payment system in operation. In the following empirical analysis, transfers are measured as including subsidies and social benefits. Grants to foreign governments, international organisations and other government units are excluded. Again the data are taken from the *Government Finance Statistics Yearbook* (2000–2006).

Governments in this model finance the expenditure by income tax revenue. In practice several taxes are used, with varying marginal rates. The tax rate variable was constructed as the ratio of tax revenue to GDP. The sources for data on tax revenue and GDP are *Government Finance Statistics Yearbook* (2000–2006) and WDI (2007) respectively. Tax revenue refers to compulsory transfers to the central government for public purposes. It contains taxes and social contributions. The group of taxes includes: tax on income, profit, capital gain; payroll and workforce; properties; goods and services; international trade and transactions, and 'other taxes'.

A central variable in the model is the ratio of the median wage to the average wage rate, $w_m/\bar{w}$. Unfortunately it is not possible to obtain data on wage rate distributions for the different countries. It is necessary to use a proxy, equal to the ratio of median to average income. The relationship between the different measures can be examined as follows. As above, let y, w and h denote earning, wage rate and hours of work respectively. Then $y = wh$ and $\log y = \log w + \log h$. Let μ_y and σ_y^2 denote the mean and variance of logarithms of y, and similarly for w. The means of logarithms are additive, so that $\mu_y = \mu_w + \mu_h$, and for the variance:

$$\sigma_y^2 = \sigma_w^2 + \sigma_h^2 + 2\sigma_{wh} \tag{3.32}$$

If w and h are lognormally distributed, y is also lognormally distributed and from the properties of the lognormal, the median and mean are:

$$y_m = \exp(\mu_w + \mu_h) \tag{3.33}$$

$$\bar{y} = \exp\left(\mu_w + \mu_h + \frac{1}{2}\sigma_y^2\right) \tag{3.34}$$

Then the earnings ratio is:

$$\frac{y_m}{\bar{y}} = \exp\left(-\frac{1}{2}(\sigma_w^2 + \sigma_h^2 + 2\sigma_{wh})\right) \tag{3.35}$$

while the wages ratio is:

$$\frac{w_m}{\bar{w}} = \exp\left(-\frac{1}{2}\sigma_w^2\right) \tag{3.36}$$

Hence:

$$\frac{w_m}{\bar{w}} = \frac{y_m}{\bar{y}}\psi \tag{3.37}$$

where:

$$\psi = \exp\left(-\frac{1}{2}\sigma_h^2 - \sigma_{wh}\right) \tag{3.38}$$

The question of importance is how ψ varies. The term σ_h^2 can reasonably be assumed to be small, so the question is whether the covariance σ_{wh} is likely to vary much between countries. Unfortunately suitable data are not available, but the above suggests that the relevant ratio of earnings can be a reasonable approximation for the ratio of median to mean wage rates.

Information on the distribution of income for the countries in the sample was obtained from the WDI (2007) and World Income Inequality Database (2007). The latter database was used to obtain data for Australia, the Czech Republic, Denmark, France, Mauritius, the Netherlands, Portugal, Slovenia and the United Kingdom. Unfortunately the income concept varies between countries. In some cases it is gross income while in others it is a net income measure.[10] This means that it was not possible to include in the following regression analyses a separate variable for the inequality of net income. However, the previous analysis has found that any independent effect of an aversion to inequality is likely to be small. Furthermore, the unit of analysis varies between the individual and the household.

Information on inequality is in the form of the Gini index, so that a transformation between the Gini measure and the required ratio must be used, as follows. It has been shown above that for a lognormal distribution with mean and variance of logarithms of μ and σ^2, the proxy for $w_m/\bar{w}$ is:

$$\frac{w_m}{\bar{w}} = \frac{e^{\mu}}{e^{\mu+\sigma^2/2}} = e^{-\frac{\sigma^2}{2}} \tag{3.39}$$

and this depends only on the variance of logarithms of income. The latter can be obtained from the Gini coefficient, $Gini$, using the lognormal property that:

$$Gini = 2N\left(\frac{\sigma}{\sqrt{2}}\right) - 1 \tag{3.40}$$

where $N\left(\sigma/\sqrt{2}\right)$ is the area contained by a standard normal distribution

---

[10]Lind (2005, pp. 116-117) discusses the possibility of a source of negative bias when net incomes are used.

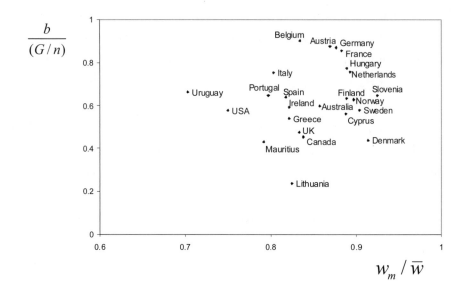

Figure 3.7: Plot of Expenditure Share Against Wage Ratio

below $\sigma/\sqrt{2}$. Hence:

$$\sigma = \sqrt{2}N^{-1}\left(\frac{Gini + 1}{2}\right) \tag{3.41}$$

where N^{-1} is the inverse function.[11]

For most countries, the Gini index is available only for selected years. Hence, the average, from available data between 2000 and 2005, was used to calculate the ratio of median to mean wage. Similarly, averages of available government expenditures and revenue over the same period were used. It was not possible to build a consistent dataset involving each of a number of consecutive years for the relevant countries.

Before reporting regression results is it useful to consider the scatter relating R and $w_m/\bar{w}$, shown in Figure 5.4. This shows substantial variation in R conditional on the wage ratio, which is expected not only because of

---

[11] Moene and Wallerstein (2001, pp. 867-868) also used earnings data and estimated the variance of log-earnings using the ratio of the ninth to the first decile, along with the assumption of lognormality.

Table 3.2: Averages of Variables for Country Groups

Group		$b/(G/n)$	t	$w_m/\bar{w}$
All	Average	0.630	0.369	0.847
	Coeff. of Variation	0.257	0.209	0.064
European	Average	0.730	0.433	0.885
	Coeff. of Variation	0.213	0.096	0.025
Non-European	Average	0.558	0.324	0.819
	Coeff. of Variation	0.228	0.196	0.066

the differences in t which cannot be represented in the same diagram, but also for reasons given above, namely that the model is clearly too simple to capture expenditure choices precisely. The diagram suggests several points. First it may be useful to investigate a role for a dummy variable relating to (continental) European countries. Second, the wage ratios are in the range from about 0.7 to a little below 0.95. Comparison with Figure 3.1 suggests that only a small average response of R to variations in $w_m/\bar{w}$ is likely. Table 3.2 provides a summary of the data in the form of means and coefficients of variation of the relevant variables. Clearly the (continental) European countries have average values of both $b/(G/n)$ and t which are noticeably above those of other countries, which also have less inequality.[12]

It would be useful to examine the specification using a sample of non-democratic countries. This is not possible because of data limitations. However, from *Government Finance Statistics* (2000–2006) comparable information on $b/(G/n)$ for Bahrain, Bhutan, China, Jordan, Kuwait and Oman were obtained. The average ratio was found to be 0.178, which is substantially lower than that of the countries shown in Table 3.2, and the coefficient of variation was 0.77, which is much higher than for all democratic countries included.

[12] As an experiment it was decided to check the regression results, reported below, if Uruguay and Lithuania were omitted in turn. There was in each case no effect on the signs of variables, though a small reduction in the standard errors was found.

3.4.2 Regression Results

Despite the highly nonlinear nature of the expression for $R = b/(G/n)$ in equation (6.24), the numerical examples suggest that it is appropriate to regress measures of R on the inverse of (proxies for) $w_m/\bar{w}$, along with t and t-squared. Furthermore, equation (6.24) suggests that it would be useful to include an interaction term, allowing for $d\left(b/(G/n)\right)/d\left(w_m/\bar{w}\right)$ to depend on t. Inspection of Figure 5.4 also suggests that a dummy variable for European countries may be appropriate.

Table 3.3: Regression Results: Dependent Variable: $b/(G/n)$

		$\frac{1}{\left(\frac{w_m}{\bar{w}}\right)}$	t	t^2	$\frac{t}{\left(\frac{w_m}{\bar{w}}\right)}$	Eur	Cons	R^2	F
1.	Coeff.	0.70	2.15	−0.85			−0.87	0.32	3.16
	t-stat	1.38	0.74	−0.22			−0.92		
2.	Coeff.	1.03	3.95	−4.31		0.19	−1.51	0.45	3.94
	t-stat	2.10	1.41	−1.08		2.14	−1.64		
3.	Coeff.	−0.25	−2.13	−2.65	4.05	0.21	0.25	0.46	3.12
	t-stat	−0.12	−0.20	−0.54	0.60	2.18	0.08		
4.	Coeff.	0.88	0.99			0.15	−0.84	0.42	4.83
	t-stat	1.86	1.76			1.86	−1.23		

Alternative regression results are reported in Table 3.3 for four alternative specifications. Importantly the above analysis suggests that $\partial R/\partial\left(w_m/\bar{w}\right)$ should be negative for all values of $\left(w_m/\bar{w}\right)$, implying that $\partial R/\partial\left(1/\left(w_m/\bar{w}\right)\right)$ should be positive. This is confirmed in all cases, remembering that in specification number 3, which contains an interaction term, the slope also depends on t.[13] Hence, these results illustrate a prediction of the model that a reduction in inequality, that is an increase in $\left(w_m/\bar{w}\right)$, is associated with a reduction in the transfer payment relative to public good expenditure. But, again as expected, this effect is relatively small. The results also illustrate the property of the model that $b/(G/n)$ has an inverse U-shaped relationship

---

[13] In specification 2, the ratio, R, reaches a peak for a tax rate of 0.46. Without the dummy variable, this value would exceed unity.

with t. Transfer payments initially increase with t, but over the higher ranges of t transfers are reduced relative to public good expenditure as a result of the negative incentive effects of further increases in the tax rate. The European dummy variable is seen to play a significant role. The addition of the interaction term, while suggested by the model, has the usual effect with such terms in that it increases the standard errors associated with other variables, as a result of the increased correlation between 'independent' variables in the regression.

This empirical finding, that a more redistributive policy (higher transfer expenditure relative to public goods) is associated with higher inequality, may be compared with those studies which find – based on a quite different model of voting over a linear tax – that higher redistributive taxation is not consistently associated with higher inequality: see the survey by Borck (2007). The present approach instead takes the size of government (the tax rate) as given and examines the resulting composition of expenditure.

3.5 Conclusions

This chapter has modelled the ratio of transfer payments to expenditure on public goods in democracies as the outcome of majority voting. A simple model was constructed in which individuals with similar preferences, but differing abilities and thus wages, vote for government expenditure on a public good, for a given proportional tax rate. Hence voting is over only one dimension and a majority voting equilibrium is shown to exist. The resulting level of a transfer payment, in the form of a basic income, is obtained from the government's budget constraint. Comparisons were made between the case where voters act entirely selfishly and where they have an aversion to net income inequality, although their private consumption and labour supply decisions are assumed to be made independently of the income distribution.

In the case where voters do not care about the income distribution, an explicit closed-form solution was found for the ratio of transfers to public good expenditure per person, expressed in terms of the ratio of the median to the arithmetic mean wage and the given tax rate. In view of the nonlinearity of this relationship, and the difficulty of obtaining a solution when inequality aversion is relevant, numerical examples were presented to illustrate the basic properties of the models.

The numerical results provided useful insights into the various relationships involved, suggesting that the ratio of transfers to public goods expenditure per person can be expressed in terms of the reciprocal of the ratio of the median to the mean wage, and is a quadratic function of the tax rate. Data for 24 democratic countries were used to estimate a cross-sectional regression, which also included a dummy for European countries. Data limitations meant that it was not possible to test for a possible role for inequality aversion, although the numerical results displayed relatively little sensitivity.

Despite the considerable data problems and the simplicity of the model, the empirical results were consistent with *a priori* expectations. In particular, reductions in inequality (an increase in the ratio of the median wage to the arithmetic mean wage) were found to be associated with reductions in transfer payments relative to public goods expenditure, at a decreasing rate. Furthermore, increases in the tax rate, from relatively low levels, are associated with increases in the relative importance of transfer payments. But beyond a certain level, further tax rate increases are associated with a lower ratio of transfers to public goods, as a result of the adverse incentive effects. The results suggest that it may be worth extending the model to include, for example, more dynamic aspects of the choice of expenditure composition. This is carried out in Chapter 5 below but, first, it is useful to consider in the next chapter a potential role for home production rather than simply a choice between work and leisure.

Chapter 4

The Role of Home Production

In the previous chapter, individuals were assumed to maximise utility, considered as a function of the consumption of private goods (or net income), leisure and the consumption of the tax-financed public good. However, there is a substantial literature on the effects of home production on labour supply, welfare and growth, with much emphasis being given to the role of joint decision making in households. Thus, the present chapter considers the potential influence of home production in the context of majority voting models of taxation and the composition of government expenditure. Its aim is to investigate how the inclusion of subsistence activities, or home production, may influence voting outcomes.

Two related questions are examined. First, majority voting over the tax rate in the familiar linear tax and transfer system is considered. This allows comparisons with earlier models of, for example, Roberts (1977) and Meltzer and Richard (1981).[1] With a proportional tax and a universal benefit, the government budget constraint implies that voting is over only one dimension, the tax rate. In this case it may, for example, be expected that there is a larger 'tax base effect' of an increase in the tax rate, compared with

---

[1]Chapter 2 above discussed the use of a stochastic voting framework, leading to maximisation of a function which resembles a social welfare function, and where closed-form solutions are generally not available. Tridimas and Winer (2005) considered probabilistic voting, with home production, using quasi-linear utility functions and concentrating on the choice of public goods and a linear income tax.

the standard model which excludes home production. The non-participation
option no longer implies that consumption is restricted to the transfer payment. The fact that individuals can substitute home production for goods
purchased in markets, as well as substituting leisure for work when the tax
rate rises, may result in a preference for relatively lower tax rates, and thus
lower transfer payments.

Second, this chapter examines the potential role of home production in
democratic choices regarding the composition of government expenditure, in
situations where there is a tax-financed pure public good in addition to a
transfer payment, conditional on a given tax rate. The framework is thus
the same as that used in the previous chapter.

It has long been established that, in the first case mentioned above – but
without home production – a majority voting equilibrium exists in which the
median voter's preferred tax rate is a function of the ratio of the median
wage rate to the arithmetic mean wage. An increase in the skewness of the
wage rate distribution (that is, a reduction in the ratio) is associated with a
higher equilibrium tax rate and therefore a more redistributive tax-transfer
system.[2] Figure 4.1 shows a standard diagram, with the basic income, or
transfer payment, on the vertical axis and the proportional tax rate on the
horizontal axis.

Individuals with lower wage rates have flatter upward sloping indifference
curves, while non-workers have horizontal indifference curves since, not pay-
ing tax, they prefer only the highest transfer possible. Each voter's preferred
position involves a tangency between the highest indifference curve and the
concave government budget constraint. Hence the lower the median relative
to the mean, the higher is the majority choice of tax rate.[3] However, empiri-

---

[2]It can be shown that the majority choice satisfies the condition, $1 - \frac{y_m}{\bar{y}} = |\eta_{\bar{y},\tau}|$, where y_m and $\bar{y}$ are respectively the median and arithmetic mean gross *income*, and $|\eta_{\bar{y},\tau}|$ is the absolute elasticity of average income with respect to the tax rate, τ. The left hand side of this expression can be interpreted as a measure of income inequality.

[3]Mueller (2003), as is usual, draws indifference curves as convex. However, it is shown

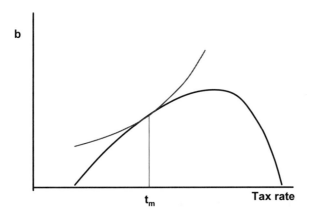

Figure 4.1: The Median Voter's Choice of Tax Rate

cal evidence regarding such a relationship, involving cross-country data, has been mixed. For a review of evidence, see Borck (2007) and Harms and Zink (2003), and on problems raised in testing this type of model empirically, see Lind (2005). In the context of time series evidence for particular countries, the variation in inequality is typically too small to establish an effect.

A similar property arises in models of the democratic choice of expenditure composition combining public goods and redistributive transfers. The previous chapter has shown that a positive relationship can be established between inequality and the proportion of expenditure devoted to the inequality-reducing transfer payment. Again cross-country empirical evidence on this relationship is equivocal.

This raises the question of whether comparisons among countries, particularly involving both developed and developing countries, where home production or subsistence activities might be thought to vary substantially, are significantly affected. The question concerns the possible extent to which differences in taxes and expenditure composition, among democratic countries, may be explained by different degrees of importance attached to subsistence

---

below that they may be slightly concave.

activities, compared with other factors such as cultural differences which are also known to vary substantially. The main aim of the present chapter is thus to consider this question. In pursuing this problem, it is also necessary to consider the precise form of specification of home production such that the models are reasonably tractable.

Section 4.1 considers voting over the tax rate in a model in which there are two goods, one of which is produced at home, in addition to leisure. The sensitivity of the choice of tax rate to the degree of importance attached to home production is examined. 'Importance' here is affected both by the preference for the home produced good in the utility function and the productivity of time spent on home production. Section 4.3 considers the case where voting concerns the division of government expenditure between transfer payments and a pure public good, conditional on a given tax rate. Again the extent to which the relationship between the majority choice of expenditure share and the ratio of the median to the arithmetic mean wage is influenced by variations in the importance of home produced goods is considered. Section 4.4 extends the analysis to allow individuals' wage rates to be affected by public good expenditure.

4.1   The Framework of Analysis

This section extends the widely used partial equilibrium model of a 'pure' tax and transfer system, where individuals have different abilities which are reflected in their wage rates. A fixed endowment of time is divided among leisure, work and home production. To obtain some idea of potential orders of magnitude, it is useful to obtain explicit solutions for the majority choice of the tax rate using a specific form for the utility function. Quasi-linear preferences are particularly simple for text-book examples. For example, Hindriks and Myles (2006, pp. 503-505) discuss majority voting where utility is consumption less (half) the square of labour supply, and show that the median voter's preferred tax rate is $(1 - y_m/\bar{y}) / \{2 - y_m/\bar{y}\}$, where y_m and $\bar{y}$ are median and arithmetic mean income respectively. Persson and Tabellini (2000) also give an example using quasi-linear preferences. However, the present chapter uses the Cobb–Douglas form, though it considers alternative specifications. The first stage is to obtain the indirect utility function, expressed in terms of the tax parameters, along with the government's budget constraint.

Suppose that individual i buys an amount, x_i, of a marketed good at price, p, and produces y_i of a home produced good using h_i units of time, according to:

$$y_i = \theta h_i^\delta \tag{4.1}$$

Other inputs into home production, arising from endowments of the individual, are subsumed into the term, θ. These endowments may include, for example, a fixed holding of land and capital goods in the form of tools. It is not required to assume that this is the same for all individuals. If the production function were to involve inputs of amounts of the market purchased good, x, the model would become significantly more complex.[4]

The individual consumes ℓ_i units of leisure and the total endowment of time is 1, so that the time devoted to paid work is $1 - \ell_i - h_i$. Using the Cobb–Douglas form, the utility function can be written:

$$U = x_i^\alpha y_i^\phi \ell_i^\gamma \tag{4.2}$$

so that, after substituting for y_i:

$$U = x_i^\alpha \left(\theta h_i^\delta\right)^\phi \ell_i^\gamma \tag{4.3}$$

Writing $\beta = \delta\phi$ and ignoring the constant θ^ϕ, this can be rewritten as:

$$U = x_i^\alpha h_i^\beta \ell_i^\gamma \tag{4.4}$$

---

[4]Greenwood *et al.* (1995) allow for the purchase of inputs, in a real business cycle model.

It is convenient below to write $\alpha + \beta + \gamma = \rho$. The standard model, which excludes home production, is thus obtained by setting $\beta = 0$. Utility therefore takes the basic Cobb–Douglas form in terms of the consumption of a market purchased good and the time devoted, separately, to leisure and home production. The latter does not generate utility directly but does so via the production function in (4.1).

If a constant elasticity of substitution utility function were used instead of (4.2), this would not, when combined with (4.1), give rise to an equivalent function in terms of hours of home production, as does (4.4). Furthermore, the constant elasticity of substitution form does not give rise to a linear relationship between earnings and the wage rate, so the government budget constraint is considerably more complex than the present case. An alternative way of looking at home production would be to suppose that instead of having two goods, one of which can be produced at home, there is just one good which may either be produced at home or purchased at price p. From the point of view of consumption, they are otherwise the same. Home and market amounts consumed are x_s and x_p respectively. Utility is thus $U_i = (x_p + x_s)^{\alpha} \ell^{1-\alpha}$, where $x_s = \theta h_s^{\delta}$. However, a problem with this formulation is that it becomes intractable.

With a tax and transfer system involving a proportional tax applied to all earnings at the rate τ, and a basic income of b, the budget constraint, where w_i is the wage rate, is:

$$px_i + w_i \left(1 - \tau\right) \left(h_i + \ell_i\right) = w_i \left(1 - \tau\right) + b = M_i \qquad (4.5)$$

where M_i is 'full income'. This is equivalent to a situation in which the individual sells all the endowment of labour time at the going wage and 'buys back' the time required for leisure and home production at a price equal to the net wage. Using the standard properties of the Cobb–Douglas utility function, involving fixed expenditure proportions, the individual's optimum values are given by:

$$x_i = \frac{\alpha}{\rho}\frac{M_i}{p} \tag{4.6}$$

$$h_i = \frac{\beta}{\rho}\frac{M_i}{w_i\left(1-\tau\right)} \tag{4.7}$$

$$\ell_i = \frac{\gamma}{\rho}\frac{M_i}{w_i\left(1-\tau\right)} \tag{4.8}$$

Thus, as expected, high-wage individuals devote relatively more time to working in the labour market, rather than taking leisure or engaging in home production. Where the opportunity cost of time is lower, it is better to spend more time in home production.

Gross earnings, $y_i = w\left(1 - h_i - \ell_i\right)$, are:

$$y_i = \left(\frac{\alpha}{\rho}\right)w_i - \left(\frac{\rho-\alpha}{\rho}\right)\left(\frac{b}{1-\tau}\right) \tag{4.9}$$

This expression takes the same form as the case where there is no home production: the only difference concerns the value of the coefficients on the wage rate and basic income. This applies only if w_i exceeds a minimum wage, $w_{\min}$, required to induce positive labour supply.

In order to obtain the government's budget constraint, aggregation must be carried out over all individuals. If $\bar{y}$ is arithmetic mean earnings, then from (4.9):

$$\bar{y} = \frac{1}{n}\sum_{w>w_{\min}}\left\{\left(\frac{\alpha}{\rho}\right)w_i - \left(\frac{\rho-\alpha}{\rho}\right)\left(\frac{b}{1-\tau}\right)\right\} \tag{4.10}$$

Let $F_1\left(w_{\min}\right)$ and $F\left(w_{\min}\right)$ denote respectively the proportion of total wage (rates) and the proportion of people with $w < w_{\min}$: these correspond to the ordinate and abscissa of the Lorenz curve of wage rates at the point where $w = w_{\min}$. Then:

$$\bar{y} = \bar{w}\frac{\alpha}{\rho}\left\{1 - F_1\left(w_{\min}\right)\right\} - \left(\frac{\rho-\alpha}{\rho}\right)\left(\frac{b}{1-\tau}\right)\left\{1 - F\left(w_{\min}\right)\right\} \tag{4.11}$$

where $\bar{w}$ is the arithmetic mean wage rate. This expression is nonlinear in view of the fact that $w_{\min}$ depends on b and τ, so it is not possible to express b as a convenient function of τ. However, the analysis is tractable if it is assumed that relatively few individuals do not work, so that F_1 and F are small and can be neglected: this produces a linear relationship between arithmetic means of y and w. This assumption in fact has a negligible effect on the shape of the government's budget constraint in the relevant region (that is, for tax parameters around those preferred by the median voter), though it may have a small effect on the absolute size of the basic income.

The government's budget constraint in this 'pure' transfer scheme is simply $b = \tau\bar{y}$, so that substituting for $\bar{y}$ and rearranging gives:

$$b = \frac{\alpha\bar{w}\tau(1-\tau)}{\rho - \alpha\tau} \tag{4.12}$$

Substituting optimal values of consumption, along with (4.12), into full income, $M_i = w_i(1-\tau) + b$, gives indirect utility, V_i, in terms of the tax rate, τ, as:

$$V_i = k\left\{w_i(1-\tau)\right\}\left(1 + \left(\frac{\bar{w}}{w_i}\right)\frac{\frac{\alpha}{\rho}\tau}{1 - \frac{\alpha}{\rho}\tau}\right)^{\rho} \tag{4.13}$$

where $k = \alpha^{\alpha}\beta^{\beta}\gamma^{\gamma}/(\rho^{\rho}p^{\alpha})$ depends on the price of goods in the market and the parameters of the utility function.

4.2 The Majority Choice of Tax Rate

Early approaches to examining the democratic choice of the size of government had to consider the existence of a majority voting equilibrium when preferences are double-peaked. Double-peaked preferences exist for some individuals because, after the point where they move to the non-participation corner solution, they prefer to see the tax rate increase until total revenue (and hence the transfer payment) reaches a maximum. Roberts (1977) showed that a voting equilibrium exists if there is hierarchical adherence (or agent monotonicity), such that the ordering of individuals by income is independent of the tax rate.[5] It is easy to show that the present model satisfies hierarchical adherence, so the median voter theorem can be invoked with the median voter being identified as the person with the median wage rate. The voting equilibrium is obtained in Subsection 4.2.1. The effects on the choice of tax rate of variations in preferences for, and the efficiency of, home production are examined in Subsection 4.2.2.

4.2.1 The Median Voter's Choice

Denoting the median wage by w_m, the majority choice of tax rate, τ_m, is the solution to $dV_m/d\tau = 0$. Differentiation of (4.13) and rearrangement give τ_m as the appropriate root of the following quadratic:

$$\tau^2 \left(\frac{\alpha}{\rho}\right)^2 \left(1 - \frac{w_m}{\bar{w}}\right) - \tau \left(1 + \frac{\alpha}{\rho} - 2\frac{\alpha}{\rho}\frac{w_m}{\bar{w}}\right) + \left(1 - \frac{w_m}{\bar{w}}\right) = 0 \qquad (4.14)$$

In order to find the majority choice of tax rate the two roots of the quadratic equation (4.14) need to be examined. Writing this quadratic as $A\tau^2 + B\tau + C = 0$, the roots are given by the standard form, $\left\{-B \pm \sqrt{B^2 - 4AC}\right\}/2A$. The term $B^2 - 4AC$ is given by:

$$B^2 - 4AC = \left(1 + \frac{\alpha}{\rho} - 2\frac{\alpha}{\rho}\frac{w_m}{\bar{w}}\right)^2 - 4\left(\frac{\alpha}{\rho}\right)^2 \left(1 - \frac{w_m}{\bar{w}}\right)^2 \qquad (4.15)$$

which, after rearranging, becomes:

$$B^2 - 4AC = \left(1 - \frac{\alpha}{\rho}\right) \left(1 + 3\frac{\alpha}{\rho} - 4\frac{w_m}{\bar{w}}\frac{\alpha}{\rho}\right) \qquad (4.16)$$

So that the two roots are:

$$\tau_m = \frac{1 + \frac{\alpha}{\rho} - 2\frac{\alpha}{\rho}\frac{w_m}{\bar{w}} \pm \sqrt{\left(1 - \frac{\alpha}{\rho}\right)\left(1 + 3\frac{\alpha}{\rho} - 4\frac{w_m}{\bar{w}}\frac{\alpha}{\rho}\right)}}{2\left(\frac{\alpha}{\rho}\right)^2 \left(1 - \frac{w_m}{\bar{w}}\right)} \qquad (4.17)$$

---

[5]Extensions within the Roberts–Meltzer–Richard framework include, for example, Galasso (2003), who considers fairness and redistribution.

It can be shown that the largest root is greater than unity since:

$$1 + \frac{\alpha}{\rho} - 2\frac{\alpha}{\rho}\frac{w_m}{\bar{w}} + \sqrt{\left(1 - \frac{\alpha}{\rho}\right)\left(1 + 3\frac{\alpha}{\rho} - 4\frac{w_m}{\bar{w}}\frac{\alpha}{\rho}\right)}$$
$$> 2\left(\frac{\alpha}{\rho}\right)^2\left(1 - \frac{w_m}{\bar{w}}\right) \tag{4.18}$$

After much manipulation it can be shown that this condition reduces to:

$$0 > \left(1 - \frac{w_m}{\bar{w}}\right)\left(\frac{\alpha}{\rho} - 1\right)\left\{\frac{\alpha}{\rho} + \frac{w_m}{\bar{w}}\left(1 - \frac{\alpha}{\rho}\right)\right\} \tag{4.19}$$

Of the three terms in parentheses, only the middle term is negative. Hence this condition always holds. Therefore only the lowest root needs to be considered.

The wage rate distribution is, as with all income distributions, positively skewed, so that $\bar{w} > w_m$. As mentioned in the Introduction, a general result in the literature on majority voting is that a reduction in $w_m/\bar{w}$, that is a movement of the median voter further below the arithmetic mean, is associated with an increase in the median voter's desired tax rate and thus transfer payment, making the system more redistributive. Redistribution is across the arithmetic mean, since the effective average tax rate is negative for $y_i < \bar{y}$ and positive for $y_i > \bar{y}$. Hence, as the median wage tends to the arithmetic mean wage, the majority choice of tax rate tends to $\tau_m = 0$. Thus it is often said that more basic inequality leads to voting for a more redistributive tax structure. In general, the ratio $w_m/\bar{w}$ is not directly a measure of inequality (since it is equal to 1 for distributions which are symmetric around $\bar{w}$), but in the case of positively skewed distributions it can be taken to reflect inequality as well as the skewness of the wage rate distribution. For example, if w is lognormally distributed as $\Lambda\left(w\,|\,\mu, \sigma^2\right)$ where μ and σ^2 are respectively the mean and variance of logarithms, it can be shown that $w_m/\bar{w}$ depends only on σ^2.

This result continues to hold where home production exists. Using the expression for the appropriate root of (4.14), it is possible to show that the derivative of the tax rate, τ_m, with respect to $w_m/\bar{w}$ is negative; that is, $\partial \tau_m/\partial (w_m/\bar{w}) < 0$. Thus, as in the basic model, reducing wage rate inequality reduces the majority choice of tax rate.

4.2.2 Variations in Beta

The question of interest here is how the existence of home production affects the choice of tax rate. As home production enters the majority choice of tax rate through the coefficient, β, the exponent on time spent in home production in the utility function, this question concerns the model's comparative static properties with respect to β. This could in principle be examined by differentiating the appropriate root of (4.14) with respect to β. Also, the slope, $\partial \tau_m/\partial (w_m/\bar{w})$, could be differentiated with respect to β, in each case bearing in mind that $\rho = \alpha + \beta + \gamma$. However, this approach does not yield unequivocal results, so that a more indirect route is needed.

Further insight can be obtained by considering individuals' preferences in (b, τ) space. The majority voting equilibrium, illustrated in Figure 4.1 and discussed above, is characterised by tangency between the median voter's highest indifference curve and the government budget constraint. With b and τ on vertical and horizontal axes respectively, any change leading indifference curves of the median voter to become steeper, and the government budget constraint (over the relevant – that is, upward sloping – range) to become flatter, has the effect of unambiguously reducing the choice of tax rate.

When β increases, both the budget constraint and indifference curves become flatter. It is thus necessary to consider the net effect of an increase in β. The indirect utility function for workers in terms of b and τ can be written (dropping subscripts for the median voter) as:

$$V_i = k \left\{ w_i \left(1 - \tau\right) \right\}^\alpha \left(1 + \frac{b}{w_i \left(1 - \tau\right)}\right)^\rho \qquad (4.20)$$

The slope of an indifference curve is:

$$\left.\frac{db}{d\tau}\right|_{V_i} = -\frac{\partial V_i/\partial \tau}{\partial V_i/\partial b}$$

$$= \frac{w_i}{\rho}\left(\alpha + \frac{(\alpha - \rho)\,b}{w_i\,(1-\tau)}\right) \tag{4.21}$$

The sign of the first derivative is undetermined, but it can be shown that over the relevant range of taxes it is increasing.

However, the negative sign of the second derivative, $-(\rho - \alpha)\,b/\rho\,(1-\tau)^2$, shows that indifference curves are slightly concave in (b, τ) space. Alternatively, writing the equation of the indifference curve as:

$$b = \left(\frac{\bar{V}_i}{k}\right)^{\frac{1}{\rho}}\{w_i\,(1-\tau)\}^{\frac{\rho-\alpha}{\rho}} - w_i\,(1-\tau) \tag{4.22}$$

the first derivative is:

$$\left.\frac{db}{d\tau}\right|_{\bar{V}_i} = -\left(\frac{\bar{V}_i}{k}\right)^{\frac{1}{\rho}}\left(\frac{\rho-\alpha}{\rho}\right) w_i^{\frac{\rho-\alpha}{\rho}}\,(1-\tau)^{\frac{-\alpha}{\rho}} + w_i \tag{4.23}$$

The sign of this is generally undetermined. However, it applies only for the range of τ for which labour supply is positive, and is therefore positive. For τ beyond the point where the individual does not work, the indifference curves become horizontal. The second derivative is:

$$\left.\frac{d^2b}{d\tau^2}\right|_{V_i} = -\frac{\alpha}{\rho}\left(\frac{\bar{V}_i}{k}\right)^{\frac{1}{\rho}}\left(\frac{\rho-\alpha}{\rho}\right) w_i^{\frac{\rho-\alpha}{\rho}}\,(1-\tau)^{\frac{-\alpha}{\rho}-1} < 0 \tag{4.24}$$

This is negative, implying that indifference curve are actually slightly concave in (b, τ) space. This property – which also holds in the basic model where there is no home production – does not seem to have been recognised in the literature, where convex indifference curves are usually drawn, as in Figure 4.1.

From (4.21), the effect of a change in β on the slope of indifference curves is:

$$\frac{d}{d\beta}\left(\left.\frac{db}{d\tau}\right|_{V_i}\right) = \frac{-\alpha w_i}{\rho^2}\left(1 + \frac{b}{w_i\,(1-\tau)}\right) < 0 \tag{4.25}$$

and for a given τ the indifference curves get flatter. A change in β also causes the government budget constraint, $b = \tau \bar{y}$, to change. The slope of this is:

$$\left. \frac{db}{d\tau} \right|_R = \bar{y} + \tau \frac{d\bar{y}}{d\tau} \tag{4.26}$$

and the effect of a change in β on this slope is:

$$\frac{d}{d\beta} \left(\left. \frac{db}{d\tau} \right|_R \right) = \frac{d\bar{y}}{d\beta} + \tau \frac{d}{d\beta} \left(\frac{d\bar{y}}{d\tau} \right) \tag{4.27}$$

From the expression for $\bar{y}$ above:

$$\frac{d\bar{y}}{d\tau} = - \left(\frac{\rho - \alpha}{\rho} \right) \frac{b}{(1 - \tau)^2} \tag{4.28}$$

and:

$$\frac{d}{d\beta} \left(\frac{d\bar{y}}{d\tau} \right) = -\frac{\alpha}{\rho^2} \frac{b}{(1 - \tau)^2} \tag{4.29}$$

Furthermore:

$$\frac{d\bar{y}}{d\beta} = -\frac{\alpha}{\rho^2} \left(\bar{w} + \frac{b}{1 - \tau} \right) \tag{4.30}$$

Hence:

$$\frac{d}{d\beta} \left(\left. \frac{db}{d\tau} \right|_R \right) = -\frac{\alpha}{\rho^2} \left(\bar{w} + \frac{b}{(1 - \tau)^2} \right) < 0 \tag{4.31}$$

Hence the government budget constraint also becomes flatter. This means that there are opposing tendencies on the preferred value of τ. The flattening of the indifference curves leads towards an increase in τ while the flattening of the budget constraint leads towards a reduction in τ. Thus the question, in determining whether the change in β leads to a reduction in the median voter's choice of τ, is whether the change (in absolute terms) in the slope of the budget constraint is greater than that of the indifference curve, at the initial τ. Since $w_m < \bar{w}$ and $0 < 1 - \tau < 1$, it can be seen that:

$$\left| \frac{d}{d\beta} \left(\left. \frac{db}{d\tau} \right|_R \right) \right| > \left| \frac{d}{d\beta} \left(\left. \frac{db}{d\tau} \right|_{V_i} \right) \right| \tag{4.32}$$

An increase in β therefore reduces τ_m.

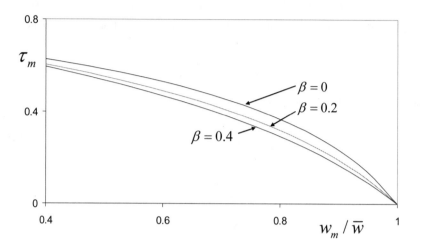

Figure 4.2: Median Voter's Preferred Tax Rate and Ratio $w_m/\bar{w}$

This is illustrated in Figure 4.2, which shows the variation in τ_m with $w_m/\bar{w}$ for a range of values of β. In producing the figure, the value of α is set to 0.7 and it is convenient to set $\gamma = 1 - \alpha$ (so that $\rho = 1 + \beta$). The introduction of home production, or an increase in β, not only reduces the value of τ_m but also involves a very slight reduction in the extent to which it varies with $w_m/\bar{w}$. An increase in β can arise from either an increase in preferences for the home produced good, ϕ, or an increase in the productivity of time spent in home production, δ. In each case there is a stronger incentive to devote more time to home production, involving a greater opportunity cost of working. The median voter thus wishes to compensate by having a slightly lower income tax rate.

It is also of interest to consider the way in which time allocation varies as β increases. An increase in β, the coefficient on home production time in utility, is expected to involve a shift away from leisure. It is shown here that it also leads to a small reduction in labour supply. First, the partial effects on leisure, ℓ, and time in home production, h, of an increase in β can be seen by differentiating the above expressions for optimal choices, giving:

$$\eta_{\ell,\beta} = \frac{\beta}{\ell}\frac{\partial\ell}{\partial\beta} = -\frac{\beta}{\rho} \tag{4.33}$$

and:

$$\eta_{h,\beta} = \frac{\beta}{h}\frac{\partial h}{\partial\beta} = 1 - \frac{\beta}{\rho} \tag{4.34}$$

Hence $\eta_{\ell,\beta} + \eta_{h,\beta} = 1$. An increase in β therefore leads to a shift from leisure towards home production, but the two changes are not equal. There is a small effect on labour supply, since:

$$
\begin{aligned}
\frac{\partial\left(1-\ell-h\right)}{\partial\beta} &= -\left(\frac{\partial\ell}{\partial\beta} + \frac{\partial h}{\partial\beta}\right) \\
&= -\frac{\alpha M_i}{\rho^2 w_i\left(1-\tau\right)} < 0
\end{aligned}
\tag{4.35}
$$

Hence, the partial effect of an increase in β is to reduce labour supply for all wage groups. However, the increase in β has been seen above to lead to a reduction in the majority choice of τ and a reduction in the value of b, since the government budget constraint becomes flatter. The latter reduction has the effect of increasing labour supply. Hence the change in labour supply resulting from both changes depends on the individual's wage rate.

These results concern the term β, but this term itself depends both on the productivity of time devoted to home production, as reflected in the coefficient, δ, as well as the relative weight, ϕ, attached to consumption of the home produced good in the utility function. But since $\beta = \delta\phi$, both these terms enter in a symmetric fashion and their effects cannot be distinguished.

4.3 Voting on the Composition of Expenditure

This section extends the model of Section 4.1 by introducing a pure public good which is tax-financed. It examines the median voter's preferred allocation of tax revenue between transfer payments and the public good. This section therefore extends the results of Chapter 3, which does not include home production. In concentrating on the composition of expenditure, the tax rate is considered to be exogenously determined, as mentioned in the Introduction. This means that there is again only one degree of freedom in choosing the transfer and public good expenditure and voting concerns just one dimension.

Consider the model in Section 4.1 which has two goods, one of which is produced at home. Suppose that, in addition, there is a tax-financed amount of a pure public good, Q_G, where the cost of production per unit is constant and equal to p_G (the price of the private marketed good is p, as above). The augmented utility function is thus:

$$U_i = x_i^\alpha h_i^\beta \ell_i^\gamma Q_G^\eta \tag{4.36}$$

A feature of the Cobb–Douglas form in this context, as mentioned above, is that it avoids a situation where expenditure per person tends to zero as population size increases.

The budget constraint facing each individual is the same as in (4.5). The utility maximising amounts, x_i, h_i and ℓ_i, are exactly the same as in equations (4.6) to (4.8) in Section 4.1. Similarly, individual i's earnings are the same as given in (4.9).

However, the form of the government's budget constraint must be modified to allow for the need to raise extra revenue to finance expenditure of $G = p_G Q_G$ on the public good. The government budget constraint becomes:

$$b = \tau \bar{y} - G/N \tag{4.37}$$

where N is the number of individuals. Hence (4.12) is easily modified by the inclusion of the term in G/N, so that:

$$b = \frac{\frac{\alpha}{\rho}\tau\bar{w} - G/N}{1 + \left(\frac{\rho - \alpha}{\rho}\right)\left(\frac{\tau}{1-\tau}\right)} \tag{4.38}$$

where again $\rho = \alpha + \beta + \gamma$. The problem here is to obtain the preferred expenditure levels of G and b for a given tax rate. The indirect utility function, modified by the addition of the public good and substituting the transfer payment from the government budget constraint (4.38), can be written in terms of the policy variable, Q_G, as:

$$V_i = \frac{k \left(\frac{1-\tau}{\rho-\alpha\tau}\right)^{\rho}}{\{w_i (1-\tau)\}^{\rho-\alpha}} \left\{ \rho w_i + \alpha\tau (\bar{w} - w_i) - \frac{p_G Q_G}{N} \right\}^{\rho} Q_G^{\eta} \qquad (4.39)$$

It can be shown that $d^2 V_i / dQ_G^2 < 0$ if $\alpha + \beta + \gamma < 1$. Hence preferences are singled-peaked and the majority choice of expenditure on public goods is obtained from $dV_m / dQ_G = 0$. This gives, after some manipulation:

$$\frac{G_m}{N} = \frac{p_G Q_{G,m}}{N} = \bar{w} \left(\frac{\eta}{\rho + \eta}\right) \left\{ \frac{w_m}{\bar{w}} + \frac{\alpha}{\rho}\tau \left(1 - \frac{w_m}{\bar{w}}\right) \right\} \qquad (4.40)$$

Hence the expenditure per capita on the public good, as a proportion of $\bar{w}$, depends on the preference parameters, the tax rate and the ratio $w_m/\bar{w}$. It increases linearly with τ and $w_m/\bar{w}$. The resulting value of b_m is given by appropriate substitution of G_m/N into (4.38):

$$b_m = \bar{w} \frac{\left(\frac{1}{\rho+\eta}\right) \left\{ \alpha\tau - \eta \frac{w_m}{\bar{w}} \left(1 - \frac{\alpha}{\rho}\tau\right) \right\}}{1 + \left(\frac{\rho-\alpha}{\rho}\right) \left(\frac{\tau}{1-\tau}\right)} \qquad (4.41)$$

and $b_m/\bar{w}$ is also a linear function of $w_m/\bar{w}$, but a nonlinear function of the exogenous tax rate, τ. An important implication of the Cobb–Douglas preferences is that this ratio does not depend on the cost of the public good per unit relative to the price of the marketed private good. Combining (7.12) and (4.40) shows that the majority choice of the ratio of the transfer payment to public good expenditure per capita, R_m, depends on the given tax rate, the preference parameters and, importantly, the ratio $w_m/\bar{w}$. Further analysis shows that $dR_m/d\,(w_m/\bar{w}) < 0$, so that increasing equality is associated with a lower R_m and hence a reduced emphasis on a redistributive expenditure share.

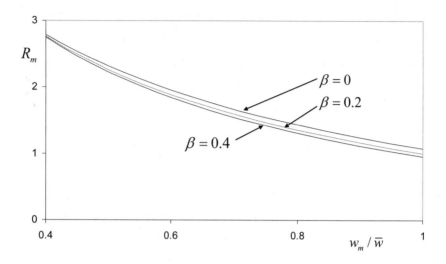

Figure 4.3: Expenditure Share and Wage Ratio

Figure 4.3 shows the relationship between R_m and $w_m/\bar{w}$, again for $\alpha = 0.7$ and $\gamma = 1 - \alpha$, for three different values of β. It can be seen that home production, as modelled here, has little effect on this relationship. Just as it involved a slightly lower tax rate, and hence transfer payment, when considering voting over the tax rate, it implies a slightly lower ratio of expenditure on transfers relative to the public good.

4.4   An Endogenous Wage Rate Distribution

This section considers the situation in which the public good expenditure affects the wage rate distribution directly. The context is still a partial equilibrium model, where interactions with the labour demand side of the economy are ignored. This may be modelled by supposing that each individual's wage depends on G, which may be thought of in terms of basic education. Suppose, for simplicity, that:

$$w_i = w_{0i}^{\theta} G^{1-\theta} \tag{4.42}$$

where w_{0i} is person i's 'basic' skill level. This specification implies that G involves an equal proportional increase in all individuals' wage rates and thus does not affect their inequality. However, a higher value of θ produces more inequality. The variance of log-wage rates is θ^2 multiplied by the variance of $\log w_0$.

As in the previous section, income taxation, at the rate τ, finances an unconditional transfer of b and the public good expenditure of G. Each individual consumes goods, x_i, priced at p per unit, along with leisure ℓ_i, and devotes h_i to home production. Again, the majority voting outcome is obtained by first deriving the indirect utility function. In the present context, the productivity enhancing public good is not considered to generate utility directly. Thus, each individual maximises:

$$U_i = x_i^\alpha h_i^\beta \ell_i^\gamma \qquad (4.43)$$

Here it is convenient to impose $1 = \alpha + \beta + \gamma$. The budget constraint is:

$$p x_i + w_i (1 - \tau) (h_i + \ell_i) = w_i (1 - \tau) + b = M_i \qquad (4.44)$$

Hence, from the standard Cobb–Douglas properties, $x_i = \alpha M_i / p$, $h_i = \beta M_i / (w_i (1 - \tau))$ and $\ell_i = \gamma M_i / (w_i (1 - \tau))$. Earnings $y_i = w_i (1 - h_i - \ell_i)$ are:

$$y_i = \alpha w_i - (1 - \alpha) \frac{b}{1 - \tau} \qquad (4.45)$$

and (if most people work), $\bar{y}$, arithmetic mean earnings, are obtained from (4.45) with $\bar{w}$, the arithmetic mean value of wage rates, instead of w_i.

Indirect utility is therefore:

$$V_i = \left(\frac{\alpha M_i}{p} \right)^\alpha \left(\frac{\beta M_i}{w_i (1 - \tau)} \right)^\beta \left(\frac{\gamma M_i}{w_i (1 - \tau)} \right)^\gamma \qquad (4.46)$$

which can be rewritten, letting $K = \left(\frac{\alpha}{p} \right)^\alpha \beta^\beta \gamma^\gamma$ as:

$$V = K (w (1 - \tau))^\alpha \left\{ 1 + \frac{b}{w (1 - \tau)} \right\} \qquad (4.47)$$

The government's budget constraint is $b + G = \tau \bar{y}$, so that the basic income in terms of G is:

$$b = \frac{\alpha \tau \bar{w} - G}{1 + (1 - \alpha) \tau / (1 - \tau)} \tag{4.48}$$

Aggregating over (4.42) gives the arithmetic mean wage rate as:

$$\bar{w} = \bar{w}_\theta^\theta G^{1-\theta} \tag{4.49}$$

where $\bar{w}_\theta = \left(\frac{1}{n} \sum w_0^\theta\right)^{1/\theta}$. Finally, substitute for $\bar{w}$ in (4.48) and then for b into (6.12) to get indirect utility in terms of G:

$$V_i = K \left(w_{0i}^\theta G^{1-\theta} (1 - \tau)\right)^\alpha \times$$
$$\left\{1 + \frac{\alpha \tau \bar{w}_\theta^\theta - G^\theta}{w_{0i}^\theta (1 - \tau) \{1 + (1 - \alpha) \tau / (1 - \tau)\}}\right\} \tag{4.50}$$

Setting $dV_i/dG = 0$, for the median voter, gives the choice of G, G_m, as:

$$G_m = \left[\frac{w_{0i}^\theta (1 - \tau) \{1 + (1 - \alpha) \tau / (1 - \tau)\} + \alpha \tau \bar{w}_\theta^\theta}{1 + \frac{\theta}{\alpha(1-\theta)}}\right]^{\frac{1}{\theta}} \tag{4.51}$$

From (4.48):

$$R_m = \frac{b_m}{G_m} = \frac{\alpha \tau \bar{w}_\theta^\theta G_m^{-\theta} - 1}{1 + \frac{(1-\alpha)\tau}{1-\tau}} \tag{4.52}$$

and using (4.51) gives, after rearrangement:

$$R_m = \frac{\frac{\theta \tau}{(1-\theta)(1-\alpha\tau)} - \left(\frac{w_{0m}}{\bar{w}_\theta}\right)^\theta}{\alpha \tau + (1 - \alpha\tau) \left(\frac{w_{0m}}{\bar{w}_\theta}\right)^\theta} (1 - \tau) \tag{4.53}$$

Direct comparisons with the previous section cannot of course be made because here the government expenditure does not enter individuals' utility functions. However, the median voter's preferred expenditure ratio b_m/G_m is again a function of the ratio of the median voter's wage rate to the arithmetic mean wage rate, since $(w_{0m}/\bar{w}_\theta)^\theta = w_m/\bar{w}$. The question of interest is whether home production has a potentially large effect on this relationship, that is, whether it is shifted substantially by variations in β.

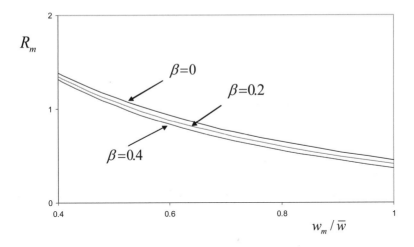

Figure 4.4: Expenditure Share and Wage Ratio with Endogenous Wages

Figure 4.4 shows the relationship between R_m and $w_m/\bar{w}$, for three different values of β, bearing in mind that $\alpha = 1 - \beta - \gamma$. In this figure $\alpha = \gamma = (1 - \beta)/2$; however, it was found that changing α and γ give similar results. It can be seen that home production has little effect on the ratio of expenditure on transfer payments to public good expenditure. Furthermore, the downward sloping profile of R_m is relatively flat, as with the model of the previous section.

4.5 Conclusions

This chapter has examined the implications of allowing for home production in modelling three types of democratic choice. First, majority voting over tax and benefit levels was examined in a pure transfer system with endogenous labour supply. Second, the choice of the share of transfer payments in total expenditure was considered in a model in which the tax rate is exogenously fixed but there is also a tax-financed pure public good. Third, the division between transfers and a public good was considered where the latter has an effect on the wage rate distribution, but does not enter individuals' utility functions directly.

The specification of home production implies that a Cobb–Douglas utility function in terms of amounts consumed of a marketed good and a home produced good (along with leisure) can be re-expressed as a function of the time devoted to home production. The analysis was simplified by the assumption that the minimum wage in the population is sufficient to ensure that all individuals work, producing a convenient form of government budget constraint which allows explicit solutions to be obtained. Both the tax rate in the first model and the expenditure share in the second model were found to depend on the ratio of the median voter's wage to the arithmetic wage. This general property has of course been established earlier for models which make no allowance for home production.

The introduction of home production in these models was found to have little effect on the democratic choice of tax and transfer levels and on the choice of expenditure composition. Attempts to examine empirically the relationship between either the level of transfers or the expenditure share and the ratio of median to average wages have produced mixed results, using cross-sectional data for a range of democratic countries. It is likely that a range of other factors are relevant in the determination of transfers and expenditure shares. The present chapter has shown that, even where the extent of home production may be expected to vary significantly, its exclusion from empirical models is not likely to significantly bias results. This negative result is in fact convenient for empirical work, given the difficulty of obtaining information regarding the time spent in home production.

Chapter 5

An Overlapping Generations Framework

It has been seen that a large theoretical literature suggests that more basic income inequality is associated with a larger extent of redistributive expenditure, although this has not been unequivocally confirmed empirically. However, the observed partial relationship between the expenditure ratio and income inequality is possibly obscured by many other factors reflecting differences in economic and demographic conditions or cultural differences across countries; see Lind (2005) and Alesina and Glaeser (2004).

In order to attempt to understand the way in which cultural factors and economic conditions may combine to influence the composition of expenditure, this chapter extends the single-period treatment of Chapter 3 by examining the division of expenditure between public goods and a transfer payment under majority voting in the context of an overlapping generations model. By taking a growth context and focusing on the expenditure composition for a given tax rate, the model allows for a wider range of factors which may contribute to cross-country variations in expenditure compositions, such as income and population growth rates and the discount factor. Cultural factors are captured by a parameter in the utility function reflecting individuals' preference for public goods relative to private goods consumption. Direct independent evidence regarding preferences for public goods is extremely difficult to obtain in view of well-known problems of preference revelation mechanisms. However, a wide range of studies take as their starting point such differences; see, for example, Haufler (1996). The transfer payment in the model is referred to as a pension, since it is received in the second period of life.[1] However, it may be thought of more broadly as a standard type of income transfer since it involves, in the present overlapping generations framework, a decision regarding income shifting between periods within the life cycle as well as intra- and inter-generational redistribution.

Members of each cohort are considered to vote on their desired pension during the retirement period, on the understanding that during the working period each cohort finances the expenditure previously agreed by the preceding cohort, and voters are aware of the nature of the government budget constraint. There is therefore a social contract in which each generation, in the retirement period, is able to benefit from the income and population growth of the following generation. The condition under which the social contract is supported by a majority of the members of any cohort involves extending the condition obtained by Aaron (1966) and Samuelson (1958). The model yields a closed-form solution for the majority choice of the ratio of transfer payments to public goods expenditure. Consistent with previous theoretical literature, the model predicts a positive relationship between income inequality and the expenditure ratio.

A numerical exercise is then implemented to examine the sensitivity of the expenditure ratio to variations in model primitives, where baseline parameter values are calibrated to the dataset for a group of democratic countries. It is found that the relationship between the expenditure ratio and the income inequality measure is quite flat over the most relevant range of income inequality. This may partly contribute to the mixed empirical results regard-

---

[1] The introduction of an additional transfer, received in the working period, would involve considerable problems arising from multidimensional voting. For alternative models of voting on pensions see, for example, Conde-Ruiz and Galasso (2005) and Walque (2005).

ing this relationship based on cross-sectional data, as summarised in Perotti (1996) and Shelton (2007). The numerical results also show that the expenditure ratio is more sensitive to variations in the tax rate and the preference parameter, and less sensitive to variations in the interest rate and growth rates of population and income.

Informed by the model, the data are re-examined. Consistent with the model, the data exhibit a significant positive relationship between tax rates and expenditure ratios, while there is no systematic partial relationship between expenditure ratios and income or population growth rates or interest rates. The parameter indicating preferences for public goods is not directly observable. However, using the explicit solution for the expenditure ratio, it is possible to obtain an indirect indication of this preference for each country considered, given that all other determinants of the expenditure ratio are observable for each country. The results show that different preferences for public goods are evident among the democratic countries considered. The US has the highest preference for public goods, corresponding to its lowest ratio of transfer payment to public goods expenditure and effective tax rate. Scandinavian countries have the lowest preference, combined with the highest expenditure ratios and tax rates. The Commonwealth countries are closely grouped in the middle. These results suggest that variations in expenditure patterns indeed reflect differences in preferences resulting from cultural differences across democratic countries. This chapter therefore provides a structural way to tackle the conjecture of Alesina and Glaeser (2004), who emphasise the importance of unobserved cultural factors in shaping the tax and expenditure policies across countries. On the other hand, by identifying differences in preferences for public goods, this study provides an alternative perspective to that taken by Alesina and Glaeser (2004), who instead focus on the role of different attitudes towards redistribution in Europe and the US in accounting for the considerable differences in their expenditure policies, though the process is not modelled formally.

This chapter is related to a large literature on political economy. Most of the literature considers one type of government expenditure, either public goods expenditure or transfer payments.[2] Several recent studies consider more than one type of government expenditure. Bearse *et al.* (2001) study majority voting over a transfer payment and public education in a static framework. Hassler *et al.* (2007) consider redistribution policy as well as provision of public goods financed by imposing a tax on the rich, which indicates the extent of redistribution, in a two-period overlapping generations model. Chapter 3 above examined majority voting over government expenditure on transfer payments as well as public goods, within a static framework. The present chapter follows this line of research, with a focus on the composition of government expenditure within an overlapping generations framework. As in previous chapters, the tax rate is taken as exogenous, which ensures voting over one dimension.

This chapter also relates to the literature on revealed preference for public goods, where estimates of the demand or preferences for public goods are obtained from survey data or voting outcomes; see Hockley and Harbour (1983) and Schram and Winden (1989) for examples. However, no comprehensive studies have been implemented to compare these preferences across countries. This chapter provides a more structural way to infer preferences for public goods for a range of democratic countries.

Section 5.1 describes some empirical evidence on expenditure ratios for a sample of democratic countries. Section 5.2 presents the model. The condition for majority support of the pay-as-you-go (PAYG) social contract is obtained, the voting equilibrium is derived, and comparative statics are examined. Section 5.3 presents some further empirical examination, informed

---

[2]For example, Tridimas (2001), Grossmann (2003) and Tridimas and Winer (2005) consider expenditure on public goods. Meltzer and Richard (1981), Grossman and Helpman (1998), Krusell and Rios-Rull (1999), Hassler *et al.* (2003), Hassler *et al.* (2005), Azzimonti *et al.* (2006) and Borck (2007) concentrate on transfer payments. The choice of government expenditure in these models is equivalent to the choice of the tax rate.

by the model, on the composition of expenditure among democracies.

5.1 Evidence on Expenditure Ratios

This section presents some empirical evidence on expenditure patterns across a sample of democratic countries. In view of the attention given to income inequality in the political economy literature, emphasis here is on the empirical relationship between the ratio of transfer payments to public goods expenditure and the ratio of median to mean income, a measure of income inequality.

It is very difficult indeed to obtain detailed comparable information on the composition of government expenditure for a wide range of countries. A dataset was constructed from *Government Financial Statistics* (2008) and other data sources, for 25 advanced democratic countries and a small group of non-democratic countries over the period 2000–2006. A major difficulty in classifying expenditure on transfers and public goods is that inadequate information about expenditure components is available. For instance, data on health and education expenditure are provided, but not all of this can be regarded as a pure public good. In the absence of clear information on the public–private mix, a specified fraction of expenditure on health and education is considered as expenditure on public goods. The ratio of total expenditure on transfers to that on public goods is calculated for three assumptions: the term R_F denotes the ratio obtained when a proportion, F, of the expenditure on health and education is included in the calculation of public goods expenditure. For example, $R_{1/2}$ refers to the ratio of total transfer expenditure to public goods expenditure, where public goods expenditure includes only one half of health and education expenditure.

Figure 5.1 shows the partial relationship between the ratio of transfer payment to public goods expenditure, $R_{1/2}$, and the ratio of median to mean income, $y_m/\bar{y}$, which are average values across the period 2000–2006. Chap-

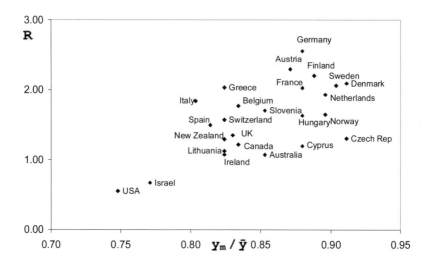

Figure 5.1: Expenditure Ratios versus Inequality Measures for a Sample of Democratic Countries

ter 3 described the procedure used for calculating the ratio of median to mean income from the Gini coefficient. A similar picture, with different absolute values of R, is obtained using a different proportion of health and education considered to be on public goods. Care must be taken in interpreting this diagram, considering the existence of differences in other relevant variables among countries. Nevertheless, Figure 5.1 suggests that there is clearly no systematic negative relationship between R and $y_m/\bar{y}$ across all these countries. For example, the US has both the lowest value of R and $y_m/\bar{y}$ (and has the lowest tax rate), while the Scandinavian countries, including Denmark, Finland, Norway and Sweden, all have much higher values of $y_m/\bar{y}$ and R. The Commonwealth countries of the UK, Australia, Canada and New Zealand are more closely grouped in the middle, showing a roughly negative relationship between R and $y_m/\bar{y}$.[3] These findings are consistent

---

[3] Further analysis reveals that the US has a higher expenditure share on every category of public goods (defence, public order and safety, economic affairs, health, education) ex-

with the mixed results documented in other empirical studies regarding the relationship between income inequality and redistribution across countries, as summarised in Perotti (1996) and Shelton (2007).

The lack of a negative relationship between R and $y_m/\bar{y}$, or in other words, a positive relationship between the expenditure ratio and income inequality, across countries does not necessarily mean that, within each country, such a relationship does not exist, once allowance has been made for a wider range of relevant variables. Unfortunately it is difficult to construct datasets showing changes over time within particular countries, and anyway it is highly likely that there would be insufficient variations in $y_m/\bar{y}$ to identify a relationship. Next, a simple overlapping generations model is presented, which allows for a range of other factors in the determination of the composition of expenditure.

5.2 The Model

This section begins by describing the overlapping generations model in which a pure public good and a transfer payment, in the form of a pension, are tax-financed on a PAYG basis. Next a condition under which a majority of each cohort supports the PAYG arrangement is established. Conditional on this social contract, the equilibrium under majority voting is characterised; in particular, the majority choice of the expenditure ratio is solved in closed form. Comparative static properties are also examined.

5.2.1 The Environment

Each individual lives for two periods, a working and a retirement period, so that the economy is populated by two overlapping cohorts in any given period. Let N_t denote the number of individuals born in period t. Individuals have identical preferences but different incomes. A young individual, i, born at time t, works in the first period and receives an exogenous income, $y_{i,t}$,

cept environment protection, compared with Scandinavian and Commonwealth countries.

which is taxed at the exogenously fixed rate τ. Young individuals have access to a storage technology, which pays a fixed rate of return, r, for every unit of goods stored in the previous period. In period t, a young individual, i, allocates disposable income between current consumption, $c_{1i,t}$, and savings through storage, $s_{i,t} \geq 0$. In retirement, the individual finances consumption of private goods, $c_{2i,t+1}$, using the unconditional and untaxed government pension, b_{t+1}, and the return on storage, $(1+r)s_{i,t}$. Government expenditures on pure public goods in t and $t+1$ are denoted as G_t and G_{t+1}.

Each individual is assumed to have the following Cobb–Douglas lifetime direct utility function, expressed in logarithmic form:

$$U_{i,t} = \log c_{1i,t} + \gamma \log Q_{G,t} + \beta \left(\log c_{2i,t+1} + \gamma \log Q_{G,t+1} \right) \qquad (5.1)$$

Here, $0 < \beta = 1/(1+\rho) < 1$ is the discount factor, ρ is the time preference rate and γ is the weight attached to the utility from the consumption of public goods, reflecting individuals' preference for public goods relative to private goods consumption. The terms $Q_{G,t}$ and $Q_{G,t+1}$ are the quantities of public goods consumed by each person at time t and $t+1$. Assume that production of public goods involves a constant unit cost, p.

To allow for population and income growth, suppose the average income of young individuals, $\bar{y}_t$, grows at a constant rate of ω, and the population grows at a constant rate, n. It is assumed that income growth involves an equal proportional change at all income levels and population growth involves an equal proportional change in population frequencies at each income level, so that ω and n are independent.

5.2.2   The Social Contract

Clearly, individuals with different incomes have different views about the PAYG arrangement. Low-income individuals may prefer a high value of the transfer b_{t+1} (and its associated high tax rate) since they are not able to save much to finance their consumption in the second period. Conversely high-income individuals could make adequate private savings during the working period and hence may prefer a low or even zero transfer (and a low tax rate). This subsection examines the condition required for the majority of each generation to be better off with the PAYG arrangement compared with a fully funded scheme in which retirement income is provided by private savings alone, thus ensuring cooperation between generations.

To compare the PAYG and fully funded schemes, assume that the two systems provide the same expenditure on public goods in each period, such that $G_t^P = G_t^F = G_t$, where a superscript, P, is used to denote values in the PAYG system, while F indicates values in the scheme with private pension funds only. So a sufficient condition for an individual's utility to be higher in the PAYG system is that lifetime income is higher.

Under the PAYG system, the present value of individual i's lifetime income is given by $(1 - \tau^P)y_{i,t} + (b_{t+1}^P/(1+r))$. Under the privately funded system where there is no transfer payment and income tax finances only the provision of public goods, individual i's lifetime income is simply $(1-\tau^F)y_{i,t}$. The tax rates in the two systems must differ, denoted as τ^F and τ^P respectively, since in the private scheme the government finances only public goods while in the PAYG system it finances public goods and the pension. Then the sufficient condition requires $(1 - \tau^P)y_{i,t} + b_{t+1}^P/(1+r) > (1 - \tau^F)y_{i,t}$, or equivalently:

$$1 + r < \frac{b_{t+1}^P}{y_{i,t}(\tau^P - \tau^F)} \tag{5.2}$$

The government budget constraint at time $t+1$ in the privately funded system is $G_{t+1} = \tau^F N_{t+1}\bar{y}_{t+1}$, and in the PAYG system it is given by $G_{t+1} + N_t b_{t+1}^P = \tau^P N_{t+1}\bar{y}_{t+1}$. Combining these two constraints gives the pension as:

$$b_{t+1}^P = (1+n)\bar{y}_{t+1}\left(\tau^P - \tau^F\right) \tag{5.3}$$

Substituting (5.3) into (5.2), and using $\bar{y}_{t+1} = \bar{y}_t(1+\omega)$ gives the following condition under which the ith individual is better off in the PAYG system:

$$(1+n)\left(1+\omega\right)\frac{\bar{y}_t}{y_{i,t}} > 1+r \qquad (5.4)$$

This can be compared with the Aaron (1966) and Samuelson (1958) condition in a model without income heterogeneity and public goods, which requires $(1+n)\left(1+\omega\right) > 1+r$. It is by ignoring cross-product terms that the condition is often stated as $r < n+\omega$. The condition in (5.4) implies that the condition for the average individual, for whom $y_{i,t} = \bar{y}_t$, is precisely the same as the Aaron–Samuelson condition.

An important feature of (5.4) is that it is independent of G, b and τ. In addition, it does not depend on the nature of individuals' preferences. Hence acceptance of the social contract by a majority of each cohort can be established prior to considerations regarding the choice of actual expenditure levels. That is, if

$$(1+n)\left(1+\omega\right)\frac{\bar{y}_t}{y_{m,t}} > 1+r \qquad (5.5)$$

the PAYG system gains majority support. For a positively skewed income distribution, median income, $y_{m,t}$, is less than the arithmetic mean income, $\bar{y}_t$: hence the greater the skewness, the more likely is the condition above to be satisfied for given values of the relevant rates. Those high-income individuals who would prefer only private funding are not allowed to 'contract out' of, or withdraw from, the social contract and the pension system. Without this compulsory element there would be an adverse selection problem arising from the gradual reduction in average income of those remaining in the system, as the richest individuals gradually contract out.

5.2.3   The Voting Equilibrium

This section examines the majority voting equilibrium, assuming that the condition required for majority support of the PAYG system, established in (5.5) above, is satisfied. Voting takes place in each period and individuals vote only on the pension to be paid during the next period. Hence, there is no incentive for members of the old cohort to vote, since their pension (which they do not finance) was determined by their vote in the previous period. Hassler *et al.* (2007) use a similar assumption, that each generation votes once only, to find the political equilibrium in an overlapping generations context. The median member of the young cohort is the decisive voter.

Normalising the price of the private consumption good to unity, the lifetime budget constraint of an individual is:

$$c_{1i,t} + \frac{c_{2i,t+1}}{1+r} = (1-\tau)y_{i,t} + \frac{b_{t+1}}{1+r} \equiv M_{i,t} \tag{5.6}$$

This allows for the fact that tax-financed public goods are non-excludable so that individuals are not charged at the point of consumption.

The consumption plans are given, using the standard properties of Cobb–Douglas utility functions, and with $s_{i,t} > 0$, as:

$$c_{1i,t} = \left(\frac{1}{1+\beta}\right) M_{i,t} \tag{5.7}$$

$$c_{2i,t+1} = \left(\frac{\beta}{1+\beta}\right)(1+r) M_{i,t} \tag{5.8}$$

The non-negativity constraint for storage is not binding for all individuals with realistic parameter values.

The indirect utility, $V_{i,t}$, is then obtained by substituting public goods consumption $Q_{G,t}$ and $Q_{G,t+1}$ from the government budget constraint, $G_t + N_{t-1}b_t = \tau N_t \bar{y}_t$, where $G_t = pQ_{G,t}$, and the optimal $c_{1i,t}$ and $c_{2i,t+1}$ into the direct utility function (8.1), giving:

$$
\begin{aligned}
V_{i,t} = \ & \log\left\{\left[(1+r)(1-\tau)y_{i,t} + b_{t+1}\right]/(1+r)\right\} \\
& + \beta \log\left\{\beta\left[(1+r)(1-\tau)y_{i,t} + b_{t+1}\right]\right\} \\
& + \gamma \log\left(\tau N_t \bar{y}_t - N_{t-1}b_t\right) + \beta\gamma \log\left(\tau N_{t+1}\bar{y}_{t+1} - N_t b_{t+1}\right) \\
& - (1+\beta)\left\{\log(1+\beta) + \gamma \log p\right\}
\end{aligned}
\tag{5.9}
$$

Voting involves only one dimension, the value of b_{t+1}. All other variables determining an individual's indirect utility are either predetermined or exogenously given. If the indirect utilities for all young individuals are single-peaked in b_{t+1}, the majority voting outcome is dominated by the median voter, who in the present context is the individual with median income, $y_{m,t}$.

Single-peakedness is guaranteed if the relationship between $V_{i,t}$ and b_{t+1} is strictly concave for all individuals, that is, if $\partial^2 V_{i,t}/\partial b_{t+1}^2 < 0$ for all i. This condition is confirmed by differentiation of (5.9). Consequently, maximising the indirect utility function with respect to b_{t+1} gives the majority choice of pension at time $t+1$, as:

$$
\begin{aligned}
b_{m,t+1} = {} & \left\{ \bar{y}_t \left(1+\beta\right)/\left(1+\beta+\beta\gamma\right) \right\} \times \\
& \left\{ (1+n)(1+w)\tau - \frac{\beta\gamma}{1+\beta}(1+r)(1-\tau)\frac{y_{m,t}}{\bar{y}_t} \right\}
\end{aligned}
\tag{5.10}
$$

The majority choice of public goods expenditure, $G_{m,t+1}$, can be solved by substituting $b_{m,t+1}$ into the government budget constraint at time $t+1$, giving:

$$
\begin{aligned}
G_{m,t+1}/N_t = {} & \bar{y}_t \left\{ \beta\gamma/\left(1+\beta+\beta\gamma\right) \right\} \times \\
& \left\{ (1+n)\left(1+w\right)\tau + (1+r)(1-\tau)\frac{y_{m,t}}{\bar{y}_t} \right\}
\end{aligned}
\tag{5.11}
$$

So the ratio of the total expenditure on pensions to that on public goods, $R_{m,t+1}$, is:

$$
\begin{aligned}
R_{m,t+1} = {} & \left\{ \left(\frac{1+\beta}{\beta\gamma}\right)(1+n)(1+w)\tau - (1+r)(1-\tau)\frac{y_{m,t}}{\bar{y}_t} \right\} \\
& / \left\{ (1+n)(1+w)\tau + (1+r)(1-\tau)\frac{y_{m,t}}{\bar{y}_t} \right\}
\end{aligned}
\tag{5.12}
$$

This result shows that $R_{m,t+1}$ depends, *inter alia*, on the ratio of median income to mean income at time t and parameters regarding population growth, income growth, the tax rate and preferences. Furthermore, an implication of Cobb–Douglas preferences is that the expenditure ratio does not depend on the constant cost of producing the public good, p, or the absolute population size. The precise form of the income distribution is irrelevant; only the *ratio* of median to mean income matters. The growth rates of population and incomes, n and ω, appear in a symmetric fashion in (8.15); they both have the same effect on $R_{m,t+1}$.

The crucial ratio, $y_{m,t}/\bar{y}_t$, is not affected by population and income growth, according to the assumption that income growth involves an equal proportional change at all income levels and population growth involves an equal proportional change in population frequencies at each income level. Hence, by equation (5.10), the majority choice of pension per old individual, $b_{m,t+1}$, grows at the same rate as average income, $\bar{y}_t$. Consequently, all endogenous variables, including total expenditure on public goods and pensions, total consumption of young and old individuals and total storage by young individuals, grow at the same rate as aggregate income, $n+\omega$. Hence, the voting equilibrium is characterised by a balanced growth path. These implications regarding balanced growth are consistent with those of neoclassical growth models with exogenous PAYG social security, despite the fact that the social security is determined by majority choice in the present model.

5.2.4   Comparative Statics

This section presents some comparative static properties of the model. The aim is to examine how total expenditure on pensions, $B_{m,t+1} \equiv N_t b_{m,t+1}$, public goods, $G_{m,t+1}$, and in particular their ratio, $R_{m,t+1}$, change in response to changes in parameters of the model. As shown in equations (5.10), (5.11) and (8.15), these relations are nonlinear. The signs of first and second derivatives of these variables with respect to each parameter are reported in Table 5.1.

A rise in $y_{m,t}/\bar{y}_t$ represents a fall in inequality. Both $B_{m,t+1}$ and $G_{m,t+1}$ are respectively linearly decreasing and increasing in $y_{m,t}/\bar{y}_t$, suggesting that higher inequality causes voters to vote for higher pension expenditure and lower public goods expenditure. Hence, the first derivative of $R_{m,t+1}$ with

Table 5.1: Comparative Statics of the Majority Choice of Expenditure on Pensions and Public Goods and Their Ratio

	$y_{m,t}/\bar{y}_t$	τ	γ	β	r	ω	n
	First Derivative						
$B_{m,t+1}$	−	+	−	−	−	+	+
$G_{m,t+1}$	+	+	+	+	+	+	+
$R_{m,t+1}$	−	+	−	−	−	+	+
	Second Derivative						
$B_{m,t+1}$	0	0	+	+	0	0	+
$G_{m,t+1}$	0	0	−	−	0	0	+
$R_{m,t+1}$	+	−	+	+	+	−	−

respect to $y_{m,t}/\bar{y}_t$ is negative. The second derivative is positive, implying that the ratio of pension expenditure to public goods increases at an increasing rate as inequality rises.

The majority choice of total expenditure on pensions and public goods depends on the tax rate, such that $B_{m,t+1}$ is linearly increasing in τ, and $G_{m,t+1}$ is linear in τ, but increases with τ only if $(1+n)(1+\omega) - (1 + r)(y_{m,t}/\bar{y}_t) > 0$. This condition is the same as that derived in (5.5) for majority support for the PAYG social security system. The majority choice of $R_{m,t+1}$ is increasing in τ unambiguously, but at a decreasing rate, if again the condition for majority support for the social contract is satisfied. These results suggest that an increase in the tax rate provides more revenue for both types of expenditure, but the increase in pension expenditure is relatively higher than the increase in public goods expenditure.

The results with respect to γ, the utility weight attached to public goods consumption in the utility function, suggest as expected that an increase in the preference for public goods unambiguously increases the total expenditure on public goods, while decreasing total expenditure on pensions and the ratio of pension to public goods expenditure. A positive second derivative of $R_{m,t+1}$ with respect to γ implies that the ratio of pension expenditure to public goods decreases at a decreasing rate as the preference for public goods rises.

Increases in the interest and time preference rates increase public goods expenditure, but decrease expenditure on pensions and its ratio to public goods expenditure. This is clear from equation (5.5): an increase in the interest rate raises the return on private savings such that individuals are more likely to prefer the privately funded scheme; that is, individuals are more likely to vote for a lower pension.

Increases in ω and n raise total expenditure on pensions and on public goods, and also their ratio. With income growth or population growth, tax revenues of the government are increased such that the government is able to spend more on both types of expenditure. However, the increase in the expenditure on pensions is higher than the expenditure on public goods because higher n and ω make individuals more likely to prefer the PAYG system, as shown in equation (5.4).

5.3   Further Empirical Examination

This section returns to the dataset covering government expenditure for a cross-sectional sample of democratic countries, discussed briefly above, making use of the analytical results.

5.3.1   Sensitivity to Parameter Values

The comparative static analysis does not show the sensitivity of the expenditure ratio with respect to changes in parameters. This subsection presents a numerical illustration of the comparative static properties which may help to identify some important factors underlying the observed variations in expenditure ratios.

To set a baseline value for each parameter, assume that the length of a time period in the model is 20 years. Using the data sample, the average annual growth rates of income and population and the real interest rate across the democracies are 0.024, 0.007 and 0.0052, giving $\omega = 0.73$, $n = 0.16$ and

$r = 0.17$ respectively. Assuming that the time preference rate is equal to the interest rate, $\rho = r$, then $\beta = 0.97$.[4] The value for the tax rate is $\tau = 0.4$, the average income tax rate across the democracies. Given the baseline values for other parameters and an average median to mean income ratio of $y_m/\bar{y} = 0.85$, γ is chosen, using (8.15), to match the average expenditure ratio for the sample ($R = 1.59$), which gives $\gamma = 0.65$.

Figures 5.2 and 5.3 illustrate variations in the relationship between $R_{m,t+1}$ and $y_{m,t}/\bar{y}_t$, for given values of the other parameters, using variations of 15 and 30 per cent changes around the baseline values. As expected, increasing $y_{m,t}/\bar{y}_t$ reduces $R_{m,t+1}$ at a decreasing rate in all diagrams, demonstrating that lower inequality is consistently associated with a lower ratio of expenditure on pensions to that on public goods. However, the relationship between R and $y_m/\bar{y}$ is also quite flat around empirically relevant values of $y_m/\bar{y}$, about 0.75 to 0.95 for the democratic countries in the sample. This may explain the weak empirical support for a positive relationship between income inequality and redistribution, as summarised in Perotti (1996) and Shelton (2007). Lind (2005) conjectures other reasons underlying the mixed empirical results.

The diagrams also show that the majority choice of R is quite sensitive to variations in the tax rate, discount factor and the utility weight attached to public goods over the most relevant range of income inequality, and less sensitive to changes in the interest rate and growth rates of population and income. This indicates the potential importance of preferences over public goods, as summarised by γ, and the tax rate, τ, in shaping the composition of expenditure for democratic countries.

---

[4] Values for ω, n and r are obtained respectively from $(1+0.024)^{20} - 1$, $(1+0.007)^{20} - 1$ and $(1+0.0052)^{20} - 1$. The value of discount factor, β, is obtained from $1/(1+0.0052)^{20}$.

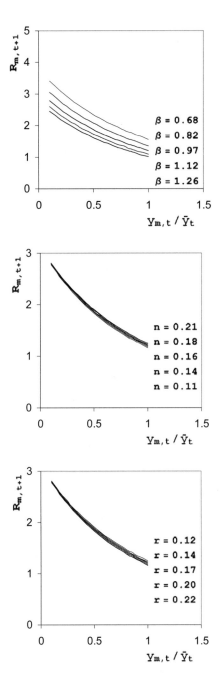

Figure 5.2: Variation in Expenditure Shares: Alternative Parameters A

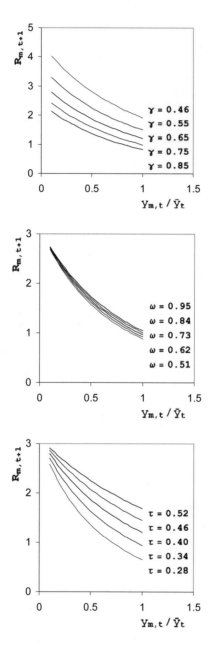

Figure 5.3: Variation in Expenditure Shares: Alternative Parameters B

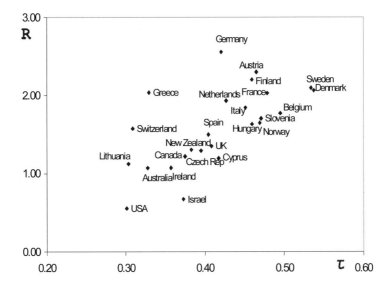

Figure 5.4: Expenditure Ratios versus Tax Rates for a Sample of Democratic Countries

5.3.2 Cross-country Comparisons

Figure 5.4 plots the expenditure ratio, $R_{1/2}$, versus the average effective tax rate, τ, for the democratic countries. Consistent with the results above, a higher ratio of expenditure on transfer payments to that on public goods is positively related to the tax rate across countries, and this partial relationship is quite significant. There are systematic differences across country groups having different cultural backgrounds. The Scandinavian group of countries has both the highest average tax rate and expenditure ratio, the US has the lowest tax rate and expenditure ratio, while the Commonwealth countries are closely grouped in the middle of the figure. The data exhibit no systematic partial relationship between expenditure ratios and income or population growth rates or interest rates, which is not surprising considering the numerical results above.

Another important factor identified in the numerical results is the parameter, γ, indicating the preference for public goods relative to private goods. Despite the fact that it is not independently observable (in view of well-known problems about preference revelation in the context of public goods), it can be inferred for each country by rearranging the analytical result in equation (8.15) to express γ in terms of other variables, which are all observable for each country.[5] Econometric estimation is not possible since time series data for each country are not available and, as mentioned earlier, they would anyway be unlikely to show sufficient variation in many of the crucial variables, in particular R and $y_m/\bar{y}$. The result in equation (8.15) is derived conditional on (5.5), the condition for majority support of the PAYG system, so it is first necessary to check if this condition holds in the data. It is found that (5.5) holds in all the democratic countries in the sample.

Table 5.2 reports summary measures, in the form of means and coefficients of variation, of relevant variables for several groups of countries. Information for each country is reported in Table 5.3. The resulting values for γ are reported in the last three columns of each table, for each assumed fraction of expenditure on health and education treated as public goods. The democratic countries are divided into various groups, within which cultural characteristics may be thought to be similar. Developing economies include the Czech Republic, Hungary and Lithuania. These belong to the group of middle-income economies in the World Development Indicator (WDI) classification which contains countries in which Gross National Income per capita in 2006 was between \$876 and \$10725. Some summary statistics for a small sample of non-democratic countries are also reported in Table 5.2. Since the majority voting model is not suitable for these countries, γ is not computed. It is clear that compared with democracies, non-democratic countries on av-

---

[5]This way of obtaining an unobservable variable using a structural model is similar to the approach used by Ingram *et al.* (1994). Unobservable shocks underlying business fluctuations are explicitly solved using a real business cycle model and observations on output, consumption and labour hours.

erage have higher income inequality, a lower tax rate and a lower ratio of transfer payments to public goods expenditure.

Table 5.2: Average and Coefficient of Variation of Variables for Country Groups

Country	$y_m/\bar{y}$	τ	$R_{1/4}$	$R_{2/4}$	$R_{3/4}$	$\gamma_{1/4}$	$\gamma_{2/4}$	$\gamma_{3/4}$
All	0.85	0.40	2.27	1.59	1.23	0.49	0.65	0.78
Democracies	(0.05)	(0.17)	(0.34)	(0.32)	(0.31)	(0.33)	(0.29)	(0.27)
Scandinavian	0.90	0.50	2.99	2.00	1.51	0.40	0.56	0.70
	(0.01)	(0.08)	(0.13)	(0.12)	(0.12)	(0.10)	(0.08)	(0.07)
Others	0.84	0.40	2.14	1.51	1.17	0.51	0.66	0.79
	(0.05)	(0.15)	(0.35)	(0.34)	(0.33)	(0.34)	(0.30)	(0.28)
Developing	0.87	0.38	1.88	1.35	1.06	0.62	0.80	0.97
	(0.05)	(0.20)	(0.20)	(0.19)	(0.19)	(0.16)	(0.16)	(0.17)
Developed	0.85	0.42	2.33	1.62	1.25	0.48	0.62	0.75
	(0.05)	(0.16)	(0.34)	(0.32)	(0.32)	(0.34)	(0.29)	(0.27)
Common-	0.84	0.38	1.71	1.23	0.95	0.51	0.67	0.80
wealth	(0.01)	(0.09)	(0.09)	(0.10)	(0.11)	(0.02)	(0.02)	(0.04)
Others	0.85	0.42	2.37	1.66	1.28	0.49	0.64	0.77
	(0.06)	(0.17)	(0.34)	(0.32)	(0.31)	(0.36)	(0.31)	(0.29)
United States	0.75	0.30	0.75	0.55	0.44	0.78	0.92	1.03
Non-	0.77	0.32	1.32	0.99	0.8			
democratic	(0.15)	(0.46)	(0.57)	(0.55)	(0.53)			

The inferred values for γ need to be treated with caution, bearing in mind also that the model uses a stylised voting process rather than modelling the more complex decision making mechanisms in practice. Nevertheless they can be regarded as indicative of relative orders of magnitude. As shown in Table 5.2, differences in the preference for public goods are evident across countries. The US has a much higher value of γ, corresponding to the fact that it has the lowest ratio of transfer payments to public goods expenditure, despite having the highest income inequality among the democracies. In contrast, the Scandinavian countries have the lowest average γ among the democratic country groups, contributing to the high ratio of transfer payments to public goods despite the relatively low degree of inequality (a value of $y_m/\bar{y}$ closer to unity). The Commonwealth countries have a γ that is comparable to the average of all democracies, but the coefficient of variation is relatively small compared with other groups, implying a similar preference over public goods among these countries.

These results suggest that variations in expenditure patterns indeed reflect differences in preferences resulting from cultural differences across democratic countries. The expenditure choice in the model corresponds to that of a selfish median voter, who has no altruistic or other motive for interpersonal redistribution via the tax and transfer system. The cultural differences indicated here thus relate purely to preferences for public goods relative to private consumption, where the latter is partly financed by the transfer payment. Asked to allocate an (exogenously determined) amount of tax revenue, US voters are inferred to prefer more to be spent on public goods relative to transfers, leaving a greater role for private saving. This study then provides an alternative perspective to that taken by Alesina and Glaeser (2004), who also emphasise the importance of cultural factors in shaping the tax and expenditure policy but instead focus on the role of different attitudes towards redistribution in Europe and the US. They summarise evidence from a *World Values Survey*, which reveals different attitudes towards redistribution in the US and Europe, as follows (2004, p. 220): 'Americans believe that they live in a mobile society in which individual effort can lift people up the social ladder. Likewise, the European welfare states are supported by European beliefs that the poor are unfortunate and would be stuck in their poverty without government intervention.' These different attitudes towards mobility and risk are seen to influence the role of social insurance (and associated redistribution via risk pooling) in different countries. However, unlike the present chapter, this process is not modelled formally in Alesina and Glaeser (2004).

To the extent that expenditure policies may actually be influenced by differential degrees of aversion to income inequality, the values of γ obtained

Table 5.3: Summary Information for All Democracies

Country	$y_m/\bar{y}$	τ	$R_{1/4}$	$R_{2/4}$	$R_{3/4}$	$\gamma_{1/4}$	$\gamma_{2/4}$	$\gamma_{3/4}$
Australia	0.85	0.33	1.53	1.07	0.82	0.51	0.66	0.79
Austria	0.87	0.47	3.55	2.30	1.70	0.30	0.44	0.56
Belgium	0.83	0.50	2.61	1.77	1.34	0.43	0.60	0.75
Canada	0.83	0.37	1.80	1.22	0.92	0.51	0.69	0.84
Cyprus	0.88	0.42	1.57	1.20	0.97	0.64	0.78	0.91
Czech Republic	0.91	0.38	1.76	1.30	1.04	0.56	0.71	0.85
Denmark	0.91	0.53	3.23	2.09	1.55	0.37	0.53	0.68
Finland	0.89	0.46	3.28	2.20	1.66	0.36	0.51	0.64
France	0.88	0.48	2.94	2.03	1.55	0.37	0.51	0.63
Germany	0.88	0.42	3.69	2.56	1.96	0.25	0.33	0.41
Greece	0.82	0.33	2.56	2.04	1.69	0.39	0.48	0.56
Hungary	0.88	0.46	2.29	1.63	1.27	0.55	0.74	0.90
Ireland	0.82	0.36	1.62	1.07	0.80	0.66	0.95	1.22
Israel	0.77	0.37	0.82	0.67	0.57	0.94	1.05	1.14
Italy	0.80	0.45	2.59	1.84	1.43	0.38	0.51	0.62
Lithuania	0.82	0.30	1.58	1.12	0.87	0.73	0.95	1.15
Netherlands	0.90	0.43	2.64	1.93	1.52	0.35	0.45	0.54
New Zealand	0.82	0.39	1.93	1.29	0.97	0.50	0.68	0.82
Norway	0.90	0.47	2.45	1.65	1.24	0.44	0.60	0.74
Slovenia	0.85	0.47	2.49	1.71	1.30	0.50	0.70	0.87
Spain	0.81	0.40	2.08	1.50	1.17	0.51	0.67	0.82
Sweden	0.90	0.54	3.01	2.06	1.57	0.42	0.60	0.75
Switzerland	0.82	0.31	2.22	1.57	1.22	0.31	0.41	0.49
United Kingdom	0.83	0.41	1.81	1.35	1.07	0.52	0.65	0.77
United States	0.75	0.30	0.75	0.55	0.44	0.78	0.92	1.03

using the present model would be modified. However, an aversion to inequality on the part of the median voter was modelled explicitly by Creedy and Moslehi (2009), in examining government expenditure in a static model which also allowed for labour supply responses to taxation. Except for very high degrees of inequality aversion, such a non-selfish desire for redistributive transfer payments was found to lead to only a small variation in the relationship between R and $y_m/\bar{y}$.

5.4   Conclusions

This chapter constructed an extension of the single-period model to consider the determinants of the composition of government expenditure in democratic countries and to what extent it may be explained by differences in economic conditions or preferences. A two-period overlapping generations model was constructed to examine the composition of expenditure under majority voting. The main focus was on public goods and a transfer payment, in the form of a pension, which are financed by exogenous income tax on a pay-as-you-go basis. The choice of expenditure is complicated by the fact that the pension involves a combination of income shifting between phases of the life cycle with both inter-generational and intra-generational transfers. The latter arises because the basic pension is unrelated to income whereas the tax is proportional to income. The former arises from the pay-as-you-go feature of financing whereby each generation can benefit from productivity and thus income growth accruing to the following generation.

The condition under which there is majority support for the social contract involved in a pay-as-you-go financing structure was established and found to be independent of the tax rate, expenditure levels and individuals' preference. Selfish individuals vote in their first period of life on the pensions to be received in their second period. Preferences are single-peaked and the decisive voter is the young individual with the median income. It was found that the majority choice of the ratio of expenditure on pensions to public goods falls at a decreasing rate when the ratio of median to mean income increases. It therefore has in common with those models which focus on the choice of tax rate the property that a higher degree of basic inequality is associated with a more redistributive structure.

However, a numerical illustration suggests that, over realistic values, differences in the ratio of transfer payments to public goods expenditure arising from differences in income inequality are likely to be small. Furthermore, the ratio is relatively sensitive to the tax rate and preference parameters (the time preference rate and weight attached to public goods in utility functions). This suggests that in a cross-sectional comparison of democratic countries, a simple relationship between redistribution and basic inequality is unlikely to be observed.

Despite the considerable data problems, an empirical examination for a sample of democratic countries illustrates that there are systematic differences in expenditure patterns across different cultural groups of countries. Using the analytical result from the model, the utility weight attached to the public good was inferred for each country, and the results suggest that different preferences are evident among these groups. Thus preference variations indicating cultural differences may play an important role in explaining the considerable differences in expenditure patterns among democratic countries.

Part III

Optimal Choice

Chapter 6

The Optimal Expenditure Composition

This Part of the present book turns from the positive analysis of majority voting over the composition of government expenditure to the normative welfare economics treatment of the optimal composition. The aim is to examine the composition of government expenditure that maximises a utilitarian social welfare function. Hence the evaluation, or social welfare, function is considered to be a function of individuals' (indirect) utilities. In this chapter, the division between expenditure on public goods and on transfer payments is examined using the simple static model introduced in Chapter 3. Thus, individuals are assumed to have similar preferences, but differing abilities and thus wages. Expenditure is financed by a proportional income tax.[1]

The analysis, while being in the tradition of optimal tax models, therefore differs from the standard problem in the optimal tax literature, which is concerned with the determination of the tax level and its associated transfer payment. The present chapter considers the optimal allocation between the two categories for a given tax rate, and thus the way in which the allocation

---

[1] This focus contrasts with the literature concerned with the optimal allocation between consumption and investment expenditure in a growth framework. In such models, a social planner, or representative agent, chooses the optimal composition of government expenditure to maximise a multi-period welfare function: for recent examples see, for example, Chen (2006), Agénor (2008), Piras (2001) and Lee (1992).

varies as the tax rate varies. As in previous chapters, the tax rate may be regarded as being determined by other considerations, for example relating to taxable capacity or 'conventional' or politically acceptable levels. With three policy instruments and a government budget constraint, there are two degrees of freedom. It would be possible to use numerical methods to carry out a two-dimensional search – over the public good expenditure and the tax rate (the transfer then being given from the government budget constraint) – to obtain the values which maximise a specified social welfare function. But the focus here is on the expenditure composition, and it turns out to be possible to derive explicit solutions which give useful insights into their determinants.

In the standard optimal tax framework, closed-form solutions are seldom available. In the present context, the solutions for expenditure components, and their ratio, are shown to depend on the ratio of a measure of location of the wage rate distribution to the arithmetic mean wage. The location measure is a welfare-weighted average of wage rates, with weights depending on the properties of the social welfare function being maximised. An approximation to the welfare-weighted average is obtained, providing explicit expressions for the expenditure components to be derived. These allow comparisons to be made with the case considered in Chapter 3, where the composition of expenditure is modelled as the outcome of majority voting.

Section 6.1 considers the optimal allocation of expenditure for an exogenous tax rate, for general forms of utility and social welfare functions. The special case of Cobb–Douglas utility functions is examined in Section 6.2, which derives the indirect utility function of each individual, expressed in terms of expenditure on the public good, the transfer payment and the given tax rate. The approximation for the welfare-weighted mean wage is derived in Section 6.3, allowing the expenditure share to be expressed explicitly in terms of the approximation for the welfare-weighted mean as a ratio of the average wage. Section 7.4 reports numerical examples, including the relationship between the composition of expenditure and the tax rate, as well as examining the effect of changes in the wage rate distribution.

6.1 The General Case

Suppose the amount of a public good, G, and a transfer payment, in the form of a tax-free basic income of b per person, is tax-financed on a pay-as-you-go basis. Each individual's labour supply, and hence taxable income, is influenced not only by the tax structure but also by the expenditure composition itself. The optimal expenditure composition is that combination of basic income and expenditure on the public good which maximises a social welfare function, subject to the government's budget constraint. The present analysis considers individualistic and 'welfarist' social welfare functions, whereby the welfare metric for each person is the utility level, which is therefore considered to be cardinal and interpersonally comparable: all individuals are assumed to have the same utility function, and differ only in facing different wage rates. Utilities are expressed in terms of individuals' indirect utilities, V_i, for $i = 1, ..., n$, and hence in terms of policy variables. Hence this section explores the optimal composition of expenditure for a social welfare function of the planner, which takes the general form:

$$W = W(V_1, ..., V_n) \qquad (6.1)$$

The objective can thus be simply stated: maximise W subject to the government budget constraint such that b is expressed as some function of G, so that $b = f(G)$. After forming the appropriate Lagrangian, the first-order conditions can easily be written down. However, they are (as in the standard optimal tax problem) deceptively simple and are actually nonlinear equations involving b and G. For present purposes it is most convenient to express the first-order conditions in terms of a standard tangency solution: that is, an optimal allocation of expenditure is obtained as a point of tangency of the highest social indifference curve which can be reached subject to the government's budget constraint.

The optimal is thus characterised by the condition:

$$\frac{db}{dG}\bigg|_t = \frac{db}{dG}\bigg|_W \tag{6.2}$$

where the left hand side of (6.2) is the slope of the budget constraint and the right hand side is the slope of a social indifference curve. The latter curves show combinations of G and b which leave W unchanged, and are thus derived by differentiating W totally with respect to public good expenditure and the transfer payment, giving:

$$dW = \left(\sum_{i=1}^n \frac{\partial W}{\partial V_i}\frac{\partial V_i}{\partial b}\right) db + \left(\sum_{i=1}^n \frac{\partial W}{\partial V_i}\frac{\partial V_i}{\partial G}\right) dG \tag{6.3}$$

Setting $dW = 0$ gives the slope of indifference curves as:

$$\frac{db}{dG}\bigg|_W = -\frac{\sum_{i=1}^n \frac{\partial W}{\partial V_i}\frac{\partial V_i}{\partial G}}{\sum_{i=1}^n \frac{\partial W}{\partial V_i}\frac{\partial V_i}{\partial b}} \tag{6.4}$$

This slope can be expressed more conveniently by defining v_i as the welfare weight attached to an increase in i's income (in the form of the basic income). This term is often referred to as the 'social marginal valuation' of i's income. Hence:

$$v_i = \frac{\partial W}{\partial V_i}\frac{\partial V_i}{\partial b} \tag{6.5}$$

and:

$$\frac{db}{dG}\bigg|_W = -\sum_{i=1}^n v_i' \left(\frac{\partial V_i/\partial G}{\partial V_i/\partial b}\right) \tag{6.6}$$

with $v_i' = v_i / \sum_{i=1}^n v_i$. The slope of social indifference curves is therefore a weighted sum of the ratio of $\partial V_i/\partial G$ to $\partial V_i/\partial b$.

Clearly further progress requires the specification of the economic structure, giving rise to the V_i and the precise form of the government's budget constraint. The most tractable approach is to assume that utility functions are Cobb-Douglas in form. This special case is examined in the following section. Other simpler tractable forms would need to be quasi-linear. More complex forms, for example even the constant elasticity of substitution case, do not allow for any of the simplifications discussed below. Numerical methods could of course be used to solve the problem for particular parameter values, but the aim here is to examine the basic form of relationships involved.

6.2 Cobb–Douglas Preferences

This section examines the tangency solution, established in the previous section, for the special case of Cobb–Douglas direct utility functions. It is necessary first to obtain the corresponding indirect utility functions, in terms of the quantity of the public good produced, the transfer payment and the tax rate. Hence labour supply, for an individual who faces a given wage rate and tax rate, and receives a non-means-tested transfer payment, must be derived. This is considered in Subsection 6.2.1. Earnings are the only source of non-transfer income and tax revenue is devoted only to the provision of the pure public good and the transfer payment. Subsection 6.2.2 obtains the resulting budget constraint facing the government, which depends on arithmetic mean wage income. This is in fact the same as in the framework considered in Chapter 3, but the results are repeated here for ease of reference. Subsection 6.2.3 then uses the tangency condition in equation (6.2) to produce an expression for the expenditure share in terms of the welfare-weighted mean income as a ratio of arithmetic mean income from earnings.

6.2.1 Indirect Utility Functions

Each individual is assumed to derive utility from consumption, c, leisure, h, and the quantity of a public good, G. Individual subscripts are omitted from c and h for convenience. By definition all individuals consume the same amount of the pure public good which must be tax-financed. Individuals have similar preferences but different productivities and therefore wage rates, w. The direct utility function is assumed to be Cobb–Douglas, so that:

$$U = c^{\alpha} h^{\beta} G^{1-\alpha-\beta} \tag{6.7}$$

The choice of Cobb–Douglas utility ensures that the choice of expenditure per person on the public good is independent of the population size. Hence it avoids the possibility that expenditure per person tends to zero as the population increases. Although all individuals consume the same amount of the public good, they do not receive the same benefits: higher-wage individuals experience higher marginal utility.

The choice of G is not determined at the individual level, since individuals cannot be excluded. The price of the private consumption good is normalised to unity, so that consumption and net earnings are equal. Suppose there is an unconditional and untaxed transfer payment of b per individual. There is a simple proportional income tax, with the rate, t, so that the price of leisure is $w(1-t)$. Therefore the form of each individual's budget constraint is:

$$c = w(1-h)(1-t) + b \tag{6.8}$$

The transfer payment per person is restricted to be positive, so that, for example, public good expenditure cannot be financed from a poll tax.

Define full income, M, as the net income obtained if all an individual's endowment of one unit of time is devoted to work, so that $M = w(1-t) + b$. The budget constraint is thus $c + hw(1-t) = M$ and, using the standard properties of the Cobb–Douglas utility function, the demand for private goods and leisure can be written as:

$$c = \alpha' M \tag{6.9}$$

$$h = \beta' \frac{M}{w(1-t)} \tag{6.10}$$

where $\alpha' = \alpha/(\alpha + \beta)$ and $\beta' = \beta/(\alpha + \beta)$. The individual works, that is $h < 1$, if the wage rate exceeds a threshold, $w_{\min}$, such that $w_{\min} = \frac{\beta'}{1-\beta'} \frac{b}{1-t}$. For those who work:

$$y_i = \alpha' w_i - \frac{\beta' b}{1 - t} \tag{6.11}$$

The indirect utility function, V, is obtained by substituting the solutions for c and h given above into the direct utility function, so that indirect utility becomes:

$$V = k \left(\frac{M}{w(1 - t)} \right)^{\alpha + \beta} G^{1 - \alpha - \beta} \tag{6.12}$$

where:

$$k = \alpha'^{\alpha} \beta'^{\beta} \left(w(1 - t) \right)^{\alpha} \tag{6.13}$$

6.2.2 The Government Budget Constraint

The government budget constraint requires that total revenue from the proportional income tax, equal to $t \sum_{i=1}^{n} y_i$ for a population of n individuals, is sufficient to finance the transfer payment, nb, and public good expenditure, pG, where p is the cost per unit of the public good, which is assumed to be fixed. If $\bar{y}$ denotes arithmetic mean earnings, then:

$$b + \frac{pG}{n} = t\bar{y} \tag{6.14}$$

In order to obtain $\bar{y}$, aggregation must be carried out over all individuals, and using (6.11):

$$\bar{y} = \frac{1}{n} \sum_{w > w_{\min}} \left\{ \alpha' w_i - \frac{\beta' b}{1 - t} \right\} \tag{6.15}$$

Letting $F_1(w_{\min})$ and $F(w_{\min})$ denote respectively the proportion of total wage (rates) and the proportion of people with $w < w_{\min}$:

$$\bar{y} = \bar{w} \alpha' \{1 - F_1(w_{\min})\} - \left(\frac{\beta' b}{1 - t} \right) \{1 - F(w_{\min})\} \tag{6.16}$$

where $\bar{w}$ denotes the arithmetic mean wage rate. This expression is highly nonlinear in view of the fact that $w_{\min}$ depends on b and t, so it is not possible to express b as a convenient function of t. However, the analysis is tractable if the following approximation is used. Assume that relatively few individuals do not work, so that F_1 and F are small and can be neglected. This produces a linear relationship between arithmetic means of y and w, whereby:

$$\bar{y} = \alpha'\bar{w} - \frac{b\beta'}{(1-t)} \tag{6.17}$$

This assumption in fact has a negligible effect on the shape of the government's budget constraint in the relevant region around the optimal point, though it may have a small effect on the absolute size of the basic income. By substituting this expression for average earnings, in (6.17), into the government budget constraint in (6.14), it is possible to express b in terms of average earnings, the tax rate and G. This gives:

$$b = \frac{t\alpha'\bar{w} - \frac{pG}{n}}{1 + \beta'\frac{t}{(1-t)}} \tag{6.18}$$

This completes the information needed to derive an expression for the optimal composition.

6.2.3   The Optimal Composition

Differentiating b, in (6.18), with respect to G, the slope of the government's budget constraint for a given tax rate is:

$$\left.\frac{db}{dG}\right|_t = -\frac{p}{n}\left(1 + \beta'\frac{t}{(1-t)}\right)^{-1} \tag{6.19}$$

This provides the left hand side of the condition in (6.2).

Differentiating (6.12) with respect to G and b and dividing gives:

$$\frac{\partial V_i/\partial G}{\partial V_i/\partial b} = \frac{(1-\alpha-\beta)}{(\alpha+\beta)G}\{w_i(1-t) + b\} \tag{6.20}$$

Therefore the slope of social indifference curves is, using (6.6), given by:

$$\left.\frac{db}{dG}\right|_W = -\frac{(1-\alpha-\beta)}{(\alpha+\beta)G}\left\{(1-t)\sum_{i=1}^{n}v_i'w_i + b\right\} \tag{6.21}$$

This is the right hand side of the tangency condition in (6.2).

Substituting (6.21) and (6.19) into (6.2), defining $\tilde{w} = \sum_i^n v_i' w_i$ as a weighted average of wage rates, with weights equal to the social marginal valuations, and substituting for b using (6.18), the optimal public good expenditure per person, G_W, can be expressed as:

$$\frac{pG_W}{n} = (1 - \alpha - \beta)\left\{\tilde{w} + t(1 - \beta')(\overline{w} - \tilde{w})\right\} \qquad (6.22)$$

The resulting optimal value of the basic income, b_W, is given by appropriate substitution into (6.18). These values apply for positive values of the social transfer, so the given tax rate must exceed the value, t_{min}, where:

$$t_{min} = \left(\frac{1}{1 - \beta'}\right)\left[1 + \left(\frac{\overline{w}}{\tilde{w}}\right)\left(\frac{\alpha + \beta}{1 - (\alpha + \beta)}\right)\right]^{-1} \qquad (6.23)$$

In addition, the tax rate is also subject to an upper limit, given the assumption that all individuals work, so that for sensible values the social transfer must remain sufficiently below the minimum wage.

The focus here is on the ratio of the transfer payment to the expenditure on the public good per person, $R_W = b_W / (pG_W/n)$, rather than absolute values. This ratio is given by:

$$R_W = \frac{1 - t}{1 - t(1 - \beta')}$$
$$\times \left[\left(\frac{1}{1 - \alpha - \beta}\right)\left\{\frac{\tilde{w}}{\overline{w}}\left(\frac{1}{t(1 - \beta')} - 1\right) + 1\right\}^{-1} - 1\right] \qquad (6.24)$$

This result shows that the ratio of the transfer payment to public goods expenditure per person depends, among other things, on the ratio of the welfare-weighted wage rate to the average wage rate.

The expression in (6.24) is highly nonlinear in $\tilde{w}/\overline{w}$ and t. However, it can be shown that $\partial R_W / \partial(\tilde{w}/\overline{w}) < 0$. Higher inequality aversion reduces $\tilde{w}$ relative to $\overline{w}$, which implies a higher ratio of expenditure on transfer payments to the public good. Hence, both higher wage inequality and inequality aversion lead to a more redistributive expenditure policy. Furthermore, it can be shown that $\partial^2 R_W/\partial t^2 < 0$, so that there is a concave relationship between R_W and t. The first derivative $\partial R_W/\partial t$ is positive for low values of t and negative for relatively higher values. This is dominated by the concave relationship between b_W and t, since $\partial G_W/\partial t$ is positive, while $\partial^2 G_W/\partial t^2 = 0$ for all relevant values of t. Hence G_W increases linearly with t. The concavity of R_W with respect to t is therefore strongly affected by the labour supply effects of taxes and transfers. Initial increases in the tax rate from a relatively low level are used to increase income redistribution by increasing the proportion of expenditure devoted to transfer payments. But beyond a certain level, the adverse incentive effects of a further increase in t reduce the optimal proportion spent on transfers.

The partial derivatives $\partial\left(G_W/n\right)/\partial\left(\bar{w}\right)$ and $\partial\left(b_W\right)/\partial\left(\bar{w}\right)$ are both positive so that an upward shift in the distribution of wage rates unambiguously increases the optimum expenditure on the public goods and transfer payment. The partial derivatives $\partial\left(G_W/n\right)/\partial\left(\tilde{w}\right)$ and $\partial\left(b_W\right)/\partial\left(\tilde{w}\right)$ are positive and negative respectively. Hence an increase in $\tilde{w}$ (with an unchanged arithmetic mean wage) has a positive effect on public goods and total expenditure, but reduces the absolute social transfer and the ratio of the transfer to public good expenditure.

6.3   The Welfare-weighted Average Wage

In examining the welfare-weighted average, $\tilde{w}$, it is clear that the social marginal valuation, $v_i = \frac{\partial W}{\partial V_i}\frac{\partial V_i}{\partial b}$, and hence the weight v_i', is highly complex even for simple forms of W. For example, suppose the social planner maximises an additive social welfare function with iso-elastic weights applied to the V_is such that:

$$W = \frac{1}{1-\varepsilon}\sum_{i=1}^{n} V_i^{1-\varepsilon} \qquad \varepsilon \neq 1, \varepsilon > 0 \qquad (6.25)$$

where ε is the degree of concavity of the weighting function and represents the degree of constant relative inequality aversion of the planner. When $\varepsilon = 1$, this becomes $W = \sum_{i=1}^{n} \log V_i$. From (6.12) the indirect utility function can be written as $V_i = k^* M_i^{\alpha+\beta}$ so that $\partial V_i/\partial b = k^* (\alpha + \beta) M_i^{\alpha+\beta-1}$ and $\partial W/\partial V_i = V_i^{-\varepsilon}$. Hence v_i is:

$$v_i = K \frac{M_i^{\alpha+\beta-1}}{M_i^{(\alpha+\beta)\varepsilon}} \tag{6.26}$$

where K is a constant. Further analysis of the solution for R_W would therefore seem to require a numerical exercise involving the use of a simulated distribution of w. It is thus worth investigating the possibility of using an approximation for $\tilde{w}$, following the kind of argument introduced in Chapter 2 above.

Suppose b is small relative to w, so that the terms involving b/w_i in the expansion of (6.26) can be neglected. This is clearly not the case for very low values of w_i, but is discussed below where a further adjustment is made. In this case an approximation, denoted $\tilde{w}_A$, for $\tilde{w} = \sum w_i (v_i/\sum v_i)$, is obtained as:

$$\tilde{w}_A = \frac{\frac{1}{n}\sum w_i^{(1+\theta)}}{\frac{1}{n}\sum w_i^{\theta}} \tag{6.27}$$

with $\theta = (\alpha + \beta)(1 - \varepsilon) - 1$. Thus $\tilde{w}$ is the ratio of two fractional moments. Further progress can be made by assuming that w is lognormally distributed as $\Lambda(y_i | \mu_t, \sigma_t^2)$, with mean and variance of logarithms of μ_t and σ_t^2 respectively. Using the properties of the lognormal moment generating function, from Aitchison and Brown (1957), it can be found that:

$$\tilde{w}_A = \exp\left(\mu + (1-\varepsilon)\frac{\sigma^2}{2}\right)\exp\left\{\sigma^2\left((\alpha + \beta)(1 - \varepsilon)\right) - 1 + \frac{\varepsilon}{2}\right\} \tag{6.28}$$

The second term in this expression is close to, but less than, unity, particularly where ε is small. In the cross-sectional inequality context, questionnaire studies involving consideration of the 'leaky bucket' experiment found values for respondents which averaged around 0.2; see Amiel *et al.* (1999). However, the use of the assumption that b can be neglected in (6.26) actually attaches too much weight to the lower wage rates, and thus imparts a downward bias to the approximation. One approach is thus to correct for this downward bias by excluding the second term in (6.28), giving:

$$\tilde{w}_A = \exp\left(\mu + (1-\varepsilon)\frac{\sigma^2}{2}\right) \tag{6.29}$$

A feature of this result in (6.29) is that $\tilde{w}_A$ is closely related to Atkinson's measure of the inequality of w. Following Atkinson (1970), let w_{ede} denote the 'equally distributed equivalent' wage, representing the equal wage which gives the same welfare as the actual distribution, using a welfare function of the form $W = \frac{1}{1-\varepsilon}\sum w_i^{1-\varepsilon}$.[2] This is the same as the above but with V_i replaced by w_i. Thus:

$$w_{ede} = \left(\frac{1}{n}\sum_{i=1}^{n} w_i^{1-\varepsilon}\right)^{\frac{1}{1-\varepsilon}} \tag{6.30}$$

Again using lognormal properties, the term $w_{ede}^{1-\varepsilon}$ has mean and variance of logarithms respectively of $(1-\varepsilon)\mu$ and $(1-\varepsilon)^2\sigma^2$, so that:

$$w_{ede} = \exp\left(\mu + (1-\varepsilon)\frac{\sigma^2}{2}\right) \tag{6.31}$$

The weighted average $\tilde{w}$ can thus be approximated by an 'equally distributed equivalent' value, since $w_{ede} = \tilde{w}_A$. The ratio of the equally distributed equivalent to the arithmetic mean wage, $\bar{w} = \exp\left(\mu + \sigma^2/2\right)$, is:

$$\frac{w_{ede}}{\bar{w}} = \left\{\exp\left(-\frac{\sigma^2}{2}\right)\right\}^{\varepsilon} \tag{6.32}$$

Furthermore, the median wage is given by $w_m = e^\mu$, whence:

$$\frac{w_m}{\bar{w}} = \exp(-\frac{\sigma^2}{2}) \tag{6.33}$$

---

[2]The Atkinson measure of inequality, A_ε, is defined as the proportional difference between the arithmetic mean wage and the equally distributed equivalent wage level, so that $A = (\bar{w} - w_{ede})/\bar{w} = 1 - w_{ede}/\bar{w}$.

The ratio $w_m/\bar{w}$ depends only on the variance of logarithms of wages. Decreasing the ratio of median to mean wage rates implies an increase in the skewness of the distribution and in this positively skewed case it also reflects an increase in inequality, as measured by σ^2. Comparison with (6.32) gives the convenient relationship:

$$\frac{w_{ede}}{\bar{w}} = \left(\frac{w_m}{\bar{w}}\right)^\varepsilon \qquad (6.34)$$

Substitution of $\tilde{w} = (w_m/\bar{w})^\varepsilon$ into (6.24) gives the ratio of expenditure on the transfer payment to public goods as a function of the ratio of median to mean wage rate. It can be shown that $\partial R_W/\partial\varepsilon > 0$. Since w_m is less than $\bar{w}$, $\log(w_m/\bar{w})$ is negative and the relationship between R_W and inequality aversion is positive. This result confirms the result discussed above that higher inequality aversion leads to a larger optimal proportion of expenditure devoted to the transfer payment.

The above results allow a direct link to be made between the optimal expenditure framework and results concerning the majority choice of the composition of expenditure. Chapter 3 above has shown that the conditions required for the median voter theory to hold are satisfied and the median voter is unambiguously identified as the individual with median wage, w_m. The resulting expenditure on the public good, G_m, was found to be:

$$\frac{pG_m}{n} = (1 - \alpha - \beta)\{w_m + t(1 - \beta')(\bar{w} - w_m)\} \qquad (6.35)$$

and of course the transfer payment, b_m, is obtained from the government budget constraint in (6.18). Hence the only difference between the two approaches concerns the wage ratio used. In the median voter model, the relevant variable is $w_m/\bar{w}$ whereas social welfare maximisation involves $\tilde{w}/\bar{w}$, the ratio of the welfare-weighted average wage to the arithmetic mean wage.

This result shows that when $\varepsilon = 1$ the optimal choice is (approximately) the same as that of the median voter. However, it is not appropriate to suggest that the median voter has inequality aversion of 1. Indeed, the majority voting outcome arises from entirely selfish behaviour where the utility of other individuals is not taken into account at all.[3]

Before considering the precise form of the relationships, it is first necessary to check, using simulations, that the approximation derived here does indeed provide a good approximation. This is examined in the following section.

6.4   The Approximation For $\tilde{w}_A$

This section provides a numerical evaluation of the approximation for the welfare-weighted mean wage, $\tilde{w}_A$. Values of expenditure components using $\tilde{w}_A = w_{ede}$ were compared with those obtained using a simulated population of size 15000 drawn at random from a lognormal distribution with $\mu = 9.0$ and $\sigma^2 = 0.5$, which imply $w_m/\bar{w} = 0.78$. Using the simulated distribution, a range of values of b were investigated: the value of b was gradually increased by 5 units. For each b the government budget constraint was used to obtain G and the resulting values were used to calculate each individual's level of utility. These were used to obtain social welfare, for the iso-elastic function with a specified inequality aversion parameter, ε. Finally, given many W measures, the maximum produces the optimal composition. To compare welfare values, the composition obtained from the approximation was used with the simulated population.

Table 6.1 gives the results for alternative values of α, β and inequality aversion, ε, with $\tau = 0.35$. These combinations produce sensible values for labour supply. The percentage difference between W using the approximation and that obtained by simulation is in each case extremely small.

---

[3]However, Chapter 3 has also shown how the majority voting outcome is modified in cases where voters do have an aversion to inequality.

Table 6.1: Optimal Composition of Expenditure in Alternative Solutions

ε	Approximation			Simulation			
	b	pG/N	R	b	pG/N	R	$\%\Delta W$
			$\alpha = 0.58,\ \beta = 0.4$				
0.2	1602.90	200.04	8.01	1625	173.09	9.39	−0.0176
0.5	1612.20	188.70	8.54	1630	166.99	9.76	−0.0077
0.8	1620.82	178.18	9.10	1635	160.89	10.16	−0.0019
			$\alpha = 0.53,\ \beta = 0.45$				
0.2	1418.78	199.86	7.10	1445	167.16	8.64	−0.0229
0.5	1428.07	188.27	7.59	1445	167.16	8.64	−0.0098
0.8	1436.70	177.51	8.09	1450	160.92	9.01	−0.0025
			$\alpha = 0.5,\ \beta = 0.45$				
0.2	1129.11	499.53	2.26	1215	416.83	2.87	−0.0684
0.5	1152.35	470.36	2.45	1205	404.28	2.98	−0.0304
0.8	1173.91	443.30	2.65	1195	391.73	3.10	−0.0079

6.5 Some Numerical Examples

In view of the form of the relationship in (6.24) between R_W and the parameters of the model, the precise nature of variations is not transparent. Hence it is useful to consider numerical examples of the sensitivity of optimal outcomes to variations in selected parameters of the model, in particular the degree of relative inequality aversion, ε, the tax rate, t, and the ratio of the welfare-weighted average wage to the arithmetic mean wage, $\tilde{w}/\bar{w}$. Using (6.34), $\tilde{w}/\bar{w}$ is obtained as $(w_m/\bar{w})^\varepsilon$ for different ε. The examples are obtained using preference parameters of $\alpha = 0.58$ and $\beta = 0.4$. These produce, with a tax rate of $t = 0.25$, a sensible proportion of time devoted to labour supply. When reporting absolute values of b and G/n, it is worth bearing in mind that the arithmetic mean and median wage rates used, expressed in annual terms, are $70000 and $60000 respectively. These are consistent with a lognormal distribution with mean and standard deviation of logarithms of hourly wage rates of 2.87 and 0.56: these are similar to those for Australia. Using the properties of the lognormal distribution the arithmetic

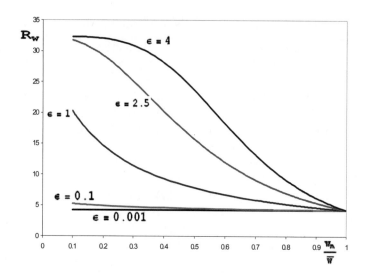

Figure 6.1: Variation in R_W with $w_m/\bar{w}$ for Different ε

mean and the median hourly wage rate are $20.64 = \exp(2.87 + 0.56/2)$ and $17.64 = \exp(2.87)$: see Aitchison and Brown (1957). Furthermore, the maximum hours per day are set at 13 to obtain annual equivalents.

Figure 6.1 shows the relationship between the ratio of expenditure on transfers to that on the public good, $R_W = b_W/(pG_W/n)$, and the wage ratio, $w_m/\bar{w}$, for the different values of ε and benchmark preference parameters, with $t = 0.25$. It illustrates the property mentioned above that the social planner's choice of R_W falls as inequality falls, that is, as $w_m/\bar{w}$ increases towards unity.

This relationship is strongly influenced by the degree of inequality aversion of the judge. When $\varepsilon = 0.1$, the optimal ratio of expenditure devoted to redistributive transfer payments to public goods is substantially less than the majority voting outcome, and is less sensitive to variations in the ratio $w_m/\bar{w}$. Where the social welfare function has a high degree of inequality aversion, Figure 6.1 shows that for $\varepsilon = 2.5$ and higher, the response of the expenditure pattern to changes in wage rate inequality is very different from that of the median voter. For high inequality aversion and high inequality the expenditure ratio is relatively high, and is insensitive to changes in the wage ratio. Thus, increasing values of $w_m/\bar{w}$ over very low ranges, that is when there is substantial inequality, has little effect on the R_W ratio. But around the range where the median is half the arithmetic mean, further increases in $w_m/\bar{w}$ (that is, reductions in inequality) have a large effect on the optimal choice of redistributive transfers relative to public good expenditure. Around that range, changes in inequality involve larger effects on the government budget constraint. In fact, the relationship between R_W and $w_m/\bar{w}$ is sigmoid for high ε, whereas that for the median voter is closer to being quadratic. Realistic values of $w_m/\bar{w}$ are around 0.8, where high values of inequality aversion are needed for differences in inequality to produce much change in the expenditure ratio.

Figure 6.2 provides further light on the effects of inequality aversion, by showing the relationship between R_W and ε for different ratios of median to mean wage rate. As expected from the analytical result, raising inequality aversion reduces the optimal ratio of expenditure on the transfer payment to public goods. From the analytical result given above, R does not necessarily increase at an increasing rate as inequality aversion increases, although it does so for the range of values shown in Figure 6.2. For the lower values of $w_m/\bar{w}$, the profiles were found to be concave over higher ranges of ε, but such high values of inequality aversion are not relevant.[4]

Figure 6.3 shows the variation in different types of government expenditure as the tax rate (considered here to be exogenous) increases. As shown in the individual figures there is an inverted U-shaped relationship between the absolute level of the transfer payment and the tax rate, and between the R_W ratio and the tax rate. Nevertheless, expenditure on public goods is linearly

---

[4]Beyond the maximum value of ε shown in the figure, aversion is close to becoming extreme, thereby corresponding to the maxi–min case.

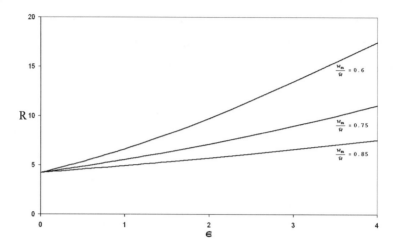

Figure 6.2: Variation in R_W with ε for Different $w_m/\bar{w}$

related to the tax rate: this was established analytically above, where it was stated that $\partial G_W/\partial t$ is positive and $\partial^2 G_W/\partial t^2 = 0$. The shapes of the various profiles are very similar for different ε values. As expected, higher inequality aversion is consistently associated with higher optimal expenditure on the transfer payment and lower expenditure on the public good. Care is needed in comparing the first two parts of the figure, in view of the fact that the scales on the vertical axes are different.

6.6   Conclusions

This chapter has examined the optimal composition of government expenditure, in terms of the ratio of transfer payments to expenditure on public goods, for a given income tax rate. A social welfare function, expressed in terms of individuals' utilities, was maximised subject to the government's budget constraint, involving a loss of one degree of freedom in policy choices. A solution to this optimal tax problem was obtained in which the optimal ratio of transfers to public good expenditure per person is expressed as a func-

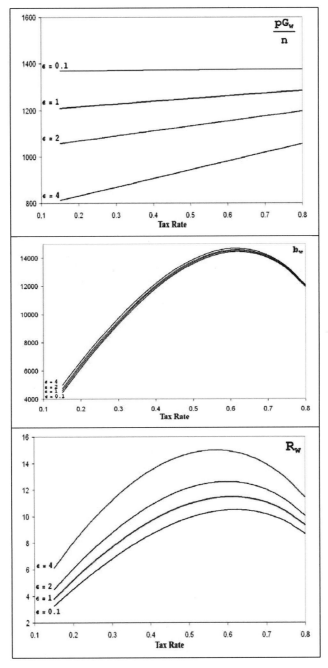

Figure 6.3: The Optimal Composition and Variations in the Tax Rate

tion of the ratio of the welfare-weighted mean wage rate to the arithmetic mean wage rate, and of the tax rate.

However, the expression for the optimal ratio is not a closed-form solution in view of the complexity of the welfare-weighted mean wage rate. Nevertheless it was shown that a useful approximation to the welfare-weighted mean is provided by the equally distributed equivalent wage rate. Using an assumption that wage rates are lognormally distributed, a simple relationship between this approximation to the welfare-weighted mean and the median wage was obtained, involving the degree of constant relative inequality aversion. The usefulness of this approximation was confirmed by simulation experiments.

Reductions in the skewness of the wage rate distribution were found to be associated with reductions in transfer payments relative to public goods expenditure, at a decreasing rate. Furthermore, increases in the tax rate, from relatively low levels, are associated with increases in the optimal ratio of transfer payments to public good expenditure. But beyond a certain level, further tax rate increases are associated with a lower ratio, in view of the adverse incentive effects whereby total revenue falls as the reduction in the tax base outweighs the effect of the increase in the tax rate.

Furthermore, a comparison of the welfare maximising expenditure composition with the majority voting outcome was made. It was shown that the difference involves the use of the ratio of median to mean wages in the voting model, compared with the welfare-weighted average wage in the optimal solution. Numerical examples were provided, showing the sensitivity of policy choices to a range of parameter values.

Chapter 7

Education, Public Goods and Transfers

This chapter extends the analysis of the previous chapter by considering the optimal allocation of government revenue among three types of expenditure. In addition to a universal transfer payment and a pure public good, the government finances expenditure on basic education, all conditional on the tax rate. These expenditures have differing effects on individuals' labour supplies, which are considered to be endogenous. The previous chapter has shown that if the choice is limited to the case of expenditure on a public good and a transfer payment, a more unequal wage rate distribution results in relatively more expenditure being devoted to the transfer payment. The question considered in this chapter is how the relationship between the composition of expenditure and basic inequality is affected by the existence of tax-financed education which raises each individual's productivity. Education is regarded as a publicly funded private good. To avoid other issues associated with educational choice, private education is not modelled here.

Judgements regarding the optimal expenditure composition have to balance the efficiency effects of education expenditure, which influences the general level but not the inequality of wage levels, with the inequality reducing effect of the unconditional transfer. An important implication of education, despite being treated as a private investment good, is that it creates a substantial fiscal spillover. Thus, the increase in human capital gives rise to higher labour supply and higher earnings, as a result of the general increase in wage rates. This in turn leads to higher income tax revenue, thereby allowing greater government expenditure on all items than would otherwise be possible. It is also somewhat inequality-increasing. The complex interactions involved mean that the nature of optimal plans is not at all obvious.

In the single-period framework, individuals are assumed to have similar preferences regarding leisure, consumption goods (net income) and the public good, but are endowed with an exogenously given ability level which differs among individuals. The education expenditure is the same for all individuals and combines with the fundamental ability level to raise the productivity of individuals, via a type of human capital production function.

It is well known that standard optimal tax models do not give rise to closed-form solutions, even for quite simple specifications of the tax structure and preferences. However, in the present context it is possible, using a convenient approximation, to obtain explicit solutions for the three expenditure levels, conditional on the tax rate. Nevertheless, the properties of the model are not immediately transparent and for this reason the analysis of comparative statics is reinforced by numerical examples.

The framework of analysis is set out in Section 7.1, which derives individuals' indirect utility functions, expressed in terms of the expenditure levels. The first-order conditions for maximisation of the welfare function, giving the optimal composition of expenditure, are set out in Section 7.2. The results depend on a welfare-weighted average of basic ability levels, resulting in nonlinear equations. Section 7.3 introduces an approximation which allows explicit, or closed-form, solutions to be obtained. Comparative static analyses are carried out in Section 7.4, which also provides some numerical examples.

7.1 The Framework of Analysis

This section describes the basic framework of analysis used. The model is static, involving a single period, and individuals' labour supplies respond to tax and expenditure changes. Individual behaviour is described in Subsection 7.1.1. The human capital production function used to generate wage rates is discussed in Subsection 7.1.2, followed in Subsection 7.1.3 by derivation of the government's budget constraint.

7.1.1 Individual Maximisation

Each individual maximises utility, U, regarded as a function of consumption, c, which, assuming the price index of private goods is normalised to 1, is equivalent to net income, leisure, h, and a tax-financed public good, Q. Assume that U takes the Cobb–Douglas form, where the individual subscript, i, is omitted for convenience:

$$U = c^{\alpha} h^{\beta} Q^{1-\alpha-\beta} \tag{7.1}$$

This widely used form has, as seen below, the convenient property in the present context that it leads to linear earnings functions relating earnings to the wage rate, thereby allowing aggregation over all individuals to be carried out relatively easily. It is shown in Section 7.2 that with this form of utility function the expenditure shares do not depend on population size. Furthermore, the shares are independent of units, and thus the average wage.

Tax revenue is obtained using a simple proportional income tax at the rate, t, and this is used to finance a basic income (a non-means-tested transfer payment) of b per person. The endowment of time is normalised to 1, so that $h \leq 1$. The individual's wage rate is w. Hence the budget constraint facing the individual is:

$$c + hw(1 - t) = w(1 - t) + b = M \tag{7.2}$$

where $M = w(1 - t) + b$ is 'full income', defined as the income that could be obtained if all of the endowment of time were devoted to work. The individual is thus considered to purchase leisure at a price equal to the net wage.

Using the standard properties of the Cobb–Douglas utility function, and defining $\alpha' = \alpha/(\alpha + \beta)$ and $\beta' = \beta/(\alpha + \beta)$, net income and leisure are:

$$c = \alpha' M \tag{7.3}$$

$$h = \beta' \left(1 + \frac{b}{w(1 - t)}\right) \tag{7.4}$$

In the standard case, expenditure on any item is the product of full income and the ratio of the relevant coefficient to the sum of coefficients. In the present context, the term $Q^{1-\alpha-\beta}$ must be treated effectively as a constant term in the utility function, because Q does not have a corresponding consumer price (only a 'tax price'). Thus, for example in (7.3), full income is multiplied by $\alpha/(\alpha + \beta)$ rather than α.

For the individual to work, w must exceed the threshold, $w_{\min}$, needed to ensure $h < 1$, where:

$$w_{\min} = \frac{b}{1 - t}\left(\frac{\beta'}{1 - \beta'}\right) \tag{7.5}$$

Gross earnings, $y = w(1 - h)$, are:

$$y = w(1 - \beta') - \frac{b\beta'}{1 - t} \tag{7.6}$$

Substituting the optimal values of c and h into the direct utility function gives indirect utility, V, as:

$$V = \left(\alpha'^{\alpha} \beta'^{\beta}\right)(w(1 - t))^{\alpha} \left(\frac{M}{w(1 - t)}\right)^{\alpha+\beta} Q^{1-\alpha-\beta} \tag{7.7}$$

7.1.2 Education and Wage Rates

The above results are expressed in terms of the individual's wage rate. However, the wage rate of each individual is itself endogenous because, in addition to financing the transfer payment and expenditure on the public good, tax revenue is used to provide public education. This involves per capita expenditure on education of E. This provides an input into a human capital production function which, along with each individual's exogenous basic ability level, w_0, generates productivity as reflected in the wage rate, w. The production function is also assumed to take the very simple Cobb–Douglas form, similar to that used by Glomm and Ravikumar (1997, p. 188), whereby:

$$w = \gamma w_0^\theta E^{1-\theta} \tag{7.8}$$

Hence the wage is proportional to a weighted average of the individual's basic ability level, w_0, and the per capita expenditure on education, E. The production function does not appear explicitly to allow for any time being spent on education, but the present approach is consistent with an assumption that each individual spends the same amount of time in education, as well as benefiting from the same government expenditure. Furthermore, this time can be regarded as coming out of time otherwise devoted to leisure, and gives the same utility as leisure. It therefore affects only the constant term in (7.8). The size of this constant term is also affected by the units of measurement and mean of logarithms, μ_{w_0}, of the basic ability level. However, it can be shown that the absolute values of γ and μ_{w_0} do not affect the optimal expenditure shares. For this reason is it most convenient simply to set $\gamma = 1$ in what follows.

The specification is similar in some respects to the kind of human capital production function used in much of the endogenous growth literature, except that it necessarily does not include either private investment by parents in their children's education or the human capital of parents. For example, the form in Blankenau *et al.* (2007, p. 393) is the same as (7.8) except that it has the human capital of the previous generation instead of w_0.[1] A

---

[1] In Capolupo (2000, p. 168), human capital accumulation is determined purely by government education expenditure and an efficiency term.

further difference is that in much of the growth literature, which involves a general equilibrium context, the labour input into an aggregate production function is defined in terms of 'effective labour' (a proportion of time devoted to labour multiplied by human capital), so that only a single wage rate needs to be determined. In the present partial equilibrium context, there is wage rate heterogeneity and individuals supply simply a number of (unadjusted) hours of labour.

The function in (7.8) has the property, again in common with many studies in the context of endogenous growth modes, that it does not specify a productivity externality. That is, individuals do not receive any benefit, in the form of a higher wage rate, from the fact that other households may have more human capital. For example, complementarities in production between low-skilled and high-skilled individuals may give rise to externalities which raise the wage received by the low-skilled individuals.[2] A specification allowing for a slightly different kind of externality is used by Angelopoulos *et al.* (2007, p. 6), and papers cited therein, where individual human capital accumulation depends on, among other things, arithmetic mean human capital. Of course, there are other types of externality arising from education which are non-economic in nature, involving social and cultural values, which are often used to justify tax-financed public education, along with market failure arguments concerning capital markets.

However, the present model contains a very important spillover effect. The tax-financed public education investment gives rise to higher incomes and hence a higher tax base. This means that the relatively low-ability individuals face a lower tax rate and receive a higher transfer payment than they would in the absence of the tax-financed investment. This is reflected in a higher social evaluation function (discussed below) which allows for both equity and efficiency considerations.

---

[2]This type of externality is explored at length in Creedy (1995), in the different context of the private decision to invest in higher education.

7.1.3 The Government Budget Constraint

All government expenditure is assumed to be financed from the proportional tax. Hence the budget constraint can be written, where n is the number of individuals and p is the constant cost per unit of producing the public good, as:

$$b + E + \frac{pQ}{n} = t\bar{y} \tag{7.9}$$

Aggregation over (7.6), and letting $F_1(w_{\min})$ and $F(w_{\min})$ denote respectively the proportion of total wage (rates) and the proportion of people with $w < w_{\min}$, gives arithmetic mean earnings, $\bar{y}$, as:

$$\bar{y} = \bar{w}(1 - \beta')\{1 - F_1(w_{\min})\} - \frac{b\beta'}{1 - t}\{1 - F(w_{\min})\} \tag{7.10}$$

where $\bar{w}$ is the arithmetic mean wage rate. The expression in (7.10) is nonlinear since $w_{\min}$ depends on the tax parameters. However, on the assumption that there are relatively few non-workers, the terms $F_1(w_{\min})$ and $F(w_{\min})$ can be neglected, giving the linear form:

$$\bar{y} = (1 - \beta')\bar{w} - \beta'\left(\frac{b}{1 - \tau}\right) \tag{7.11}$$

Substituting into (7.9) and rearranging gives the transfer payment expressed in terms of E and Q, reflecting the fact that only two of the policy variables can be chosen independently. Thus:

$$b = \frac{t\bar{w}(1 - \beta') - (E + pQ/n)}{1 + \beta't/(1 - t)} \tag{7.12}$$

The average wage rate can be expressed in terms of basic abilities and public expenditure on education. Using (7.8):

$$\bar{w} = E^{1-\theta}(\frac{1}{n}\sum_{i=1}^{n} w_{0,i}^{\theta}) \tag{7.13}$$

and writing $\bar{w}_\theta = \frac{1}{n}\sum_{i=1}^{n} w_{0,i}^{\theta}$ as the moment of order θ (about the origin):

$$\bar{w} = E^{1-\theta}\bar{w}_\theta \tag{7.14}$$

This can be substituted into (7.12) to give:

$$b = \frac{tE^{1-\theta}\bar{w}_\theta(1-\beta') - (E+pQ/n)}{1+\beta't/(1-t)} \qquad (7.15)$$

The government budget constraint therefore involves a loss of one degree of freedom in the choice of policy instruments.

7.2   The Optimal Composition of Expenditure

The social planner is modelled as selecting values of Q, E and b, for an exogenously given tax rate, in order to maximise a social welfare function, W, of the additive form:

$$W = \sum_{i=1}^{n} W(V_i) \qquad (7.16)$$

subject to the government's budget constraint in (7.9), and where indirect utility can be written as $V_i = V(Q, E, b|t)$. Form the Lagrangian:

$$\mathcal{L} = \sum_{i=1}^{n} W(V_i) + \lambda\left[t\bar{y} - b - E - pQ/n\right] \qquad (7.17)$$

The first-order conditions are thus:

$$
\begin{aligned}
\frac{\partial \mathcal{L}}{\partial b} &= \sum_i \frac{\partial W}{\partial V_i}\frac{\partial V_i}{\partial b} + \lambda\left[t\frac{\partial \bar{y}}{\partial b} - 1\right] = 0 \\
\frac{\partial \mathcal{L}}{\partial Q} &= \sum_i \frac{\partial W}{\partial V_i}\frac{\partial V_i}{\partial Q} + \lambda\left[t\frac{\partial \bar{y}}{\partial Q} - \frac{p}{n}\right] = 0 \\
\frac{\partial \mathcal{L}}{\partial E} &= \sum_i \frac{\partial W}{\partial V_i}\frac{\partial V_i}{\partial E} + \lambda\left[t\frac{\partial \bar{y}}{\partial E} - 1\right] = 0 \\
\frac{\partial \mathcal{L}}{\partial \lambda} &= t\bar{y} - b - E - pQ/n = 0 \qquad (7.18)
\end{aligned}
$$

Write $\frac{\partial W}{\partial V_i}\frac{\partial V_i}{\partial b} = v_i$, the marginal 'social' value attached to an increase in i's income. Furthermore:

$$\frac{\partial W}{\partial V_i}\frac{\partial V_i}{\partial Q} = v_i\frac{\partial V_i/\partial Q}{\partial V_i/\partial b} \qquad (7.19)$$

and:

$$\frac{\partial W}{\partial V_i} \frac{\partial V_i}{\partial E} = v_i \frac{\partial V_i/\partial E}{\partial V_i/\partial b} \tag{7.20}$$

From (7.10) the partial derivatives in (7.18) are $\partial \bar{y}/\partial b = \beta'/(1-t)$ and $\partial \bar{y}/\partial Q = 0$ and $\partial \bar{y}/\partial E = (1-\beta')(1-\theta)\bar{w}_\theta E^{-\theta}$. Therefore, the first three first-order conditions above can be rewritten:

$$\sum_i v_i = \lambda \left(1 - \beta'\frac{t}{1-t}\right) \tag{7.21}$$

$$\sum_i v_i \frac{\partial V_i/\partial Q}{\partial V_i/\partial b} = \lambda \frac{p}{n} \tag{7.22}$$

$$\sum_i v_i \frac{\partial V_i/\partial E}{\partial V_i/\partial b} = \lambda \left\{1 - t(1-\beta')(1-\theta)\bar{w}_\theta E^{-\theta}\right\} \tag{7.23}$$

A procedure for solving these equations, along with the budget constraint, is presented in the following subsection. Expressions for the optimal value of Q in terms of E, and of b in terms of E and Q, are derived: these can be used to obtain Q and b.

7.2.1 Solving the First-order Conditions

This subsection derives explicit (closed-form) solutions for the policy variables, Q, b and E, conditional on the income tax t. First, it is necessary to obtain expressions for the ratios of partial derivatives of the indirect utility function. Substituting for $w = \gamma w_0^\theta E^{1-\theta}$ and $M = w(1-t)+b$ into (7.7), the indirect utility function can be written, again omitting i subscripts for convenience, as:

$$V = \left(\alpha'^\alpha \beta'^\beta\right)\left(w_0^\theta E^{1-\theta}(1-t)\right)^{-\beta}\left(w_0^\theta E^{1-\theta}(1-t)+b\right)^{\alpha+\beta} Q^{1-\alpha-\beta} \tag{7.24}$$

The three partial derivatives of V with respect to Q, b and E are:

$$\frac{\partial V}{\partial Q} = \frac{(1-\alpha-\beta)V}{Q} \tag{7.25}$$

$$\frac{\partial V}{\partial b} = \frac{(\alpha+\beta)V}{M} \tag{7.26}$$

$$\frac{\partial V}{\partial E} = \frac{(\alpha + \beta)(1 - \theta)(1 - t) wV}{EM} - \frac{\beta (1 - \theta) V}{E}$$

$$= \frac{(1 - \theta) V}{E} \left(\frac{(\alpha + \beta)(1 - t) w}{M} - \beta \right) \qquad (7.27)$$

Hence the required ratios are:

$$\frac{\partial V/\partial Q}{\partial V/\partial b} = \frac{(1 - \alpha - \beta) M}{(\alpha + \beta) Q} \qquad (7.28)$$

and:

$$\frac{\partial V/\partial E}{\partial V/\partial b} = \frac{(1 - \theta) M}{E} \left(\frac{w(1 - t)}{M} - \beta' \right)$$

$$= \frac{(1 - \theta)}{E} \{ w(1 - t)(1 - \beta') - \beta'b \} \qquad (7.29)$$

Substituting (7.29) and (7.28) into the relevant first-order conditions gives:

$$\sum_i \frac{v(1 - \alpha - \beta) M}{(\alpha + \beta) Q} = \lambda \frac{1}{n} \qquad (7.30)$$

$$\sum_i \frac{v(1 - \theta)}{E} \{ w(1 - t)(1 - \beta') - \beta'b \} = \lambda \left\{ 1 - tE^{-\theta} \tilde{w}_\theta (1 - \beta')(1 - \theta) \right\} \qquad (7.31)$$

Solutions for optimal Q and b can be obtained as follows. Consider first the two-dimensional choice of b and Q, for given E. This is equivalent to the requirement that a social indifference curve is tangential to the budget constraint, which is obtained by dividing (7.30) by (7.21). Writing $v'_i = v_i / \sum_i v_i$ gives:

$$\sum_i v' \{ w(1 - t) + b \} = \left(\frac{\alpha + \beta}{1 - \alpha - \beta} \right) \frac{pQ/n}{\left(1 - \beta' \frac{t}{1-t} \right)} \qquad (7.32)$$

However, using (7.8) to substitute for w, the left hand side of (7.32) becomes:

$$\sum_i v' \{ w(1 - t) + b \} = b + (1 - t) E^{1-\theta} \sum_i v' w_0^\theta \qquad (7.33)$$

Let $\tilde{w}_\theta = \sum_i v'_i w_{0,i}^\theta$, a welfare-weighted average of w_0^θ (the weighted moment of order θ about the origin). Hence, rearrangement of (7.32) gives:

$$b = \left(\frac{\alpha + \beta}{1 - \alpha - \beta} \right) \frac{pQ/n}{\left(1 - \beta' \frac{t}{1-t} \right)} - (1 - t) E^{1-\theta} \tilde{w}_\theta \qquad (7.34)$$

This result expressed the basic income in terms of the expenditure on the public good and on education per person. Using the government budget constraint, that is setting (7.34) equal to (7.15) and rearranging, gives:

$$\frac{pQ}{n} = \frac{E^{1-\theta}\left\{\tilde{w}_\theta + t\left(1 - \beta'\right)\left(\bar{w}_\theta - \tilde{w}_\theta\right)\right\} - E}{1 + \frac{\alpha+\beta}{1-\alpha-\beta}\left(\frac{1-t(1-\beta')}{1-t(1+\beta')}\right)} \tag{7.35}$$

This result can be simplified as follows. Denoting the denominator by Ψ^{-1}, it can be seen that Ψ can be expressed as:

$$\Psi = \frac{(1 - \alpha - \beta)}{\left(1 + \frac{2\beta t}{1-t(1+\beta')}\right)} \tag{7.36}$$

Furthermore, define $\hat{w}_\theta$ as the weighted average:

$$\hat{w}_\theta = \tilde{w}_\theta\left(1 - t\left(1 - \beta'\right)\right) + t\left(1 - \beta'\right)\bar{w}_\theta \tag{7.37}$$

This allows (7.35) to be written more succinctly as:

$$\frac{pQ}{n} = \Psi\left(E^{1-\theta}\hat{w}_\theta - E\right) \tag{7.38}$$

This expresses pQ/n in terms of E only. A corresponding solution for b in terms of E can be obtained by substituting for pQ/n, using (7.38), into (7.15), whereby:

$$b = \frac{1-t}{1-t\left(1-\beta'\right)}\left[\left\{t(1-\beta')\bar{w}_\theta - \Psi\hat{w}_\theta\right\}E^{1-\theta} + E\left(\Psi - 1\right)\right] \tag{7.39}$$

It therefore remains to solve for E, as follows. Consider, for given Q, the choice between b and E, involving a tangency solution between a social indifference curve and the budget constraint, when taking the two dimensions b and E. Thus, divide (7.31) by (7.21), and again use (7.8) to express wage rates in terms of basic abilities and education expenditure, to get:

$$\frac{1-\theta}{E}\left[(1-t)\left(1-\beta'\right)E^{1-\theta}\tilde{w}_\theta - \beta'b\right] = \frac{1 - tE^{-\theta}\bar{w}_\theta(1-\beta')\left(1-\theta\right)}{1 - \beta'\frac{t}{1-t}} \tag{7.40}$$

Further rearrangement gives:

$$(1-t)\left(1-\beta'\right)\left(1-\theta\right)E^{-\theta}\left[\tilde{w}_\theta + t\left\{\bar{w}_\theta - \left(1+\beta'\right)\tilde{w}_\theta\right\}\right] =$$

$$(1 - t) + (1 - \theta)\, \beta' \left\{ 1 - t\,(1 + \beta') \right\} \frac{b}{E} \tag{7.41}$$

However, from the result for b in terms of E in (7.39), the required ratio in (7.41) becomes:

$$\frac{b}{E} = \frac{(1 - t)\left[\left\{ t(1 - \beta')\bar{w}_\theta - \Psi\hat{w}_\theta \right\} E^{-\theta} + (\Psi - 1) \right]}{1 - t\,(1 - \beta')} \tag{7.42}$$

Hence, collecting terms in $E^{-\theta}$ and rearranging gives:

$$E^\theta = (1 - \theta) \times$$
$$\frac{(1 - \beta') \left\{ 1 - t\,(1 - \beta') \right\} H - \beta' \left\{ 1 - t\,(1 + \beta') \right\} \left\{ t(1 - \beta')\bar{w}_\theta - \Psi\hat{w}_\theta \right\}}{\left\{ 1 - t\,(1 - \beta') \right\} + (1 - \theta)\,\beta'\,(\Psi - 1)\left\{ 1 - t\,(1 + \beta') \right\}} \tag{7.43}$$

Where H is:

$$H = \tilde{w}_\theta \left\{ 1 - t\,(1 + \beta') \right\} + t\bar{w}_\theta \tag{7.44}$$

This is not a weighted average of the two terms involving w. Taking the right hand side of (7.43), dividing numerator and denominator by $1 - t\,(1 + \beta')$, and using the fact that:

$$\frac{1 - t\,(1 - \beta')}{1 - t\,(1 + \beta')} = \frac{(1 - \alpha - \beta)\,(\Psi^{-1} - 1)}{\alpha + \beta} \tag{7.45}$$

the solution for E is given by the result in (7.43).[3] The resulting value of E can then be substituted into (7.38) to obtain the optimal value of Q. Finally, these values of E and Q can be used in (7.34) to obtain the basic income, b.

Finally, writing total government expenditure as $T = pQ/n + b + E$ gives, after simplification:

$$T = \frac{E^{1-\theta}\,(t\bar{w}_\theta(1 - \beta')\,(1 - t) + \beta't\Psi\hat{w}_\theta) + \beta'tE(1 - \Psi)}{1 - t(1 - \beta')} \tag{7.46}$$

Total tax revenue is $t\bar{y}$, and comparing this with $pG/n + b + E$ provides a useful independent check on computations, such as those reported below.

---

[3] Alternatively it is possible to write $E^{-\theta} = \frac{(1-\alpha-\beta)(\Psi^{-1}-1)+(1-\theta)\beta(\Psi-1)}{(1-\theta)(A_1\tilde{w}_\theta + A_2\bar{w}_\theta)}$, where $A_1 = (1 - \alpha - \beta)\,(1 - \beta')\,\Psi^{-1}\,(1 - t\,(1 + \beta')) + \beta t\Psi\,(1 - t\,(1 - \beta'))$ and $A_2 = (1 - \alpha - \beta)\,(1 - \beta')\,\Psi^{-1}t - \beta t(1 - \beta') + \beta t^2\Psi\,(1 - \beta')$. Unfortunately $A_1 + A_2 \neq 1$.

The ratio of each expenditure component to total expenditure can then be obtained.

It is easily seen that the resulting complex expressions are independent of the population size. However, these expressions do not represent 'closed form' solutions because of their nonlinearity and the complex form taken by $\tilde{w}_\theta$, which depends on the welfare weights and thus the form of the social welfare function used. Further progress can be made using an explicit form for W and an approximation for $\tilde{w}_\theta$ which allows explicit solutions to be obtained, making the properties of the model clearer. This is examined in the following section.

7.3 The Welfare Weights

In examining the welfare-weighted average, $\tilde{w}_\theta$, it is clear that the term $v_i = \frac{\partial W}{\partial V_i} \frac{\partial V_i}{\partial b}$, and hence the weight v_i', is highly complex even for simple forms of W. For example, suppose the social planner maximises an additive social welfare function with iso-elastic weights applied to the V_i such that:

$$
\begin{aligned}
W &= \frac{1}{1-\varepsilon} \sum_{i=1}^{n} V_i^{1-\varepsilon} & \varepsilon \neq 1, \varepsilon > 0 \\
&= \log y & \varepsilon = 1
\end{aligned}
\tag{7.47}
$$

where ε is the degree of concavity of the weighting function and represents the degree of constant relative inequality aversion of the planner. Hence $\partial W / \partial V_i = V_i^{-\varepsilon}$ and substituting for V from (7.24), along with $\partial V_i / \partial b$ from (7.26) gives an awkward expression for $\frac{\partial W}{\partial V_i} \frac{\partial V_i}{\partial b}$. The present section therefore follows the approach used earlier (in Chapters 2 and 6) to obtain an approximation for the welfare-weighted average.

It can be shown that, if b is relatively small (in comparison with average earnings), a reasonable approximation to $\tilde{w}_\theta$ can be based on an equally distributed equivalent measure. In general for the variable x, the 'equally distributed equivalent' value, x_e, is the value which, if obtained by everyone, gives the same welfare, defined in terms of x, as the actual distribution. This concept is associated with the Atkinson measure of inequality, A, which is expressed as the proportional difference between the arithmetic mean and the equally distributed equivalent value, so that:

$$A = 1 - \frac{x_e}{\bar{x}} \tag{7.48}$$

Using an iso-elastic welfare function, such as (7.47), expressed in terms of x, x_e is:

$$x_e = \left(\frac{1}{n} \sum_{i=1}^{n} x_i^{1-\varepsilon} \right)^{\frac{1}{1-\varepsilon}} \tag{7.49}$$

Furthermore, if x is lognormally distributed as $\Lambda(\mu, \sigma^2)$, then $x^{1-\varepsilon}$ is lognormally distributed as $\Lambda((1-\varepsilon)\mu, (1-\varepsilon)^2 \sigma^2)$, and using the result for the arithmetic mean of a lognormal variable (see Aitchison and Brown, 1957), (7.49) becomes:

$$x_e = \exp\left(\mu + (1-\varepsilon)\frac{\sigma^2}{2} \right) \tag{7.50}$$

Hence if w_0 is assumed to be lognormally distributed as $\Lambda(\mu_{w_0}, \sigma^2_{w_0})$, then:

$$\bar{w}_\theta = \exp\left(\theta\mu_{w_0} + \frac{1}{2}\theta^2\sigma^2_{w_0} \right) \tag{7.51}$$

and:

$$\tilde{w}_\theta = \exp\left(\theta\mu_{w_0} + \frac{1}{2}(1-\varepsilon)\theta^2\sigma^2_{w_0} \right) \tag{7.52}$$

This allows the implications of alternative degrees of inequality aversion to be examined.

Using these results it is possible to show, after much manipulation, that the mean of logarithms, μ_{w_0}, does not appear in expressions for the expenditure ratios, E/T, $(pQ/n)/T$ and b/T. It is clearly convenient that these ratios do not depend on the unit of measurement, though of course the absolute values do depend on μ_{w_0}.

7.4 Numerical Examples

Previous sections have obtained explicit results regarding the optimal values of expenditure components. However, the complexity of the expressions means that the comparative static properties are not transparent. The present section therefore uses numerical examples to reinforce discussion of the model's properties. First, suitable parameter values for calibration are outlined, after which the effects of varying a range of parameters are examined. These include the elasticity of the wage rate with respect to basic ability, θ, the inequality of the basic ability level, $\sigma^2_{w_0}$, the degree of inequality aversion of the judge, ε, and the exogenously fixed tax rate, t.

7.4.1 Calibration of the Model

In selecting basic parameter values it is necessary first to ensure that they give rise to sensible values of the proportion of time devoted to labour supply. Using preference parameters of $\alpha = 0.5$ and $\beta = 0.4$, along with a tax rate of $t = 0.35$, the proportion of time devoted to labour supply, at the arithmetic mean wage rate, is around 0.58. Furthermore, it is necessary to consider values of θ which, along with other parameters, give rise to positive values of the transfer payment, b, and reasonable absolute and relative values of expenditure. In the following numerical examples, θ is allowed to vary between 0.75 and 1: the latter corresponds to the case where education expenditure has no role in generating ability levels.[4]

As a benchmark case, individuals' basic ability levels, w_0, are assumed to follow a lognormal distribution with variance of logarithms, $\sigma^2_{w_0} = 0.36$ and mean of logarithms, $\mu_{w_0} = 3$, remembering that the latter affects only absolute values of expenditure.

In calibrating this type of model it is difficult to obtain obvious empirical counterparts. For example it may be thought that estimates of labour

---

[4]Strictly, results are undefined for $\theta = 1$, so the upper limit in practice is set at 0.999.

supply elasticities could be used, but there is no single elasticity from which calibration can be based. The approach adopted with this kind of exercise is to ensure that the orders of magnitude of certain important variables make sense, such as the labour supplied by the individual with arithmetic mean wage rate, and typical values of expenditure on consumption. Extensive sensitivity analyses were carried out to ensure that results presented are fully representative and do not arise from pathological cases. With the benchmark parameters mentioned here, the absolute values of expenditure on education, public goods and the transfer payment in all reported results have reasonable magnitudes, in relation to approximate observed values. As mentioned earlier, an independent check on total tax revenue, resulting from arithmetic mean earnings, and the sum of expenditure on education, public goods and the transfer payment, confirmed both the accuracy of the analytical expression and the computations.

7.4.2   Comparative Statics

Consider first the influence of σ_w^2 on the optimal composition of government expenditures. From the human capital production function (7.8) the variance of logarithms of wage rates is $\sigma_w^2 = \theta^2 \sigma_{w_0}^2$ and is not affected by E, which is the same for everyone. It is, however, influenced by θ, which also governs the extent to which education expenditure contributes to human capital, $1 - \theta$. In the following discussion, it is convenient to define the term $G = pQ$ as the expenditure on the public good.

A higher value of $\sigma_{w_0}^2$ has two effects. First, *ceteris paribus*, it increases the arithmetic mean value of w and hence average earnings.

$$\bar{w} = \exp\left(\mu_w + \sigma_w^2\right) = \exp\left(\theta \mu_{w_0} + (1 - \theta)\log E + 0.5\theta^2 \sigma_{w_0}^2\right) \qquad (7.53)$$

This gives rise to a higher total revenue, which allows all types of expenditure to increase. The higher E also reinforces the effect on average earnings, though it is moderated somewhat by the increase in b. Second, an inequality averse planner makes the expenditure pattern more redistributive, so that b increases relative to G/n and E. Hence optimal $(G/n)/T$ and E/T fall, despite their absolute increase, while b/T increases. However, all these effects are relatively small given that $\sigma_{w_0}^2$ is only a small component of the arithmetic mean wage.

The way in which optimal shares vary as $\sigma_{w_0}^2$ increases is shown in Figure 7.1. The top panel illustrates variations in the share of expenditure on education, E/T, with changes in $\sigma_{w_0}^2$; the middle panel shows how the ratio of optimal public goods expenditure per person to total expenditure, $(G/n)/T$, varies; and the lower panel shows how the share of transfer payments varies with $\sigma_{w_0}^2$. In each case the variations are obtained for an inequality aversion coefficient of $\varepsilon = 0.8$, and profiles are shown for four values of the parameter, θ. The effects of variations in $\sigma_{w_0}^2$ are seen to be similar for all values of θ. That is, profiles of optimal expenditure components and shares, as $\sigma_{w_0}^2$ varies, are simply shifted upwards or downwards by increases or decreases in θ.

An increase in inequality aversion, ε, does not have a similar effect to that of an increase in basic inequality, $\sigma_{w_0}^2$, because the latter affects arithmetic mean earnings and hence tax revenue. The increase in ε increases the difference between $\tilde{w}_\theta$ and $\bar{w}_\theta$. The desire for a more redistributive policy on the part of the planner leads to an increase in b, in absolute and relative terms, at the expense of E and Q. Thus b and b/T increase while Q, E, $(G/n)/T$ and E/T all fall slightly. Again, these effects are small and are similar for all values of θ. The three panels of Figure 7.2 show in turn the relationship between ε and the optimal E/T, $(G/n)/T$ and b/T, again for different values of θ. In each case the variation in the budget share, as inequality aversion increases, is small. Hence different planners may have very different degrees of inequality aversion and yet would display little disagreement concerning optimal expenditure shares. It is clear that the value of θ, influencing the role of education in generating ability levels, is much more important. This

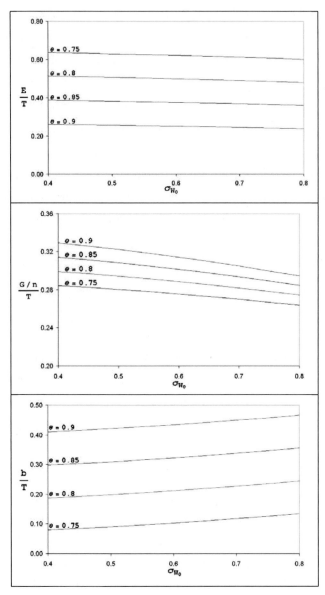

Figure 7.1: The Optimal Composition and Variations in the Variance of Initial Wage

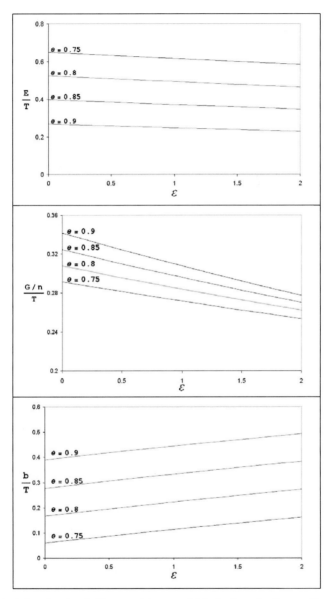

Figure 7.2: The Optimal Composition and Variations in Inequality Aversion

is discussed next.

The effect of an increase in θ is to produce an investment effect. This arises from the fact that a higher θ implies that education is less effective in raising the average level of productivity. This leads to the planner reducing E in absolute terms. In the limit, a value of $\theta = 1$ means that education plays no role in determining w, so that there is no point in investing in education and optimal E falls to zero. Hence the investment effect of variations in θ can be expected to be quite substantial. The consequent reduction in education spending, in absolute and relative terms as θ increases, leaves more tax revenue available for spending on transfer payments and the public good, despite the associated reduction in average earnings. However, the reduction in average earnings via the term $(1 - \theta) \log E$ is modified to a small extent by the effect of higher θ in raising $\bar{w}$ for given E, via the terms $\theta \mu_{w_0}$ and $0.5 \theta^2 \sigma_{w_0}^2$ in equation (7.53). The last term is similar to the effect of increasing inequality, while the effect on $\bar{w}$ operating via μ_{w_0} is known to have no effect on relative orders of magnitude. Figure 7.3 shows the variation in optimal E/T, $(G/n)/T$ and b/T with θ, while Figure 7.4 shows the variation in the absolute levels of E, G/n and b.

These diagrams show that the overall effect of increasing θ is to reduce optimal E and E/T while raising G, b, G/T and b/T. In view of the significant investment effect of variations in θ, this parameter has a much larger effect on policy variables than inequality aversion or basic inequality. The ratios appear to be approximately linearly related to θ, but this property is far from evident from the corresponding analytical expressions.

The above discussion relates to changes in parameters and their effects on optimal expenditure patterns for a given tax rate, which is assumed to be set exogenously. Clearly, a minimum value of t is necessary in order to ensure that the transfer payment is positive, given that some non-transfer expenditure is carried out, otherwise the inequality-reducing benefit becomes the equivalent of a regressive poll tax. It is useful to consider how the optimal

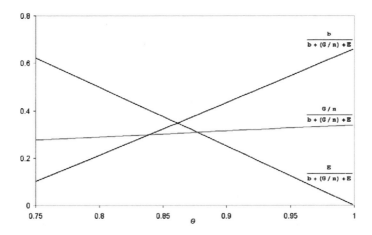

Figure 7.3: Variations in the Optimal Shares of Expenditure on Education, Public Goods and Transfer Payment as θ Varies

composition varies as the tax rate varies. First, the incentive effect of an increasing tax rate, *ceteris paribus*, reduces average earnings. Initially, the increasing 'tax rate' effect of a higher rate outweighs the falling 'tax base' effect, so that total revenue rises. However, for higher tax rates, further increases lead to a reduction in total revenue as the falling tax base effect dominates. This kind of effect is of course familiar. Hence an inequality averse planner would raise the transfer payment as the tax rate is increased – but only to the extent that this is made possible by the revenue effect. It has been mentioned that increasing the tax rate has a disincentive effect on labour supply, thereby reducing average earnings. The return from investing in education is therefore lower, so an increase in t has the effect of lowering the optimal value of E. The effect of increasing b and reducing E means that eventually as the tax rate is increased, Q can in principle turn negative: such a 'public bad' does not make sense in the present framework, thereby imposing an upper limit on the tax rate. The relationships between the tax rate and the optimal share of expenditure on education, public goods and

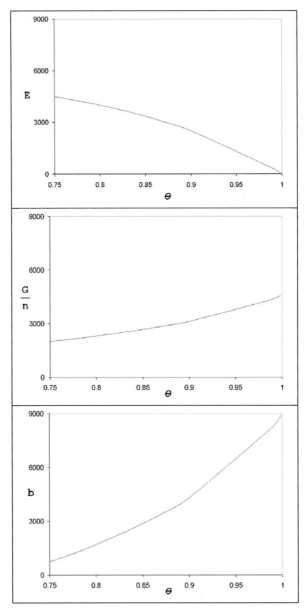

Figure 7.4: The Optimal Composition and Variations in Efficiency Parameter
θ

transfer payments are shown in the three panels of Figure 7.5. In each case variations are illustrated for four different values of the parameter, θ, in the education production function.

7.5 Conclusions

This chapter has examined the optimal allocation of tax revenue among a universal transfer payment, a pure public good and expenditure on education. Using a single-period framework, individuals were assumed to have similar preferences but to be endowed with an exogenously given heterogeneous ability level. The education expenditure raises the productivity of individuals, via a type of human capital production function. The social welfare function was based on individuals' (indirect) utilities, and reflecting a degree of relative inequality aversion. Judgements regarding optimal expenditure therefore have to balance the efficiency effects of education expenditure (which does not reduce wage rate inequality) with the inequality-reducing effect of the transfer. In this framework, education creates a substantial fiscal spillover whereby the increase in human capital gives rise to higher labour supply earnings and thus higher income tax revenue, thereby allowing greater government expenditure on all items than would otherwise be possible. Explicit solutions were obtained for the expenditure levels. However, in view of the complexity of the expressions, comparative static properties of the model were reinforced by numerical examples.

A higher inequality of exogenous ability levels was found to increase average earnings. The higher total revenue allows all types of expenditure to increase. Higher inequality aversion makes the expenditure pattern more redistributive, so that the transfer payment increases relative to public good and education expenditure, despite their absolute increase. However, these effects are relatively small.

The desire for a more redistributive policy leads to an increase in transfer

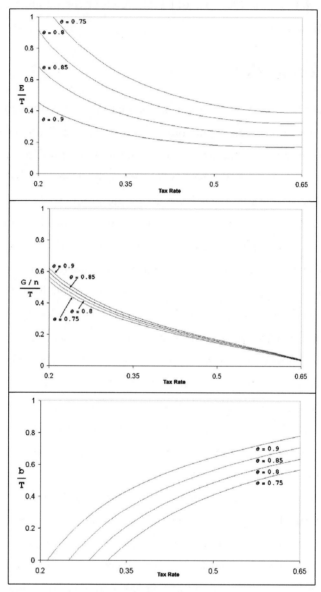

Figure 7.5: Optimal Expenditure Shares and Variations in the Tax Rate

payments in absolute and relative terms, at the expense of the other two components. The variation in budget shares, as inequality aversion increases, is small. Hence different independent judges may have very different degrees of inequality aversion and yet would display little disagreement concerning optimal expenditure shares.

The effect of an increase in the coefficient on basic ability in the human capital production function (the elasticity of the wage with respect to basic ability) is to produce an investment effect. First, it implies that education is less effective in raising the average level of productivity, which leads to the planner reducing education spending in absolute terms. Ultimately, as the coefficient approaches unity, education plays no role, so the investment effect of such variations is expected to be substantial. The consequent reduction in education spending, in absolute and relative terms, leaves more tax revenue available for spending on transfer payments and the public good, despite the associated reduction in average earnings. In view of the significant investment effect of variations in this elasticity, this parameter has a much larger effect on policy variables than inequality aversion or basic inequality.

Chapter 8

The Overlapping Generations Context

This chapter returns to the overlapping generations framework set out in Chapter 5. Instead of considering majority voting outcomes, this chapter, as with others in this Part of the book, carries out a normative exploration of the expenditure mix which would be chosen by a utilitarian judge having a degree of inequality aversion. The framework of analysis is that of the choice of expenditure on non-rival and non-excludable public goods and transfer payments, in the form of an unconditional pension, in a growing economy with overlapping generations. Expenditure is tax-financed on a pay-as-you-go basis. The utilitarian judge is regarded as maximising a social welfare function expressed in terms of the (indirect) utilities of heterogeneous individuals, subject to the pay-as-you-go financing constraint. By taking a growth context and focusing on the expenditure composition for a given tax rate, the model allows for a range of factors other than the judge's inequality aversion which may contribute to the division of expenditure, such as consumers' preferences, tax and interest rates, and the growth rates of income and population. The transfer payment in the model is referred to as a pension, since it is received in the second period of life. However, it may be thought of more broadly as a standard type of income transfer since it involves a decision regarding income shifting between periods within the life cycle as well as intra- and inter-generational redistribution.

A number of recent studies emphasise the importance of unobserved cultural factors in shaping tax and expenditure policies. Alesina and Glaeser (2004), on the basis of cross-national survey data, conjecture that different preferences for a more equal income distribution in Europe and the US may play an important role in accounting for the considerable differences in their expenditure policies. Corneo and Grüner (2002), using a large international survey, present empirical evidence of systematic differences across countries in the preference for redistributive policies. This chapter helps to understand, using a structural model, the way in which different views regarding inequality may influence the composition of expenditure.

The optimal expenditure ratio, defined as the ratio of transfer payments (the pension) to public goods expenditure, is shown to depend on a welfare-weighted mean income in relation to arithmetic mean income, along with individuals' preferences for public goods, the discount rate, population and income growth rates, and the tax rate. However, a closed-form solution for the expenditure ratio is not available, as the welfare-weighted mean income in general depends on the choice of pension expenditure. A useful approximation is therefore considered for the welfare-weighted mean income, using an explicit form for the welfare function. This produces an approximate solution for the optimal expenditure ratio, and simulations show that the approximation performs well. Comparative statics based on the approximate solution are shown to accord with expectations. In particular, a higher inequality aversion gives rise, *ceteris paribus*, to the transfer payment forming a larger proportion of total government expenditure.

It is of course unreasonable to suggest that, in practice, expenditure decisions arise from the optimising plans of a single omniscient and omnipotent judge. However, it is of interest to consider the hypothetical question of what value judgements could be considered to be implicit in the observed expenditure policies of countries. The approximate closed-form solution for the optimal expenditure ratio allows an implied value of inequality aversion to be obtained for a range of countries, given data for other determinants of the expenditure ratio for each country. The results show that different degrees of inequality aversion are evident among the countries examined. The average implied inequality aversion for Scandinavian countries is consistently higher than that of Commonwealth countries, while the US has a lower degree of inequality aversion than average Scandinavian and Commonwealth countries. These results are consistent with Lambert *et al.* (2003), who measure the degree of inequality aversion for a large sample of countries from income inequality indexes. Germany has the highest implied inequality aversion among all countries. Significant inequality aversion in Germany was also found in Lambert *et al.* (2003) and Schwarze and Härpfer (2007), where the latter use regional life-satisfaction data to estimate inequality aversion in Germany. These results suggest that variations in expenditure patterns could possibly reflect different social preferences regarding inequality which may result from cultural differences across countries. This study then provides a structural way to investigate the conjecture of Alesina and Glaeser (2004).

In view of the complexity of decision making in practice and the frequent need for compromises, it is typically far from straightforward to 'reconstruct' the values which may be implied by actual policies. The evaluation of implicit values can thus help to judge the consistency of actual policies with certain stated objectives of policy makers and commentators. This study therefore relates to a large literature which attempts to recover implicit value judgements in government tax and expenditure policies. For example, early attempts to impute a value of inequality aversion implicit in government tax decisions include Christiansen and Jansen (1978) and Stern (1977). See also Mera (1969), Moreh (1981) and Brent (1984). Ravallion (1988) examined inequality aversion implicit in regional disbursement policies. More recent studies include Madden (1992, 1995) and Cragg (1991) in the context of indi-

rect taxes, and Oliver and Spadaro (2004) and Spadaro (2007) in the context
of direct taxation. By examining the shape of the implicit welfare function,
Spadaro (2007) found that it was concave, thereby supporting the idea that
tax policy could be regarded as the outcome of an optimising process. Implicit values in the choice of adult equivalent scales were examined by van
de Ven and Creedy (2005). Schwarze and Härpfer (2007) and Lambert *et al.*
(2003), as mentioned above, provide empirical examinations of attitudes towards inequality. By using a structural model to infer inequality aversion for
a range of countries, the present study obtains results which are consistent
with these earlier studies.

The chapter is arranged as follows. Section 8.1 describes the economic
environment. Section 8.2 examines the optimal choice of expenditure of the
utilitarian judge. Section 8.3 describes the approximation which produces the
closed-form solution for the expenditure ratio and discusses the comparative
statics. Implicit value judgements for a range of countries are investigated
in Section 8.4.

8.1   The Economic Environment

This section describes the overlapping generations model in which a pure
public good and a transfer payment, in the form of a pension, are tax-financed
on a pay-as-you-go basis.

Each individual is assumed to live for two periods, a working and a retirement period, so that the economy is populated by two overlapping cohorts in
any given period. Let N_t denote the number of individuals born in period t.
Individuals have identical preferences but are heterogeneous with respect to
incomes. A young individual i, born at time t, works in the first period and
receives an exogenously fixed income, $y_{i,t}$. Income is taxed at rate τ, which
is the same for all individuals and is assumed to be exogenously determined.
In period t, young individual i allocates disposable income between current

consumption, $c_{1i,t}$, and savings, $s_{i,t}$. In the second period of life, the individual finances consumption of private goods, $c_{2i,t+1}$, using the unconditional and untaxed pension from the government, b_{t+1}, and the return on savings, $(1+r)s_{i,t}$, where r is the constant interest rate at which individuals can borrow or lend. The price of the private consumption goods is normalised to unity, so that c also denotes private consumption expenditure.

The quantity of pure public good in period t is denoted as Q_t, which can be consumed by all individuals in period t. Assume that the production of public goods involves a constant unit cost, p. Then government expenditure on public goods in t is simply $G_t \equiv pQ_t$.

Suppose all individuals have Cobb–Douglas preferences, expressed for person i as:

$$U_{i,t} = c_{1i,t} c_{2i,t+1}^{\beta} Q_t^{\gamma} Q_{t+1}^{\gamma\beta} \tag{8.1}$$

where $0 < \beta = 1/(1+\rho) < 1$ is the discount factor, ρ is the time preference rate and γ is the utility weight attached to consumption of public goods, reflecting the preference for public goods relative to private goods.

In view of the inter-generational transfers in addition to the income shifting and intra-generational redistribution, it is desirable to allow for population and income growth. Suppose the average income of young individuals grows at a constant rate of ω over time, and there is constant growth, at the rate n, in the population. It is assumed that income growth involves an equal proportional change at all income levels and that population growth involves an equal proportional change in population frequencies at each income level, so that ω and n are independent.

8.2 The Utilitarian Optimal Choice

This section investigates the optimal choice of expenditure by a utilitarian judge who aims to maximise a social welfare function. It begins by describing each individual's consumption and saving choice conditional on government expenditures, which yields indirect utility as a function of those expenditures. It then defines the social welfare function in terms of individual utilities and characterises the optimal expenditure ratio, defined as the ratio of total expenditure on pensions to that on public goods, that maximises the social welfare function.

From Section 8.1, the lifetime budget constraint of individual i is given by:

$$c_{1i,t} + \frac{c_{2i,t+1}}{(1+r)} = (1-\tau)y_{i,t} + \frac{b_{t+1}}{(1+r)} \equiv M_{i,t} \tag{8.2}$$

This form allows for the fact that tax-financed public goods are non-excludable so that individuals are not charged at the point of consumption. The consumption plans, conditional on the values of public expenditure and the pension, are given, using the standard properties of Cobb–Douglas utility functions, as:

$$c_{1i,t} = M_{i,t}/(1+\beta), \quad c_{2i,t+1} = \beta(1+r)M_{i,t}/(1+\beta) \tag{8.3}$$

So the indirect utility function, $V_{i,t}$, is:

$$V_{i,t} = \left(\frac{M_{i,t}}{1+\beta}\right)\left(\frac{\beta(1+r)M_{i,t}}{(1+\beta)}\right)^{\beta} Q_t^{\gamma} Q_{t+1}^{\gamma\beta} \tag{8.4}$$

The utilitarian judge, recognising that individuals' consumption and saving decisions are conditional on its expenditure choices, chooses a sequence of expenditures on public goods and pensions, $\{b_{t+1}, G_{t+1}\}_{t=0}^{\infty}$, ($b_0$ and G_0 are given), to maximise a social welfare function, subject to the government budget constraint in every period.

In the pay-as-you-go financing structure, income tax revenue in each period must be sufficient to finance the transfer payments to those currently retired along with the public good. Hence, at time t the government budget constraint, where $\bar{y}_t$ denotes arithmetic mean income, is given by:

$$G_t + N_{t-1}b_t = \tau N_t \bar{y}_t \tag{8.5}$$

The social welfare function is defined as the following discounted sum of all generations' utilities:

$$SW = \sum_{t=-1}^{\infty} \delta^t W_t \qquad (8.6)$$

where δ is the judge's discount factor, which could be different from private individuals' discount factor, β. The social welfare associated with generation t, W_t, is defined as a function of utilities of all individuals born in period t:

$$W_t = W\left(V_{1,t}, ..., V_{i,t}, ... V_{N_t,t}\right) \qquad (8.7)$$

where $V_{i,t}$ is defined in (8.4), and the function W is time-invariant, individualistic and Paretean. To ensure the problem is well defined, it is also assumed that W is additively separable, and strictly increasing and (weakly) concave in each of its arguments.[1]

A simplification arises from the fact that the imposition of pay-as-you-go financing as well and two-period overlapping generations nature of the model ensure that maximisation of the social welfare function in (8.6) is equivalent to the maximisation of W_t in every period t. This property also arises because there is no income shifting between other 'disconnected' generations, only those overlapping at any time.

Then the first-order conditions for choice of b_{t+1}, for $t = 0, 1, \ldots$, are given by:

$$\sum_{i=1}^{N_t} \frac{\partial W_t}{\partial V_{i,t}} \left(\frac{\partial V_{i,t}}{\partial b_{t+1}} + \frac{\partial V_{i,t}}{\partial G_{t+1}} \frac{dG_{t+1}}{db_{t+1}} \right) = 0 \qquad (8.8)$$

Define $v_{i,t} = (\partial W_t/\partial V_{i,t})(\partial V_{i,t}/\partial b_{t+1})$ as the welfare weight attached to an increase in i's pension income. Then:

$$\sum_{i=1}^{N_t} \frac{\partial W_t}{\partial V_{i,t}} \frac{\partial V_{i,t}}{\partial G_{t+1}} = \sum_{i=1}^{N_t} v_{i,t} \left(\frac{\partial V_{i,t}/\partial G_{t+1}}{\partial V_{i,t}/\partial b_{t+1}} \right) \qquad (8.9)$$

---

[1]The social welfare function defined this way is consistent with requirements for time-consistent policy. See Calvo and Obstfeld (1988) and Ambler (2000) for further discussion on this issue in overlapping generations models. A simple form of W_t adopted by many studies, such as Ghiglino (2000), defines W_t as the weighted sum of lifetime utilities of individuals in cohort t.

Hence, writing $\tilde{v}_{i,t} = v_{i,t}/\sum_{i=1}^{N_t} v_{i,t}$, where $\sum_{i=1}^{N_t} \tilde{v}_{i,t} = 1$ and noting that from the government budget constraint in (8.5), $dG_{t+1}/db_{t+1} = -N_t$, substitution in (8.8) for each t gives:

$$\sum_{i=1}^{N_t} \tilde{v}_{i,t} \left(\frac{\partial V_{i,t}/\partial G_{t+1}}{\partial V_{i,t}/\partial b_{t+1}} \right) = \frac{1}{N_t} \tag{8.10}$$

This result does not depend on the precise form of V or W, but further progress can be made using (8.4) above, which gives:

$$\frac{\partial V_{i,t}}{\partial G_{t+1}} = \frac{\beta\gamma V_{i,t}}{G_{t+1}} \tag{8.11}$$

$$\frac{\partial V_{i,t}}{\partial b_{t+1}} = \frac{(1+\beta)\, V_{i,t}}{(1+r)(1-\tau)y_{i,t} + b_{t+1}} \tag{8.12}$$

Substituting into (8.10) and writing $\tilde{y}_t = \sum_i^{N_t} \tilde{v}_{i,t} y_{i,t}$ gives:

$$\frac{\beta\gamma\left\{(1+r)(1-\tau)\tilde{y}_t + b_{t+1}\right\}}{(1+\beta)\, G_{t+1}} = \frac{1}{N_t} \tag{8.13}$$

The term $\tilde{y}_t$ is a welfare-weighted average of individual incomes with weights, $\tilde{v}_{i,t}$. Substituting the government budget constraint into (8.13) gives the optimal per capita expenditure on the pension, b_{t+1}. Therefore the ratio of expenditure on pensions to total expenditure, $B_{t+1} \equiv N_t b_{t+1}/(\tau N_{t+1} \bar{y}_{t+1})$, is given by:

$$B_{t+1} = \frac{1}{(1+\beta+\beta\gamma)} \left\{ (1+\beta) - \beta\gamma \frac{(1+r)(1-\tau)}{\tau(1+n)(1+\omega)} \frac{\tilde{y}_t}{\bar{y}_t} \right\} \tag{8.14}$$

The share of total expenditure on public goods, $G_{t+1}/\tau N_{t+1} \bar{y}_{t+1}$, is thus simply obtained as $1 - B_{t+1}$. Therefore the ratio of total expenditure on pensions to that on public goods, R_{t+1}, is:

$$R_{t+1} = \frac{((1+\beta)/\beta\gamma)(1+n)(1+\omega) - (1+r)(\frac{1-\tau}{\tau})(\tilde{y}_t/\bar{y}_t)}{(1+n)(1+\omega) + (1+r)(\frac{1-\tau}{\tau})(\tilde{y}_t/\bar{y}_t)} \tag{8.15}$$

This result shows how the optimal expenditure ratio, R_{t+1}, depends, *inter alia*, on the ratio of the welfare-weighted mean income to the arithmetic mean income at time t as well as parameters regarding population growth, income growth, the tax rate and preferences. The expenditure ratio does not depend on the constant cost of producing the public good, p. This property arises from the Cobb–Douglas form of utility functions. The distinction between G and Q is nevertheless made here for transparency. This optimal choice is characterised by a balanced growth path, along which all aggregate endogenous variables grow at the same rate as aggregate income, and per capita variables grow at the same rate as average income.

The expression in (8.15) cannot of course be regarded as providing a closed-form solution for the expenditure ratio, as the welfare-weighted mean income in general depends on the value of b. However, a useful approximation is considered in the following section, using an explicit form of the welfare function, which makes use of a basic approach introduced in earlier chapters.

8.3 Approximating the Optimal Expenditure Ratio

This section shows how an approximation for the optimal expenditure ratio can be obtained by approximating the welfare-weighted average income, $\tilde{y}_t$, using a widely adopted social welfare function which takes the iso-elastic form:

$$W_t = \frac{1}{1-\varepsilon} \sum_{i=1}^{N_t} V_{i,t}^{1-\varepsilon} \tag{8.16}$$

where $\varepsilon \geq 0$ denotes relative inequality aversion of the judge. For $\varepsilon = 1$ this takes the form $W_t = \sum_{i=1}^{N_t} \log V_{i,t}$. The case of $\varepsilon = 0$ corresponds to an absence of inequality aversion and gives the 'classical utilitarian' welfare function

Thus $\partial W_t / \partial V_{i,t} = V_{i,t}^{-\varepsilon}$ and obtaining $\partial V_{i,t}/\partial b_{t+1}$ from (8.4), the welfare weights, $v_{i,t} = (\partial W_t/\partial V_{i,t})(\partial V_{i,t}/\partial b_{t+1})$, are:

$$v_{i,t} = \frac{(1+\beta)\left(\frac{\beta^\beta(1+r)^\beta Q_t^\gamma Q_{t+1}^{\beta\gamma}}{(1+\beta)^{(\beta+1)}}\right)^{1-\varepsilon}}{(1+r)}\left((1-\tau)y_{i,t} + \frac{b_{t+1}}{(1+r)}\right)^{\beta-\varepsilon(1+\beta)} \tag{8.17}$$

This form is clearly intractable, but it is reasonable to suppose that b_{t+1} is small relative to $y_{i,t}$.[2] In this case an approximation, $\tilde{y}_{A,t}$, for the welfare-weighted mean is obtained as the ratio of two fractional moments:

$$\tilde{y}_{A,t} = \frac{\frac{1}{N_t} \sum y_{i,t}^{1+\beta-\varepsilon(1+\beta)}}{\frac{1}{N_t} \sum y_{i,t}^{\beta-\varepsilon(1+\beta)}} \tag{8.18}$$

Suppose further that $y_{i,t}$ is lognormally distributed as $\Lambda(y_{i,t}|\,\mu_t, \sigma_t^2)$, with mean and variance of logarithms of μ_t and σ_t^2 respectively. The vth moment is given by $\mu_v = \exp\left(v\mu + v^2\sigma^2/2\right)$, and thus $\bar{y} = \mu_1 = \exp\left(\mu + \sigma^2/2\right)$; see Aitchison and Brown (1957). Using these properties, it can be found that:

$$\frac{\tilde{y}_{A,t}}{\bar{y}_t} = \exp\left[\{2\beta - 2\varepsilon\,(1+\beta)\}\,\frac{\sigma_t^2}{2} \right] \tag{8.19}$$

Higher ε therefore reduces $\tilde{y}_{A,t}$ relative to $\bar{y}_t$, by giving a lower weight to higher incomes. The classical utilitarian case of $\varepsilon = 0$ gives rise to $\tilde{y}_t/\bar{y}_t = \exp\left(2\beta\right)$. Using (8.19) to approximate $\tilde{y}_t/\bar{y}_t$ in (8.14) and (8.15) gives a closed-form solution for the transfer as a proportion of total expenditure and the expenditure ratio. From (8.14) it can be seen that the transfer B could be negative if γ is sufficiently large while ε is sufficiently low, implying a poll tax.

Before carrying out comparative static analyses, it is necessary to conduct simulation exercises to investigate whether the approximation derived here works well. These are reported in the following subsection.

8.3.1   Testing the Approximation

This subsection tests the value of the approximation derived in Section 8.3. Hence values of the expenditure components using the approximation $\tilde{y}_A$ were compared with those obtained using a simulated population of size

---

[2] Data on pension expenditure are not available. However, the total expenditure on transfers, including pension, accounts for about 20 per cent of GDP on average for the countries examined below. Furthermore, the simulations show that the approximation works well even with $b/\bar{y}$ around 0.25.

15000 drawn at random from a lognormal distribution with $\mu = 9.0$ and $\sigma^2 = 0.32$. This implies $y_m/\bar{y} = 0.85$, which is the average for the sample of countries used in previous chapters. Using the simulated distribution, a range of values of b_{t+1} were investigated. For each b_{t+1} the government budget constraint was used to obtain G_{t+1} and the resulting values were used to calculate each individual's level of utility. These were then used to obtain social welfare, using the iso-elastic function with a specified inequality aversion parameter, ε. Finally, given a number of W_t measures for different b_{t+1}, the maximum was determined, giving the optimal composition. Table 8.1 gives the results for a range of degrees of inequality aversion, with other parameters set at the average of the sample reported in Table 8.3. These results show that the approximation gives values of expenditure levels and ratios which are close to those obtained using a large simulated population.

Table 8.1: Composition of Government Expenditure: Alternative Solutions

	Approximation			Simulation		
ε	b_{t+1}	B_{t+1}	R	b_{t+1}	B_{t+1}	R
			$\gamma = 0.9$			
1.81	2813	0.51	1.03	2660	0.48	0.93
2.01	2935	0.53	1.13	2730	0.49	0.97
2.21	3042	0.55	1.22	2790	0.50	1.01
			$\gamma = 1$			
1.81	2537	0.46	0.85	2420	0.44	0.78
2.01	2740	0.50	0.98	2530	0.46	0.84
2.21	2908	0.53	1.11	2630	0.48	0.91
			$\gamma = 1.10$			
1.81	2419	0.44	0.77	2280	0.41	0.70
2.01	2557	0.46	0.86	2350	0.42	0.74
2.21	2680	0.48	0.94	2420	0.43	0.77

8.3.2   Comparative Static Properties of the Model

It is now possible to discuss comparative static properties of the model. Examination of (8.15), using (8.19) to approximate $\tilde{y}_t/\bar{y}_t$, shows that a higher

tax rate is associated with a greater proportion of expenditure being devoted
to transfer payments, whereby R_{t+1} is increasing in τ at a decreasing rate.
An increase in the tax rate gives the government more income to spend
on both types of expenditure, but the increase in pension expenditure is
relatively higher than the increase in public goods expenditure.[3] Population
and income growth have similar effects, as they appear in (8.15) together in
the form $(1+n)(1+\omega)$: they are perfect substitutes for each other. Increases
in ω and n increase the share of expenditure on pensions and decrease the
share of expenditure on public goods, and also their ratio. With income
growth or population growth, tax revenues of the government are increased
such that the government is able to spend more on both types of expenditure.
However, the increase in the expenditure on pensions is higher than the
expenditure on public goods.

An increase in the interest rate has a negative effect on the share of
expenditure on pensions and on the ratio of pensions to public goods, but
it increases total expenditure on public goods. A higher interest rate leads
to more private savings by individuals at a young age. This results in a
higher public goods expenditure and a lower ratio of pensions to public goods
expenditure.

An increase in income inequality, as measured by σ^2, reduces $\tilde{y}_A/\bar{y}$, from
(8.19), and thus increases the proportion of expenditure devoted to the pension. Hence more basic inequality implies a more redistributive expenditure
policy. This result is consistent with models examining majority voting over
the tax rate, with an unconditional transfer payment, in which a uniform result is that more basic inequality leads to the choice of a more redistributive
tax and transfer structure; for example, see Meltzer and Richard (1981). Sim-
ilarly, an increase in inequality aversion, ε, also reduces $\tilde{y}_A/\bar{y}$ and therefore
raises the share of expenditure on redistribution.

---

[3]However, in Chapter 3 a concave relationship between the share of transfers and the
tax rate was found, arising from adverse incentive effects of the tax and transfer system.

The comparative static results with respect to the weight attached to public goods, γ, suggest that an increase in the preference for public goods unambiguously increases the share of expenditure on public goods, but decreases the share of expenditure on pensions and the ratio of pensions to public goods expenditure. Analytic results relating to β were found to be equivocal, but the numerical results reported below demonstrate that both B and R fall as β increases.

A numerical exercise is implemented to illustrate the comparative static properties and further examine the sensitivity of the optimal expenditure ratio with respect to changes in parameters. The baseline values for parameters τ, r, β, ω, n and σ^2 were set to the average of the sample. The baseline value for γ is 1. The baseline value for ε is the average implied ε across the sample countries for $\gamma = 1$ (Table 8.4). The following section describes how ε is calculated. The parameter variations considered are 10 and 20 per cent changes around the baseline values. Table 8.2 reports the values of B and R as parameters vary around their baseline values. In each case only one parameter at a time is varied, with all other parameters kept at their baseline values.

Table 8.2: Share of Pension Expenditure and Expenditure Ratio for Alternative Parameter Values

		τ	r	β	ω	n	σ^2	ε	γ
	-20%	0.433	0.502	0.526	0.480	0.491	0.461	0.416	0.569
	-10%	0.468	0.499	0.509	0.489	0.493	0.479	0.459	0.531
B	Baseline	0.496	0.496	0.496	0.496	0.496	0.496	0.496	0.496
	$+10\%$	0.519	0.493	0.485	0.502	0.498	0.511	0.526	0.463
	$+20\%$	0.538	0.490	0.476	0.509	0.500	0.525	0.551	0.432
	-20%	0.764	1.007	1.108	0.924	0.965	0.856	0.711	1.319
	-10%	0.879	0.995	1.038	0.957	0.974	0.920	0.850	1.133
R	Baseline	0.984	0.984	0.984	0.984	0.984	0.984	0.984	0.984
	$+10\%$	1.079	0.972	0.941	1.009	0.993	1.045	1.111	0.862
	$+20\%$	1.165	0.960	0.908	1.037	1.002	1.105	1.229	0.760

The results show that the share of expenditure on pensions, public goods and their ratio are quite sensitive to variations in the tax rate, the weight attached to public goods, the variance of the distribution of income and the discount factor. They are less sensitive to changes in the interest rate and the growth rates of population and income. The expenditure ratio is most sensitive to variations in ε around the baseline value. For the classical utilitarian welfare function, that is for $\varepsilon = 0$, and other parameters at their baseline values, it is found that the resulting expenditure on transfers as a proportion of total expenditure is 0.056, and the expenditure ratio is 0.060. An absence of inequality aversion therefore implies some expenditure on redistributive transfer payments. This arises because the social welfare function is a simple sum of indirect utilities which are in turn concave functions of transfer income. Hence there is a benefit from income shifting. Similarly, in standard static optimal tax models the optimal tax, and thus transfer, is positive even when $\varepsilon = 0$.

8.4   Implicit Inequality Aversion

This section considers the following hypothetical question. Supposing that actual expenditure policies were determined by a utilitarian judge of the type considered above, what degree of inequality aversion is implied? This type of question has previously been considered in the context of static models of taxation. Actual policy making is of course far too complicated to be captured by such a simple model, and in practice value judgements are extremely difficult to articulate precisely and thus are never expressed explicitly by policy makers. But information about implicit value judgements can provide a useful input into rational policy analysis.

The present framework allows an implied value, $\hat{\varepsilon}$, of inequality aversion to be obtained. Using the approximation for $\tilde{y}_A/\bar{y}$ in (8.19) above, $\hat{\varepsilon}$ is, after some rearrangement:

$$\hat{\varepsilon} = \frac{1}{1+\beta} \left(\beta + \left(\frac{1}{2} \right) \frac{\log(\tilde{y}_A/\bar{y})}{(-\sigma_t^2/2)} \right) \tag{8.20}$$

For the lognormal distribution, median income is $y_m = e^{\mu}$, so the ratio of median to mean income is given by $\log(y_m/\bar{y}_t) = -\sigma_t^2/2$. Hence (8.20) can be seen to involve a ratio of two terms consisting of logarithms of income ratios, one containing the welfare-weighted mean and the other involving the median income.

From equation (8.14), it is possible to express $\tilde{y}/\bar{y}$, and hence $\tilde{y}_A/\bar{y}$, for the relevant period in terms of β, γ, τ, n, ω, r and the share of pension expenditure, B. However, a problem is raised by the difficulty of obtaining detailed comparable data on the composition of government expenditure for a wide range of countries. A major difficulty in the present context is that inadequate information about expenditure components is available. Ideally, separate details regarding pension expenditure are required, but only aggregate expenditure on transfer payments can be obtained: the use of the aggregates effectively requires an assumption that the composition of transfers is similar across countries.[4] Hence the results presented here should be treated with much caution.

The data are as follows. The OECD Social Expenditure Database covers 30 OECD countries for the period 1980–2005. The share of social expenditure as a percentage of total expenditure is obtained from this dataset. Social expenditure includes Old age, Survivors, Incapacity-related benefits, Health, Family, Active labour market programmes, Unemployment, Housing and Other social policy areas.[5]

---

[4] Also, not all non-transfer expenditure is on pure public goods. Furthermore, much of transfer expenditure is in practice endogenous since, without a universal transfer, governments only set levels and qualifying conditions for the receipt of benefits, not total expenditure.

[5] Aggregated data are described in http://stats.oecd.org/OECDStatDownloadFiles/ _OECDSOCX2007InterpretativeGuide_En.pdf, sections 3.3, Annex 1 and Annex 4.

The source of data for growth rates in income and population, and real interest rates, is World Development Indicators (2007). Data for interest rates in the US, UK and Austria were obtained respectively from websites of Federal Reserve Bank of USA, Bank of England and Central Bank of Austria. Suppose the annual average growth of GDP per capita is x per cent, and the length of a time period in this overlapping generation model is 20 years. The required adjusted growth rate is obtained as $(1+x)^{20}-1$. The same approach was used for population growth and the interest rate for each country. Also, by assuming that the time preference rate is equal to the real interest rate, $\rho = r$, the discount factor for each country, β, is obtained from $1/(1+r)^{20}$.

The tax rate is obtained from World Development Indicators (2007), which includes tax revenue as well as social contributions. The ratio of tax revenue to GDP includes compulsory transfers to the central government for public purposes. The ratio of social contributions to GDP includes social security contributions by employees, employers and self-employed individuals, and other contributions whose source cannot be determined. They also include actual or imputed contributions to social insurance schemes operated by governments.

Data on Gini inequality measures were obtained from World Development Indicators (2007) and World Income Inequality Database (2007). Unfortunately, the income concept varies across countries. In some countries gross income is considered and in others it is net income. Suppose income follows the lognormal distribution with mean and variance of logarithms of income, μ and σ^2. This variance can be obtained from the Gini index using $\sigma = \sqrt{2}\Phi^{-1}(\frac{Gini+1}{2})$, where Φ^{-1} is the inverse function of the standard normal cumulative distribution; see Aitchison and Brown (1957, p. 13). Since for most of the countries the Gini index is available only for selected years, the average of available years between 2000 and 2006 was used to calculate the ratio of median to mean income. Consequently, averages of growth of GDP per capita, population growth, the real interest rate, government expenditures and revenues were computed over the same period.

Information cannot be obtained concerning the value of γ, the relative weight attached to public goods in the utility function. Independent evidence on preferences for public goods is obviously notoriously difficult to obtain in view of the well-known problems of preference revelation with non-rival and non-excludable goods. It is possible only to obtain, for a given country at any time, a value of $\tilde{y}/\bar{y}$ conditional on an assumed value of γ. Hence, the sensitivity of results to variations in γ is examined. In considering sensible values for γ, it was decided to use a 'benchmark case' of $\gamma = 1$; that is, consumers have the same preference for public goods as for private goods. Then variations of 10 per cent and 20 per cent around this value were considered. The results reported here are for the extreme case where individuals' preferences are assumed to be the same in all countries. However, comparisons can be made across columns.

Tables 8.4 and 8.5 show the implied values of inequality aversion, ε, for each country in the sample.[6] For each value of γ the countries are ranked in increasing order, that is from low implied inequality aversion to high implied aversion. Furthermore, the countries are divided into various groups. The Scandinavian countries include Denmark, Finland and Norway. The group of Commonwealth countries includes the UK, Australia, Canada and New Zealand.

From the generally large values of implied aversion reported in Table 8.4, it seems highly likely that the inability to measure a more restricted concept of transfer payments has imparted a significant upward bias. It is therefore perhaps more useful to concentrate on the relative orders of magnitude for different countries. There is much consistency in the rankings as γ is varied. The average implied inequality aversion for Scandinavian countries is consis-

---

[6]The values may be considered as conditional estimates based on a single year, and therefore having no degrees of freedom. As mentioned above, information for each country is not available for all years. Furthermore, there is relatively little variation in the income distribution over time.

Table 8.3: Summary Information for Each Country and Group of Countries

Country	B	τ	r	β	ω	n	$Gini$	σ^2
Australia	0.50	0.25	0.11	0.90	0.46	0.30	30.56	0.31
Austria	0.53	0.36	0.27	0.79	0.39	0.10	29.15	0.28
Belgium	0.52	0.41	0.15	0.87	0.39	0.10	32.97	0.36
Canada	0.44	0.19	-0.12	1.14	0.47	0.21	32.56	0.35
Czech Republic	0.45	0.30	-0.14	1.16	1.37	0.01	25.33	0.21
Denmark	0.50	0.33	0.17	0.86	0.38	0.07	23.80	0.18
Finland	0.51	0.35	-0.03	1.03	0.83	0.06	26.88	0.24
France	0.54	0.40	0.18	0.85	0.33	0.14	27.50	0.25
Germany	0.57	0.28	0.36	0.74	0.32	0.01	28.31	0.26
Greece	0.44	0.34	-0.02	1.02	1.17	0.07	34.27	0.39
Hungary	0.44	0.34	0.41	0.71	1.27	-0.04	28.43	0.27
Iceland	0.38	0.29	0.88	0.53	0.74	0.33	25.00	0.20
Ireland	0.46	0.31	-0.55	2.24	1.23	0.45	34.28	0.39
Italy	0.51	0.35	-0.14	1.17	0.19	0.11	36.03	0.44
Netherlands	0.45	0.37	0.14	0.88	0.38	0.09	26.33	0.23
New Zealand	0.48	0.31	1.02	0.50	0.49	0.27	33.70	0.38
Norway	0.51	0.37	0.61	0.62	0.45	0.15	25.79	0.22
Poland	0.50	0.29	0.79	0.56	1.31	-0.03	34.49	0.40
Spain	0.53	0.26	-0.07	1.08	0.52	0.34	34.66	0.40
Switzerland	0.54	0.18	0.05	0.95	0.31	0.15	33.68	0.38
United Kingdom	0.51	0.36	0.39	0.72	0.56	0.10	33.00	0.35
United States	0.44	0.18	0.05	0.95	0.36	0.21	40.81	0.57
Scandinavian Countries								
Average	0.51	0.35	0.25	0.84	0.55	0.09	25.49	0.21
Coeff. of Variation	0.02	0.06	1.33	0.25	0.44	0.51	0.06	0.13
Commonwealth Countries								
Average	0.48	0.28	0.35	0.82	0.49	0.22	32.46	0.35
Coeff. of Variation	0.06	0.26	1.42	0.34	0.10	0.39	0.04	0.08
All Countries								
Average	0.49	0.31	0.20	0.92	0.63	0.15	30.80	0.32
Coeff. of Variation	0.09	0.21	1.83	0.39	0.60	0.89	0.14	0.30

Table 8.4: Implied Inequality Aversion for Gamma of 0.8, 0.9 and 1

$\gamma = 0.8$		$\gamma = 0.9$		$\gamma = 1$	
Country	ε	Country	ε	Country	ε
Ireland	0.30	Ireland	0.49	Ireland	0.68
Greece	0.35	Greece	0.57	Greece	0.79
Hungary	0.44	Hungary	0.79	Hungary	1.13
Czech Republic	0.49	Czech Republic	0.90	Czech Republic	1.30
Iceland	0.61	Iceland	1.08	Iceland	1.50
Belgium	0.99	Belgium	1.30	Belgium	1.60
Netherlands	1.01	Poland	1.36	Poland	1.61
Poland	1.08	UK	1.42	Italy	1.67
UK	1.11	Netherlands	1.42	US	1.71
Finland	1.16	Italy	1.44	UK	1.72
NZ	1.19	NZ	1.47	NZ	1.73
Italy	1.20	US	1.56	Netherlands	1.81
US	1.41	Finland	1.60	Spain	2.01
Spain	1.43	Spain	1.72	Finland	2.05
Norway	1.51	Canada	1.93	Canada	2.16
France	1.54	Norway	2.02	Australia	2.42
Austria	1.68	France	2.02	Austria	2.49
Canada	1.69	Austria	2.09	Norway	2.50
Australia	1.77	Australia	2.10	France	2.50
Denmark	2.30	Denmark	2.86	Switzerland	3.33
Switzerland	2.69	Switzerland	3.01	Denmark	3.41
Germany	3.24	Germany	3.73	Germany	4.21
Scandinavian Countries					
Average	1.66		2.16		2.65
Coefficient of Variation	0.35		0.30		0.26
Commonwealth Countries					
Average	1.44		1.73		2.01
Coefficient of Variation	0.24		0.20		0.17
All Countries					
Average	1.33		1.68		2.01
Coefficient of Variation	0.56		0.47		0.42

Table 8.5: Implied Inequality Aversion for Gamma of 1, 1.1 and 1.2

$\gamma = 1.1$		$\gamma = 1.2$	
Country	ε	Country	ε
Ireland	0.87	Ireland	1.09
Greece	0.99	Greece	1.20
Hungary	1.45	Hungary	1.75
Czech Republic	1.68	US	1.98
US	1.85	Czech Republic	2.07
Poland	1.86	Poland	2.09
Belgium	1.90	Italy	2.16
Iceland	1.90	Belgium	2.20
Italy	1.91	NZ	2.21
NZ	1.98	Iceland	2.27
UK	2.01	UK	2.29
Netherlands	2.19	Netherlands	2.55
Spain	2.31	Canada	2.61
Canada	2.38	Spain	2.64
Finland	2.50	Finland	2.97
Australia	2.74	Australia	3.07
Austria	2.89	Austria	3.29
Norway	2.96	Norway	3.41
France	2.99	France	3.50
Switzerland	3.66	Switzerland	4.01
Denmark	3.94	Denmark	4.48
Germany	4.71	Germany	5.24
Scandinavian Countries			
Average	3.14		3.62
Coefficient of Variation	0.24		0.21
Commonwealth Countries			
Average	2.28		2.54
Coefficient of Variation	0.16		0.15
All Countries			
Average	2.35		2.69
Coefficient of Variation	0.39		0.37

tently higher than that of Commonwealth countries, and the former are more homogeneous, as shown by the lower coefficient of variation. The relative positions of the two groups of countries accord with expectations. Countries within each group become more homogeneous with regard to the implicit inequality aversion as γ is increased. This can be seen by the reduction in the coefficient of variation within each group.

A notable change in ranking by implied inequality aversion, as γ is increased, is for the US. This country moves from around the middle to around the bottom quartile, which is perhaps more consistent with *a priori* expectations. Germany has the highest implied inequality aversion for all values of γ, which may perhaps be regarded as consistent with its 'social-market model'. Significant inequality aversion in Germany was also found by Schwarze and Härpfer (2007). Furthermore, Lambert *et al.* (2003) suggested that countries which have lower population growth tend to have higher inequality aversion, and indeed Germany has a much lower population growth rate than the other countries examined. Similarly, Scandinavian countries have relatively low population growth rates. Exceptions to this result are for the former communist countries of Hungary, Poland and the Czech Republic, which have low population growth rates combined with relatively low implicit inequality aversion. The low implied inequality aversion for Ireland is consistent with the findings of Madden (1992, 1995), although his results were confined to implications of indirect tax structures.

8.5 Conclusions

This chapter examined the optimal composition of government expenditure, as chosen by an independent utilitarian judge, in the two-period overlapping generations model introduced in Chapter 5. The focus was on public goods and a transfer payment, in the form of a pension, which are financed by income tax on a pay-as-you-go basis. The choice of expenditure to maximise a social welfare function is complicated by the fact that the pension involves a combination of income shifting between phases of the life cycle with both inter-generational and intra-generational transfers. The latter arises because the basic pension is unrelated to income whereas the tax is proportional to income. The former arises from the pay-as-you-go feature of financing whereby each generation can benefit from productivity and thus income growth accruing to the following generation. This modelling framework, despite its simplicity, therefore offers useful insights into the nature of the policy choices involved.

The analysis is a normative exercise in welfare economics rather than a positive attempt to explain differences in the composition of government expenditure in different countries. There is no suggestion that policies are actually based on the maximisation of a clearly stated social welfare function. The same point of view is of course taken in all models which examine optimal policies, however defined. Nevertheless it is of interest to consider what values are implied by actual policies, using a 'what if' approach. Thus, if outcomes are considered as arising from maximisation of a welfare function, what extent of inequality aversion do they reveal?

Expressions for the choice of expenditure levels and their ratio were found to depend on the ratio of a welfare-weighted average income to arithmetic mean income in each generation. This welfare-weighted arithmetic mean income level was shown to depend on the degree of relative inequality aversion of the judge. Using an approximation for this welfare-weighted mean income, it was thus possible to produce, for a range of countries, implicit values of the inequality aversion parameter, conditional on assumed preferences of individuals for public goods relative to private goods. The implicit values of inequality aversion, revealed by the policies of different countries, were generally found to accord with expectations and also consistent with previous studies. However, their absolute values are likely to be biased upwards by the difficulty of measuring the transfer payments (the pension) modelled here.

Part IV

A General Equilibrium Model

Chapter 9

A General Equilibrium OLG Model

In the dynamic overlapping generations model, used in Chapters 5 and 8, a partial equilibrium framework was adopted in which the incomes of individuals during the working period and the rate of interest were exogenously given. The present chapter extends this model to allow factor prices to be endogenously determined. Instead of assuming a given distribution of income in any period, each individual is endowed with an exogenous ability level in terms of 'efficiency units' of labour. The wage rate per efficiency unit, along with the rate of interest, is then determined within the model via a production function.

As in Chapter 5, this chapter investigates majority voting over the division of government expenditure between public goods and pensions in the context of a dynamic general equilibrium model with overlapping generations of heterogeneous individuals. The fact that the interest rate is endogenous means that in this chapter the effect of expenditure policies on capital accumulation and total output can be studied. Moreover, the effects on total output of inequality can be examined in this framework. The earlier partial equilibrium analysis abstracted from the interaction between forward-looking decisions, such as investment and the policy choice.

The analytical procedure used is as follows. First, the special case is examined where government policies relating to taxes and the composition of expenditure are exogenous. Second, the case where the composition of government expenditure is an outcome of majority voting is considered. In both cases the general equilibrium approach allows analysis of the effects on the interest rate, the wage rate and savings of taxation and the composition of government expenditure. Consequently, the effect on total capital and total output as well as the future level of pensions can be studied.

This chapter relates to another strand of the literature which looks at the relationship between inequality and growth. Perotti (1996) surveys the relationship between income distribution and growth, and suggests that inequality affects growth in four different ways. These are through endogenous fiscal policy, socio-political instability, human capital investment with borrowing constraints, and endogenous fertility. This chapter follows the first group of studies and links inequality and growth within the endogenous policy framework.

Another line of research considers voting on taxation and growth. Persson and Tabellini (1992, 1994) and Alesina and Rodrik (1994), with some differences in the specification of their models, find that high inequality increases the demand for redistribution through higher taxation. Consequently, a high tax rate leads to a low after-tax return on saving and this results in low aggregate investment and thereby low growth. Benabou (2002) presents a model with voting and imperfect capital markets and shows the link between inequality and growth. The general equilibrium framework allows the link between inequality, redistributive policy and capital accumulation to be studied. A negative relationship between inequality and GDP per capita is obtained but, in the present study, it is not possible to link inequality and growth since the model does not have endogenous growth.

In Chapter 5, where the interest rate was assumed to be exogenous, it was shown that the pay-as-you-go social security scheme receives the support of a majority of each cohort if the product of population growth, income growth and the ratio of mean to median income exceeds the interest rate. In the present general equilibrium context, total private savings in pay-as-you-go and fully funded schemes are different. Hence, total capital and the private return on savings are different in these schemes. In the present chapter, inter-generational redistribution decreases the capital stock. Therefore, the return on capital, the interest rate, is higher and the wage rate is lower in a pay-as-you-go scheme compared with a fully funded scheme. This implies that the general equilibrium environment provides redistribution in favour of individuals with high capital income. This is consistent with Boldrin and Rustichini (2000), Galasso (1999) and Cooley and Soares (1999), who construct general equilibrium models where a pay-as-you-go scheme is implemented and is sustainable. Galasso (1999) constructs an overlapping generations model where agents are identical within a cohort but heterogeneous across cohorts. Population growth is constant and there are age-specific survival probabilities. Cooley and Soares (1999) also construct a general equilibrium overlapping generations model where individuals live for four periods and there is heterogeneity across cohorts. In the present chapter there is heterogeneity within a cohort and it is assumed that a pay-as-you-go scheme is implemented and is supported politically.

In the present dynamic context, the ratio of transfer payments to total expenditure is found to depend negatively on the preference for public goods in individuals' utility functions and the share of capital in production, and positively on the tax rate. In particular, it is shown that more inequality (a lower ratio of median to mean innate ability or income) gives rise *ceteris paribus* to a higher ratio of expenditure on pensions to total expenditure. As discussed in previous chapters, this result is consistent with earlier models examining majority voting over the tax rate, with an unconditional transfer payment.

The chapter is arranged as follows. Section 9.1 describes the framework of analysis. Section 9.2 examines the competitive equilibrium under exogenous policies. This provides a benchmark with which to compare capital accumulation and total output when the composition of government expenditure is endogenous. Consequently, the difference between the benchmark model and the outcome of majority voting can be studied. Section 9.3 characterises the voting equilibrium. Closed-form solutions for the share of expenditure on pensions cannot be obtained. However, the comparative static properties are examined and illustrated numerically. In Section 9.4, the effect of an interest-income tax are examined.

9.1   The Economic Environment

This section describes the overlapping generations environment with a public sector, along with the form of the government budget constraint and the production side of the economy. Subsection 9.1.1 begins by describing the individuals' consumption and saving choices conditional on government expenditures. This yields total savings as a function of the transfer payment and the tax rate. A public consumption good enters the utility function of individuals who operate both as economic agents and voters. Subsection 9.1.2 then describes the government budget constraint. The public good and expenditure on pensions are financed by income taxation, under a balanced budget. Finally, Subsection 9.1.3 describes the production side of the economy and the market clearing conditions. It characterises the endogenous wage and interest rates.

9.1.1   The Consumption Side

Consider a dynamic general equilibrium model with overlapping generations of heterogeneous individuals, who have different economic abilities or skills when they are born. All individuals are assumed to live for two periods, a working and a retirement period. Hence, the economy is populated by two overlapping cohorts in any given period. A young individual, i, born at time,

t, does not have any wealth and has one unit of labour which is inelastically supplied in the first period. Omitting i subscripts for convenience, economic ability is measured in terms of efficiency units, e_t, at time, t, and has a continuous distribution with $e_t^h \leq e_t \leq e_t^l$ and density $f(e_t)$. Therefore, the average skill level at time t is $\bar{e}_t = \int_{e_t^l}^{e_t^h} e_t f(e_t) de_t$.

Suppose the average ability of young individuals grows at a constant rate of ω over time, so that:

$$\frac{\bar{e}_{t+1}}{\bar{e}_t} = 1 + \omega \qquad (9.1)$$

Also, there is positive and constant growth, at the rate n, in the population, so that:

$$\frac{N_{t+1}}{N_t} = 1 + n \qquad (9.2)$$

where N_t denotes the number of individuals born in period t.

The wage per efficiency unit of labour at time t is denoted w_t. Therefore, the income of an individual i at time t is $e_{i,t} w_t$, which is heterogeneous across individuals because of differences in abilities. A young individual, i, at time t, pays proportional income tax at the rate τ_t, and spends disposable income on consumption, $c_{1i,t}$, and savings, $s_{i,t}$. In the second period of life, all individuals receive the unconditional and untaxed pension from the government, b_{t+1}. In addition, an individual i receives a return on savings of $r_{t+1} s_{i,t}$, where r_{t+1} is the interest rate at time $t + 1$. In the second period of life, older individuals finance their consumption of private goods, $c_{2i,t+1}$, from these two sources of income (interest income and the pension). The price of the consumption good is normalised to unity, so that c denotes private consumption expenditure. For simplicity, it is assumed here that there is no tax on interest income. The effect of introducing an interest-income tax is considered in Section 9.4.

Although there is heterogeneity in innate ability, individuals have identical preferences. The utility function for person i is:

$$U_{i,t} = \log c_{1i,t} + \gamma \log Q_{G,t} + \beta \left(\log c_{2i,t+1} + \gamma \log Q_{G,t+1} \right) \qquad (9.3)$$

where $Q_{G,t}$ and $Q_{G,t+1}$ are the consumption of public goods in the first and second periods of life respectively, and γ is the weight attached to the consumption of public goods. Hence, a non-productive public good is considered in this chapter.[1] In addition, $0 < \beta = 1/(1+\rho) < 1$ is the discount factor, where ρ is the time preference rate. The lifetime budget constraint is:

$$c_{1i,t} + \frac{c_{2i,t+1}}{1 + r_{t+1}} = (1 - \tau_t)e_{i,t}w_t + \frac{b_{t+1}}{1 + r_{t+1}} \equiv M_{i,t} \qquad (9.4)$$

where $M_{i,t}$ is the present value of lifetime income of individual i. The choice of public goods at time t and $t+1$ is not determined at the individual level, since individuals cannot be excluded. It is determined along with the pension via a democratic process. The maximisation problem of an individual i under the lifetime budget constraint gives the optimal consumption in the first, $c_{1i,t}^*$, and second period, $c_{2i,t+1}^*$ as:

$$c_{1i,t}^* = \frac{M_{i,t}}{(1 + \beta)} \qquad (9.5)$$

and:

$$c_{2i,t+1}^* = \frac{\beta(1 + r_{t+1})M_{i,t}}{(1 + \beta)} \qquad (9.6)$$

Hence, optimal planned private savings of young individual, i, $s_{i,t}^*$, with ability level, $e_{i,t}$, are:

$$s_{i,t}^* = \frac{\beta(1 - \tau_t)e_{i,t}w_t}{1 + \beta} - \frac{b_{t+1}}{(1 + r_{t+1})(1 + \beta)} \qquad (9.7)$$

The optimal savings of individual i depend positively on the interest rate, that is, the return on savings made from time t to $t+1$. In addition, optimal savings depend negatively on the pension received in period $t + 1$. This indicates that a higher level of public saving, reflected in a higher pension level, reduces the incentive of individuals for private saving.[2] Increasing the

---

[1] On models in which public goods affect the production function, see Grossmann (2003) and Koulovatianos and Mirman (2005).

[2] Assuming perfect capital markets, high-income individuals may prefer a low, or even zero, transfer while making positive savings during the working period. Conversely, some low-income people may wish to vote for a high value of transfer, part of which is used to repay a loan in the first period while the remainder finances consumption in the second period.

tax rate decreases the disposable income for individual i by $e_{i,t}w_t$. Hence, income taxation is more costly for an individual with a higher level of ability.

The aggregate savings level of all retired individuals at time t, denoted S_t^*, is:

$$S_t^* = \sum_{i=1}^{N_{t-1}} s_{i,t-1}^* = \frac{N_{t-1}}{(1+\beta)} \left(\beta(1-\tau_{t-1})\bar{e}_{t-1}w_{t-1} - \frac{b_t}{1+r_t} \right) \tag{9.8}$$

It is clear that increasing tax and total pension decreases total savings. Changing the tax rate and the pension level affects savings through capital availability and the interest rate, as discussed in Section 9.4.

9.1.2 The Government

The government provides public goods, runs the social security system and imposes a linear tax on the income of young workers at the fixed rate τ_t, which is assumed to be exogenously determined. Total expenditure on pensions and public goods expenditure in each period is financed on a pay-as-you-go basis. There is no asymmetric information and the government can observe labour productivity. Hence, the government budget constraint at time t is given by:

$$G_t + N_{t-1}b_t = \tau_t N_t \bar{e}_t w_t \tag{9.9}$$

where total government expenditure on pure public goods at time t is denoted by G_t. It is equal to $PQ_{G,t}$, where P denotes constant cost of producing one unit of the public good.

Individuals vote on the composition of government expenditure for given tax. In this chapter it is assumed that voters vote on the share of redistributive expenditure in total expenditure, instead of total redistributive expenditure. This is for analytical tractability in the present general equilibrium model. Suppose the share of expenditure on pensions in total expenditure, at time t is δ_t. Therefore, the share of total expenditure on public goods is $1 - \delta_t$. The per capita unconditional and untaxed pension that each old individual at time t receives is given by:

$$b_t = \delta_t \tau_t \left(1+n\right) \bar{e}_t w_t \qquad (9.10)$$

In addition, expenditure on public goods as share of total expenditure becomes $G_t = (1 - \delta_t)\tau_t N_t \bar{e}_t w_t$.

9.1.3　The Production Side

This subsection starts by examining the market clearing conditions for labour and capital at time t. Let total labour input in efficiency units be denoted by $L_t = N_t \bar{e}_t$, where N_t is number of young at time t and $\bar{e}_t$ is average innate ability. An important assumption is that full depreciation of capital is assumed. This means that the quantity of capital is equal to total saving in each period.[3] Substituting the unconditional and untaxed pension from (9.10) into total optimal saving (9.8) gives the total capital at time t. Therefore we have:

$$K_t = \frac{N_{t-1}}{(1+\beta)} \left(\beta(1 - \tau_{t-1})\bar{e}_{t-1} w_{t-1} - \frac{\delta_t \tau_t \left(1+n\right) \bar{e}_t w_t}{1+r_t} \right) \qquad (9.11)$$

where K_t denotes the quantity of physical capital at time t. Suppose firms produce single goods according to the following Cobb–Douglas production function in this economy:

$$F(K_t, L_t) = K_t^\alpha L_t^{1-a} \qquad (9.12)$$

Individuals can lend at the rate r, but the rental paid to the owners of capital needs to allow for the depreciation rate. Thus the capital rental is r plus the depreciation rate, and the latter is by assumption equal to 1. Therefore, setting the price and marginal revenue of output equal to unity, factor payments are given by:

$$1 + r_t = \alpha K_t^{\alpha-1} L_t^{1-\alpha} \qquad (9.13)$$

$$w_t = (1 - \alpha) K_t^\alpha L_t^{-\alpha} \qquad (9.14)$$

---

[3]This simplifies the mathematics and enables an analytical solution to be obtained.

9.2 Equilibrium with Exogenous Government Policy

This section explores capital accumulation and output when the tax rate and the share of redistributive expenditure are exogenous. The results are subsequently compared with those where composition of government expenditure is an outcome of voting. As explained in Section 9.1, markets are competitive and capital and labour earn their marginal revenue products. The market clearing condition for labour indicates that $L_t = N_t \bar{e}_t$. Moreover, the market clearing condition for capital was obtained in equation (9.11), which shows that total savings of the old generation is equal to total capital in each period. Substituting the wage at time t and $t-1$ as well as the interest rate at time t into (9.11) gives, after some manipulation, the capital accumulation equation as:

$$k_t = \frac{\beta(1 - \tau_{t-1})(1 - \alpha) k_{t-1}^\alpha}{(1+n)(1+\omega)\left((1+\beta) + \delta_t \tau_t \left(\frac{1-\alpha}{\alpha}\right)\right)} \tag{9.15}$$

where k_t is capital per unit of effective labour. The relationship between the share of redistributive expenditure and accumulation of capital is:

$$\frac{\partial k_t}{\partial \delta_t} = -\frac{\beta(1 - \tau_{t-1})\tau_t \left(\frac{1-\alpha}{\alpha}\right)(1 - \alpha) k_{t-1}^\alpha}{(1+n)(1+\omega)\left((1+\beta) + \delta_t \tau_t \left(\frac{1-\alpha}{\alpha}\right)\right)^2} < 0 \tag{9.16}$$

Also the second derivative of k_t with respect to δ_t is:

$$\frac{\partial^2 k_t}{\partial \delta_t^2} = -\frac{2\beta(1 - \tau_{t-1})\tau_t^2 \left(\frac{1-\alpha}{\alpha}\right)^2 (1 - \alpha) k_{t-1}^\alpha}{(1+n)(1+\omega)\left((1+\beta) + \delta_t \tau_t \left(\frac{1-\alpha}{\alpha}\right)\right)^3} > 0 \tag{9.17}$$

These results show that a higher share of redistributive expenditure reduces k_t, at an increasing rate, since it increases the public savings (for the pension) and private savings are lower.

The steady-state level of capital per unit of effective labour can be obtained from (9.15). Assuming that in the steady-state, $\tau_t = \tau_{t-1} = \tau$ and $\delta_t = \delta$, the steady-state of capital per unit of effective worker becomes:

$$k^* = \left(\frac{\beta(1 - \tau)(1 - \alpha)}{(1+n)(1+\omega)\left((1+\beta) + \delta\tau \left(\frac{1-\alpha}{\alpha}\right)\right)}\right)^{\frac{1}{(1-\alpha)}} \tag{9.18}$$

and capital per unit of labour is constant over time, while total labour, L_t, and total capital, K_t, grow at the rate $\omega + n$.

The partial derivative $\partial k^*/\partial \delta$ is negative. Hence, an increase in the share of expenditure on redistribution has a negative effect on the steady-state level of capital per unit of effective labour. A rise in the share of expenditure on pensions thus increases the steady-state interest rate (and reduces the wage rate). The partial derivative $\partial k^*/\partial \tau$ is also negative. The relationship between the tax rate and capital per unit of effective labour can be seen from (9.7) and the fact that an increase in the total government size reduces disposable incomes and consequently savings. This is only the direct effect of tax on capital accumulation. The indirect effect is through the share of redistribution and is analysed in the next section, where the share of redistributive expenditure is endogenous as the outcome of voting.

9.3   Collective Choice

This section examines the majority voting equilibrium. First, the indirect utility function is obtained and it is shown that preferences are single-peaked, confirming that a voting equilibrium exists. Next, the comparative static properties of the majority voting outcome are examined.

9.3.1   Single-peakedness of Preferences

Voting takes place in each period and individuals vote only on the share of redistributive expenditure from total expenditure to be paid during the next period, for a given tax rate.[4] Suppose the condition required for the majority

---

[4]Suppose young individuals at time t vote on the share of redistributive expenditure at t for a given tax rate. The capital stock at t depends on the share of expenditure on pensions at t and affects the wage and interest rate at t and $t+1$ respectively. Hence, the share of redistributive expenditure affects lifetime income. It can be shown that young voters at time t choose a zero level of redistribution if they vote on redistributive expenditure at time t. This result is similar to a partial equilibrium case where the interest and wage rate are exogenous.

of each generation to be better off with the pay-as-you-go arrangement is satisfied, thus ensuring cooperation between generations. Since the preferences
are selfish, there is no incentive for members of the old cohort to vote. Those
currently retired do not have a second vote over their pension, which they
do not finance, since this has already been determined by their vote in the
previous period.[5] The median member of the young cohort is the decisive
voter.

The indirect utility function is obtained by substituting the optimal consumption of young and old into the direct utility function, and is:

$$V_{i,t} = \log\left(\frac{M_{i,t}}{1+\beta}\right) + \beta \log\left(\frac{\beta r_{t+1} M_{i,t}}{(1+\beta)}\right) + \gamma\left(\log Q_{G,t} + \beta \log Q_{G,t+1}\right) \quad (9.19)$$

The values of $Q_{G,t}$ and $Q_{G,t+1}$ can be expressed in terms of share of expenditure on public goods at time t and $t+1$ since voters are aware of the nature
of the government budget constraint. Substituting r_{t+1}, w_t and w_{t+1} gives,
after some manipulation:

$$
\begin{aligned}
V_{i,t} =\ & (1+\beta) \log\left\{ \alpha(1+\beta) + \tau_{t+1}(1-\alpha)\delta_{t+1}\left(1 + \beta\left(\frac{\bar{e}_t}{e_{i,t}}\right)\right)\right\} \\
& - (1 + \beta\alpha(\gamma+1)) \log\left\{\alpha(1+\beta) + \delta_{t+1}\tau_{t+1}(1-\alpha)\right\} \\
& + \beta\gamma \log\left\{1 - \delta_{t+1}\right\} + \varphi
\end{aligned}
\quad (9.20)
$$

where φ depends on variables and parameters that are either exogenously
given or predetermined. From (9.20), it is clear that voting involves only one
dimension, the share of expenditure on pensions, δ_{t+1}.

It is necessary to establish that preferences are single-peaked. The first
derivative of the indirect utility of an individual i with respect to the share
of expenditure on pensions is given by:

$$\frac{\partial V_{i,t}}{\partial \delta_{t+1}} = \frac{(1+\beta)}{HR_i + \delta_{t+1}} - \frac{\beta\gamma}{1 - \delta_{t+1}} - \frac{(1 + \beta\gamma\alpha + \alpha\beta)}{H + \delta_{t+1}} \quad (9.21)$$

---

[5]This assumption is consistent with a number of studies. For example, Hassler *et al.*
(2007) use a similar assumption, that each generation votes once only, to find the political
equilibrium in an overlapping generations context.

where $R_i = \left\{1 + \beta \left(e_{i,t}/\bar{e}_t\right)^{-1}\right\}^{-1}$ and $H = \alpha \left(1 + \beta\right)/(1-\alpha)\tau_{t+1}$. The second derivative is expressed as the following:

$$\frac{\partial^2 V_{i,t}}{\partial \delta_{t+1}^2} = -\frac{(1+\beta)}{(HR_i + \delta_{t+1})^2} + \frac{(1+\beta\gamma\alpha + \alpha\beta)}{(H + \delta_{t+1})^2} - \frac{\beta\gamma}{(1 - \delta_{t+1})^2} \qquad (9.22)$$

The last term in this expression is always negative, and by using the first-order condition the sign of the first two terms can be shown to be negative. From the first-order condition:

$$\frac{(1+\beta)}{HR_i + \delta_{t+1}} - \frac{(1 + \beta\alpha \left(\gamma + 1\right))}{H + \delta_{t+1}} = \frac{\beta\gamma}{1 - \delta_{t+1}} \qquad (9.23)$$

Therefore, the left hand side of the above equation is positive. In addition, $1/(HR_i + \delta_{t+1})$ is greater than $1/\left(H + \delta_{t+1}\right)$, since R_i is positive and less than one. Consequently:

$$\frac{(1+\beta)}{(HR_e + \delta_{t+1})^2} > \frac{(1 + \beta\alpha \left(\gamma + 1\right))}{(H + \delta_{t+1})^2} \qquad (9.24)$$

Hence, the second derivative of indirect utility with respect to the share of redistributive expenditure is negative. This guarantees that preferences are single-peaked and consequently a voting equilibrium exists.

9.3.2   Majority Voting Equilibrium

The strictly concave relationship between $V_{i,t}$ and δ_{t+1} is a sufficient condition and guarantees that a voting equilibrium exists and the majority voting outcome is dominated by the median voter, who is the individual with the median innate ability, $e_{m,t}$, in the present context. Consequently, maximising the median voter's indirect utility function, $V_{m,t}$, with respect to share of redistributive expenditure gives the majority choice of share of expenditure on pension at time $t + 1$, $\delta_{m,t+1}$. The first-order condition is:

$$\frac{\partial V_{m,t}}{\partial \delta_{m,t+1}} = \frac{(1+\beta)}{HR_e + \delta_{m,t+1}} - \frac{\beta\gamma}{1 - \delta_{m,t+1}} - \frac{(1 + \beta\gamma\alpha + \alpha\beta)}{H + \delta_{m,t+1}} = 0 \qquad (9.25)$$

where $R_m = \left\{1 + \beta \left(e_{m,t}/\bar{e}_t\right)^{-1}\right\}^{-1}$ and $H = \alpha \left(1 + \beta\right)/(1 - \alpha)\tau_{t+1}$. Rearranging the expression above gives a quadratic equation in terms of the share of expenditure on pension $\delta_{m,t+1}$ and can be summarised by the following expression:

$$A\delta_{m,t+1}^2 + B\delta_{m,t+1} + C = 0 \qquad (9.26)$$

where A, B and C depend on the preference parameter, tax rate, share of capital in production and ratio of median to mean ability and respectively are:

$$
\begin{aligned}
A &= -\beta\left(1-\alpha\right)\left(\gamma+1\right) \\
B &= -A - \beta\gamma\left[1 + H\left(1 + \left(H+1\right)R_m\right)\right] - C \\
C &= \left\{\left(1+\beta\right) - \left(1 + \beta\gamma\alpha + \alpha\beta + \beta\gamma H\right)R_m\right\}H \qquad (9.27)
\end{aligned}
$$

Hence, $\delta_{m,t+1} = \left(-B \pm \sqrt{\Delta}\right)/2A$, where $\Delta = B^2 - 4AC$. These results are not straightforward. However, further insights can be obtained by using the data for a sample of democratic countries. It is possible to show, for all countries in the sample, that the first root is negative and the second root is positive and less than one. This result is obtained for a range of 30 per cent around the data. Suppose the time preference rate is equal to the interest rate, so that $\rho = r$. Then β is obtained for each country in the sample. Given data on τ, δ, β and $e_m/\bar{e}$ and for α between 0.2 and 0.5, the weight attached to the public good is inferred for each country using the closed-form solution (9.25). Next, two roots are obtained from $\left(-B \pm \sqrt{\Delta}\right)/2A$.

The above result shows that the voting equilibrium for the share of redistributive expenditure depends on the tax rate, the weight attached to public goods, time preference and the share of capital in production. In addition, the ratio of redistributive expenditure to total expenditure is independent of population and ability growth rates. Moreover, the share of expenditure on pensions depends only on the ratio of median to mean ability. This implies that the absolute levels (or units of measurement) are not relevant and the distribution of ability affects the majority choice of the share of redistributive expenditure.

9.3.3   Some Comparative Statics

Despite the fact that the closed-form solution for $\delta_{m,t+1}$ is not straightforward, from (9.25) it is possible to show that the ratio of expenditure on the pension to total expenditure is constant over time. Therefore, total expenditure on the pension grows with constant rate of $n + \omega$.

The comparative static properties can be investigated using implicit differentiation. Suppose $F(\delta_{m,t+1}, e_{m,t}/\bar{e}_t, \tau_{t+1}, \beta, \gamma, \alpha) = \partial V_{m,t}/\partial \delta_{m,t+1}$. Thus the derivative of F with respect to $\delta_{m,t+1}$, $F_{\delta_{m,t+1}}$, is $\partial^2 V_{m,t}/\partial \delta^2_{m,t+1}$. Since preferences are single-peaked, $F_{\delta_{m,t+1}}$ is negative.

The ratio of median to mean ability can be interpreted as income inequality, because all individuals supply one unit of labour inelastically in the first period of their life. Moreover, wage rate is the marginal product of total labour in efficiency units. An increase in the ratio of median to average ability, where the former is less than the latter, implies a decrease in inequality. The relationship between inequality and the ratio of redistributive expenditure to total expenditure, by using implicit differentiation, is:

$$
\frac{d\delta_{m,t+1}}{d\left(e_{m,t}/\bar{e}_t\right)} = -\frac{F_{e_{m,t}/\bar{e}_t}}{F_{\delta_{m,t+1}}} = \frac{\dfrac{(1+\beta)H\beta(e_{m,t}/\bar{e}_t)^{-2}\left\{1+\beta(e_{m,t}/\bar{e}_t)^{-1}\right\}^{-2}}{\left(H\left\{1+\beta(e_{m,t}/\bar{e}_t)^{-1}\right\}^{-1}+\delta_{m,t+1}\right)^2}}{\partial^2 V_{m,t}/\partial \delta^2_{m,t+1}} < 0 \qquad (9.28)
$$

This result shows that increasing $e_{m,t}/\bar{e}_t$, or decreasing inequality, causes voters to choose a lower share of expenditure on redistribution and a higher share on the public good. In other words, less inequality leads to lower redistributive expenditure. As shown in Section 9.2, there is a negative relationship between the share of redistributive expenditure and the steady-state level of capital per unit of effective labour. Consequently, inequality slows capital accumulation and output per unit of effective labour.

The relationship between the weight attached to public goods in the utility function and the share of redistributive expenditure is:

$$\frac{d\delta_{m,t+1}}{d\gamma} = -\frac{F_\gamma}{F_{\delta_{m,t+1}}} = \frac{\left(\frac{\beta}{1-\delta_{t+1}} + \frac{\alpha\beta(1-\alpha)\tau_{t+1}}{\alpha(1+\beta)+\delta_{m,t+1}\tau_{t+1}(1-\alpha)}\right)}{\partial^2 V_{m,t}/\partial\delta_{m,t+1}^2} < 0 \qquad (9.29)$$

This result suggests that higher preferences for public goods causes individuals to vote unambiguously on a lower share of expenditure on redistribution and a higher share of expenditure on public goods. In this general equilibrium framework it is possible to see how the weight attached to the public good affects the steady-state of capital and output. Raising the weight attached to public good decreases the share of redistributive expenditure and hence increases capital accumulation, as shown in (9.18).

Similarly, we can use the implicit differentiation to find $d\delta_{m,t+1}/d\tau_{t+1}$ and $d\delta_{m,t+1}/d\alpha$ as follows:

$$\frac{d\delta_{m,t+1}}{d\tau_{t+1}} = -\frac{F_{\tau_{t+1}}}{F_{\delta_{m,t+1}}} = -\frac{\frac{\alpha(1+\beta)}{(1-\alpha)\tau_{t+1}^2}\left(\frac{(1+\beta)R_m}{(HR_e+\delta_{m,t+1})^2} - \frac{1+\beta\gamma\alpha+\alpha\beta}{(H+\delta_{m,t+1})^2}\right)}{\partial^2 V_{m,t}/\partial\delta_{m,t+1}^2} > 0 \quad (9.30)$$

$$\frac{d\delta_{m,t+1}}{d\alpha} = -\frac{F_\alpha}{F_{\delta_{m,t+1}}} = \frac{\frac{(1+\beta)\left\{\frac{(1+\beta)R_m}{\left(HR_e+\delta_{m,t+1}\right)^2} - \frac{1+\beta\alpha(1+\gamma)}{\left(H+\delta_{m,t+1}\right)^2}\right\}}{(1-\alpha)^2\tau_{t+1}} + \frac{\beta(\gamma+1)}{(H+\delta_{m,t+1})}}{\partial^2 V_{m,t}/\partial\delta_{m,t+1}^2} < 0$$

$$(9.31)$$

These results show that the sign of $F_{\tau_{t+1}}$ and F_α both depend on $\frac{(1+\beta)R_m}{(HR_e+\delta_{t+1})^2} - \frac{1+\beta\alpha(1+\gamma)}{(H+\delta_{t+1})^2}$, which has an ambiguous sign. From the condition for single-peakness it is known that $\frac{1+\beta}{(HR_e+\delta_{t+1})^2} > \frac{1+\beta\gamma\alpha+\alpha\beta}{(H+\delta_{t+1})^2}$, but R_e, $1/\left(1+\beta\left(e_{m,t}/\bar{e}_t\right)^{-1}\right)$, is less than one. However, in a sample of advanced democratic countries, this condition is checked and shown to be positive for all countries in the sample.[6]

The comparative static result with respect to the tax rate suggests that an increase in the tax rate raises the share of expenditure on pensions. This

---

[6]Assuming that the time preference rate is equal to the interest rate, $\rho = r$, so β is obtained for each country in the sample. Given data on τ, δ, β and $e_m/\bar{e}$ and for α between 0.2 and 0.5, the weight attached to public good is obtained from closed-form solution (9.25) for all countries in the sample. Afterwards, the condition $\frac{(1+\beta)R_e}{(HR_e+\delta_{t+1})^2} - \frac{(1+\beta\alpha(1+\gamma))}{(H+\delta_{t+1})^2}$ is checked for different γ corresponding to different α for all countries.

can be understood from the fact that the public good is non excludable and non rival. Moreover, when young individuals pay a higher tax rate in the first period, they prefer to receive higher redistribution in the second period so that they support a higher share on redistribution. In Section 9.2 it was found that there is a negative relationship between the tax and the steady-state of capital per unit of worker (9.18) when the share of expenditure is exogenous. It is possible to show that this negative relationship is obtained in this case where the share of redistributive expenditure is an outcome of majority voting.

The result with respect to α suggests that an increase in the share of capital in total output has a negative effect on the share of redistributive expenditure in total expenditure. This result can be understood from the fact that higher α means that capital is more important and increasing the share of pension or public saving reduces the total private saving or total capital. The relationship between share of capital in the production, α, and composition of government expenditure can only be analysed in a general equilibrium environment where factor prices are endogenous. Koulovatianos and Mirman (2005) study the effect of share of capital on the tax rate in a simple growth model with heterogeneity in productivity of capital. They show that voters vote on the lower tax in an economy with a higher share or productivity of capital.

9.3.4 Numerical Illustrations

It is of interest to consider the potential effects of changes in parameters and find the sensitivity of the ratio of redistributive expenditure with respect to changes in parameters. Suppose the length of a time period in the model is 20 years. Consider a set of benchmark values which are the averages over the sample of democratic countries, to be discussed in the next section, where for each country the value used is the annual average over the period 2000–2006.

The baseline value for the tax is 0.37. Assuming that the time preference rate is equal to the interest rate, $\rho = r$, then the baseline value for β is 0.93.[7] The baseline value for share of capital in production, α, is 0.3. The baseline value for weight attached to public goods is set at $\gamma = 0.45$. This value of γ produces $\delta = 0.49$ for $e_m/\bar{e} = 0.7$, $\tau = 0.37$ and $\alpha = 0.3$, which are average values for the sample. The closed-form solution, equation (9.25), is used for calculating γ.

Figures 9.1 and 9.2 illustrate variations in the relationship between share of redistributive expenditure, δ, and inequality, for given values of the other parameters. As expected, an increasing ratio of median to mean income reduces δ in all figures, highlighting the finding that higher equality is consistently associated with a lower ratio of pension expenditure to total expenditure. However, over the most relevant range of inequality, the response is very low.

The parameter variations considered are 15 and 30 per cent changes around the baseline value. By taking percentage variations it is possible to make statements about the relative sensitivity to different parameter changes. The diagrams show that the majority choice of δ is quite sensitive to variations in the tax rate, share of capital in production and the weight of public goods in the utility function, and less sensitive to changes in the discount factor.

9.4 An Interest Income Tax

This section studies the robustness of the results when the government levies a labour tax on young workers and a capital tax on old individuals. The incentive regarding income shifting from the first to the second period of life is changed by imposing a tax on capital income. The current young are

---

[7]The annual average real interest over the period 2000–2006 is used for each country to calculate the time preference rate. Then, the value of β is obtained from $1/(1+r)^{20}$ for each country, which assumes a 20 year period.

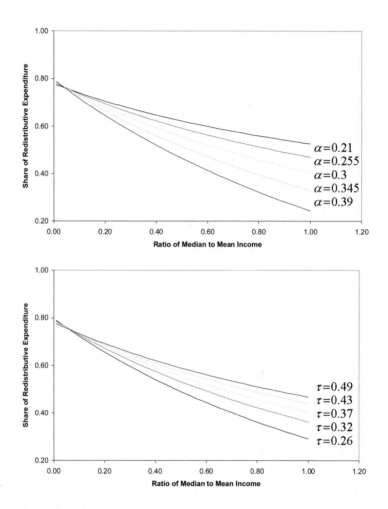

Figure 9.1: Variation in Expenditure Ratio for Alternative Tax Rate, Share of Capital

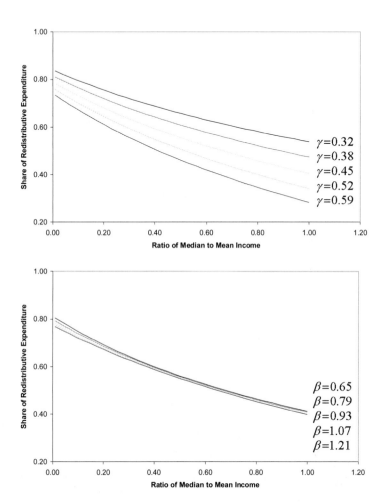

Figure 9.2: Variation in Expenditure Ratio for Alternative Preference Parameters

aware that the next generation will pay labour income tax and tax on their return on savings to finance expenditure on their pension as well as provision of public goods in the next period.

Suppose the wage income tax rate and the capital income tax rate are the same in each period. Therefore, the budget constraint of the old generation changes and an individual i, at time $t + 1$, receives the after-tax return on private savings, $(1 - \tau_{t+1})r_{t+1}s_{i,t}$. The lifetime budget constraint for an individual i becomes:

$$c_{1i,t} + \frac{c_{2i,t+1}}{(1 - \tau_{t+1})(1 + r_{t+1})} = (1 - \tau_t)e_{i,t}w_t + \frac{b_{t+1}}{(1 - \tau_{t+1})(1 + r_{t+1})} \equiv M_{i,t} \tag{9.32}$$

Preferences are the same as (9.3). It can be found that the optimal savings of individual i are given by:

$$s_{i,t}^* = \frac{\beta(1 - \tau_t)e_{i,t}w_t}{(1 + \beta)} - \frac{b_{t+1}}{(1 - \tau_{t+1})(1 + r_{t+1})(1 + \beta)} \tag{9.33}$$

The equilibrium condition of the capital market implies that the capital stock in period t is equal to the total savings of the young in period $t-1$. Hence, by again assuming full depreciation of capital, total capital at time t becomes:

$$K_t = \frac{N_{t-1}}{(1 + \beta)}\left(\beta(1 - \tau_{t-1})\bar{e}_{t-1}w_{t-1} - \frac{b_t}{(1 - \tau_t)(1 + r_t)}\right) \tag{9.34}$$

Both labour and capital taxes decrease saving over time and thus depress the long run capital stock, as can be seen by the negative relationship between K_t and tax rate at time t and $t-1$.

The production technology and factor pricing are the same as described above, but the government budget constraint at time t is now:

$$G_t + N_{t-1}b_t = \tau_t K_t^\alpha L_t^{1-a} \tag{9.35}$$

Hence, the share of expenditure on the pension in total expenditure is equal to $\delta_t \tau_t K_t^\alpha L_t^{1-a}$. Substituting the share of redistributive expenditure from the government budget constraint as well as w_t, w_{t-1} and r_t into (9.34), after some manipulation, gives capital accumulation as:

$$k_t = \frac{\beta(1 - \tau_{t-1})(1 - \alpha)}{\left(1 + \beta + \frac{\delta_t}{\alpha}\frac{\tau_t}{1 - \tau_t}\right)(1 + n)(1 + w)} k_{t-1}^\alpha \tag{9.36}$$

where k_t denotes capital per unit of effective labour. By assuming that in the steady-state $\tau_t = \tau_{t-1} = \tau$ and $\delta_t = \delta$, the steady-state of capital per effective worker becomes:

$$k^* = \left(\frac{\beta(1 - \tau)(1 - \alpha)}{\left(1 + \beta + \frac{\delta}{\alpha}\frac{\tau}{1 - \tau}\right)(1 + n)(1 + w)}\right)^{\frac{1}{(1-\alpha)}} \tag{9.37}$$

It can be shown that $\partial k^*/\partial\delta < 0$ and $\partial^2 k^*/\partial\delta^2 > 0$, which imply that a higher share of redistributive expenditure reduces capital per unit of effective labour, by increasing the rate.[8] Moreover, $\partial k^*/\partial\tau$ is negative because an increase in tax reduces lifetime disposable income.

Indirect utility is obtained by appropriate substitution as:

$$
\begin{aligned}
V_{i,t} &= (1 + \beta) \log\left(X + \beta\tau_{t+1}\delta_{t+1}\left(e_{i,t}/\bar{e}_t\right)^{-1}\right) - (\beta\alpha(1 + \gamma) + 1) \log(X) \\
&\quad + \beta\gamma \log(1 - \delta_{t+1}) + \chi
\end{aligned}
\tag{9.38}
$$

where $X = (1 - \tau_{t+1})\alpha(1 + \beta) + \delta_{t+1}\tau_{t+1}$ and χ depends on variables and parameters that are either exogenously given or predetermined. Therefore, the first-order condition for utility maximisation becomes:

$$
\begin{aligned}
\frac{\partial V_{i,t}}{\partial\delta_{t+1}} &= \left(\frac{(1 + \beta)\left(1 + \beta\left(e_{i,t}/\bar{e}_t\right)^{-1}\right)}{X + \beta\tau_{t+1}\delta_{t+1}\left(e_{i,t}/\bar{e}_t\right)^{-1}} - \frac{(\beta\alpha(1 + \gamma) + 1)}{X}\right)\tau_{t+1} - \frac{\beta\gamma}{1 - \delta_{t+1}} \\
&= 0
\end{aligned}
\tag{9.39}
$$

The sufficient condition for preferences to be single-peaked is $\partial^2 V_{i,t}/\partial\delta_{t+1}^2 < 0$. It is not possible to establish this analytically in the present case, but it is

---

[8] This can be understood from the fact that a higher share of redistributive expenditure in total expenditure means higher per capita public saving. A rising pension reduces savings and long run capital per unit of effective labour.

found to hold using parameters relating to a sample of democratic countries, as discussed earlier.

The majority choice of the share of redistributive expenditure, $\delta_{m,t+1}$, is the median voter's choice, that is, the solution to $\partial V_{m,t}/\partial \delta_{m,t+1}$. As in the basic model, the analytical solution for $\delta_{m,t+1}$ is not straightforward. However, the comparative static properties can be studied by using the implicit function theorem. It is possible to show that the derivative of the share of redistributive expenditure, $\delta_{m,t+1}$, with respect to $e_{m,t}/\bar{e}_t$ is negative; that is, $\partial \delta_{m,t+1}/\partial(e_{m,t}/\bar{e}_t) < 0$. Thus, as in the basic model, reducing inequality reduces the majority choice of ratio of redistributive expenditure to total expenditure. Inequality influences the share of expenditure on redistribution which influences the capital stock and GDP per unit of effective labour in this case. In addition, there is a negative relationship between the share of redistributive expenditure and the weight attached to public goods in the utility function, so that $\partial \delta_{m,t+1}/\partial \gamma < 0$. Hence, the comparative static results are robust when the framework is extended to include taxation on labour and capital simultaneously.

9.5   Conclusions

This chapter has extended the analysis in Chapter 8 by examining the composition of government expenditure, as the outcome of majority voting, in a dynamic general equilibrium environment. As in the earlier chapter, the main focus was on public goods and a pension, where the tax-financed expenditure is financed on a pay-as-you-go basis. Individuals work during the first period of life, supply one unit of labour inelastically, pay a proportional tax on their income, and either save or borrow. During the second period of life, the retirement period, they receive the tax-financed transfer payment and they have their own savings.

Consideration of the choice of tax-financed public good expenditure and the level of a pension is substantially complicated by the fact that the pension involves a combination of income shifting between phases of the life cycle with both inter-generational and intra-generational transfers. The latter arises because the basic pension is unrelated to income whereas the tax is proportional to income, and the former arises from the pay-as-you-go feature of financing.

Using the majority voting approach, selfish individuals vote in the first period on the share of redistributive expenditure to be received in the next period, given the tax rate and full information about the nature of the government's budget constraint. Therefore, voting is over one dimension. It was found that preferences are single-peaked and the decisive voter is the young individual with the median ability, or income, since the old cohort does not have any incentive to vote on the next period's share of redistributive expenditure.

The comparative static results of this majority choice show that the ratio of pension expenditure to total expenditure falls when the ratio of median to mean ability, or income, increases. This implies that a lower degree of basic inequality is associated with a less redistributive structure. This result is similar to other models of voting on the tax rate, although the present study examined voting on the composition of government expenditure. Moreover, it was shown that the ratio of transfer payments to total expenditure depends negatively on the preference for public goods and the share of capital in the production, and it depends positively on the tax rate. The share of expenditure on pensions is independent of the population and income growth.

The general equilibrium approach provides an environment for examining the effects of inequality on redistributive expenditure and, subsequently, on capital accumulation and output per capita. It was shown analytically that there is a negative relationship between inequality and output per unit of effective labour. This is related to the literature which studies the relationship between inequality and growth. Another finding is that a rising tax rate decreases capital accumulation where redistributive expenditure is both exogenous or an outcome of majority voting.

Numerical illustrations demonstrated that the share of redistributive expenditure is relatively flat for realistic values of the income ratio. In addition, the ratio of expenditure on pensions to total expenditure is more sensitive to changes in the weight attached to public goods, the tax rate and the share of capital in production compared with changes in the discount factor.

Bibliography

[1] Aaron, H. (1966) The social insurance paradox. *The Canadian Journal of Economics and Political Science*, 32, pp. 371–374.

[2] Acemoglu, D. and Robinson, J.A. (2007) *Economic Origins of Dictatorship and Democracy.* Cambridge: Cambridge University Press.

[3] Agénor, P.R. (2008) Fiscal policy and endogenous growth with public infrastructure. *Oxford Economic Papers*, 60, pp. 57–87.

[4] Aghion, P. and Durlauf, S. (2005) *Handbook of Economic Growth Volume 1B.* New York: Elsevier.

[5] Aitchison, J.A. and Brown, J.A.C. (1957) *The Lognormal Distribution.* Cambridge: Cambridge University Press.

[6] Alesina, A. and Glaeser, E.L. (2004) *Fighting Poverty in the US and Europe: a World of Difference.* Oxford: Oxford University Press.

[7] Alesina, A. and Rodrik, D. (1994) Distributive politics and economic growth. *Quarterly Journal of Economics*, 109, pp. 465–490.

[8] Allen, R.G.D. and Bowley, A. (1935) *Family Expenditure.* London: P.S. King.

[9] Ambler, S. (2000) Optimal time consistent fiscal policy with overlapping generations. *Center for Research on Economic Fluctuations and Employment (CREFE) Working Paper* No. 111.

[10] Amiel, Y., Creedy, J. and Hurn, S. (1999) Measuring attitudes towards inequality. *Scandinavian Journal of Economics*, 101, pp. 83–96.

[11] Angelopoulos, K., Malley, J. and Philippopoulos, A. (2007) Public education expenditure, growth and welfare. *CESifo Working Paper*, No. 2037.

[12] Atkinson, A.B. (1970) On the measurement of inequality. *Journal of Economic Theory*, 2, pp. 244–263.

[13] Azzimonti, M., De Francisco, E. and Krusell, P. (2006). Median-voter equilibria in the neoclassical growth model under aggregation. *Scandinavian Journal of Economics*, 108, pp 587–606.

[14] Bearse, P., Glomm, G. and Janeba, E. (2001) Composition of government budget, non-single peakedness, and majority voting. *Journal of Public Economic Theory*, 3, pp. 471–481.

[15] Benabou, R. (2002) Tax and education policy in a heterogeneous-agent economy: what levels of redistribution maximize growth and efficiency? *Econometrica*, 70, pp. 481–517.

[16] Bernasconi, M. and Profeta, P. (2007) Redistribution or education? The political economy of the social race. *CESifo Working Paper Series*, CESifo Working Paper No. 1934.

[17] Blankenau, W.F., Simpson, N.B. and Tomljanovich, M. (2007) Public education expenditures, taxation, and growth: linking data to theory. *American Economic Review*, 97, pp. 393–397.

[18] Boldrin, M. and Rustichini, A. (2000) Political equilibria with social security. *Review of Economic Dynamics*, 3, pp. 41–78.

[19] Borck, R. (2007) Voting, inequality and redistribution. *Journal of Economic Surveys*, 21, pp. 90–109.

[20] Borck, R. (2008) Central versus local education finance: a political economy approach. *International Tax and Public Finance*, 15, pp. 338–352.

[21] Borge, L.-E. and Rattsø, J. (2004). Income distribution and tax structure: empirical test of the Meltzer–Richard hypothesis. *European Economic Review*, 48, pp. 805–826.

[22] Brent, R.J. (1984) On the use of distributional weights in cost–benefit analysis: a survey of schools. *Public Finance Quarterly*, 12, pp. 213–230.

[23] Calvo, G. and Obstfeld, M. (1988) Optimal time-consistent fiscal policy with finite lifetimes: analysis and extensions. In *Economic Effects of the Government Budget* (ed. by E. Helpman, A. Razin and E. Sadka). Cambridge, MA: MIT Press.

[24] Capolupo, R. (2000) Output taxation, human capital and growth. *Manchester School*, 68, pp. 166–183.

[25] Chen, B.-L. (2006) Economic growth with an optimal public spending composition. *Oxford Economic Papers*, 58, pp. 123–136.

[26] Conde-Ruiz, J.I. and Galasso, V. (2005). Positive arithmetic of the welfare state. *Journal of Public Economics*, 89, pp. 933–955.

[27] Conde-Ruiz, J.I. and Profeta, P. (2007) The redistributive design of social security systems. *Economic Journal*, 117, pp. 686–712.

[28] Cooley, T.F. and Soares, J. (1999) A positive theory of social security based on reputation. *Journal of Political Economy*, 107, pp. 135–160.

[29] Corneo, G. and Grüner H.P. (2002) Individual preferences for political redistribution. *Journal of Public Economics*, 83, pp. 83–107.

[30] Coughlin, P. (1982) Pareto optimality of policy proposals with probabilistic voting. *Public Choice*, 39, pp. 427–433.

[31] Coughlin, P. and Nitzan, S. (1981) Directional and local electoral equilibria with probabilistic voting. *Journal of Economic Theory*, 24, pp. 226–239.

[32] Cragg, M. (1991) Do we care? A study of Canada's indirect tax system. *Canadian Journal of Economics*, 24, pp. 124–143.

[33] Creedy, J. (1995) *The Economics of Higher Education: An Analysis of Taxes versus Fees*. Aldershot: Edward Elgar.

[34] Creedy, J. (1996) *Fiscal Policy and Social Welfare*. Cheltenham: Edward Elgar.

[35] Creedy, J. and Moslehi, S. (2009) Modelling the composition of government expenditure in democracies. *European Journal of Political Economy*, 25, pp. 42–55.

[36] Creedy, J. and Moslehi, S. (2010a) The role of home production in voting over taxes and expenditure. *Australian Journal of Labour Economics*, 13, pp. 81–97.

[37] Creedy, J. and Moslehi, S. (2010b) The optimal composition of government expenditure among transfers, education and public goods. *Hacienda Pública Española*, 194, pp. 41–64.

[38] Creedy, J. and Moslehi, S. (2011) The optimal division of government expenditure between public goods and transfer Payments, *Australian Economic Papers* (forthcoming).

[39] Creedy, J. and van de Ven, J. (2000) Retirement incomes: private savings versus social transfers. *Manchester School*, 68, pp. 539–551.

[40] Creedy, J., Amiel, Y. and Hurn, S. (1999) Measuring attitudes towards inequality. *Scandinavian Journal of Economics*, 101, pp. 83–96.

[41] Creedy, J., Li, S.M. and Moslehi, S. (2010a) The composition of government expenditure: economic conditions and preferences, *Economic Inquiry*, 49, pp. 94–107.

[42] Creedy, J. Li, S.M. and Moslehi, S. (2010b) Inequality Aversion and the Optimal Composition of Government Expenditure, *Macroeconomic Dynamics*, 14, pp. 291–306.

[43] Croix, D. and Michel, P. (2002) *A Theory of Economic Growth: Dynamics and Policy in Overlapping Generations.* Cambridge: Cambridge University Press.

[44] Devarajan, S., Swaroop, V. and Zou, H. (1996) The composition of public expenditure and economic growth, *Journal of Monetary Economics*, 37, pp. 313–344.

[45] Dolmas, J. (2008) What do majority-voting politics say about redistributive taxation of consumption and factor income? Not much. Federal Reserve Bank of Dallas, Working Paper No. 0814.

[46] Epple, D. and Romano, R. (1996) Ends against the middle: determining public service provision when there are private alternatives. *Journal of Public Economics*, 62, pp. 297–325.

[47] Fernandez, R. and Rogerson, R. (1995) On the political economy of education subsidies. *Review of Economic Studies*, 62, pp 249–262.

[48] Galasso, V. (1999) The US social security system: what does political sustainability imply? *Review of Economic Dynamics*, 2, pp. 698–730.

[49] Galasso, V., (2003). Redistribution and fairness: a note. *European Journal of Political Economy*, 19, pp. 885–892.

[50] Ghiglino, C. (2000) Optimal policy in OG models. *Journal of Economic Theory*, 90, pp. 62–83.

[51] Glomm, G. and Ravikumar, B. (1992) Public versus private investment in human capital endogenous growth and income inequality. *Journal of Political Economy*, 100, pp. 813–834.

[52] Glomm, G. and Ravikumar, B. (1997) Productive government expenditures and long-run growth. *Journal of Economic Dynamics and Control*, 21, pp. 183–204.

[53] Greenwood, J., Rogerson, R. and Wright, R. (1995) Household production in real business cycle theory. In *Frontier of Business Cycle Research* (ed. by T.F. Cooley), pp. 157–174. New Jersey: Princeton University Press.

[54] Grossman, G.M. and Helpman, E. (1998) Intergenerational redistribution with short-lived governments. *Economic Journal*, 108, pp. 1299–1329.

[55] Grossmann, V. (2003) Income inequality, voting over the size of public consumption, and growth. *European Journal of Political Economy*, 19, pp. 265–287.

[56] Harms, P. and Zink, S. (2003) Limits to redistribution in a democracy: a survey. *European Journal of Political Economy*, 19, pp. 651–668.

[57] Hassler, J., Krusell, P., Storesletten, K. and Zilibotti, F. (2005) The dynamics of government. *Journal of Monetary Economics*, 52, pp. 1331–1358.

[58] Hassler, J., Mora, J., Storesletten, K. and Zilibotti, F. (2003) The survival of the welfare state. *American Economic Review*, 93, pp. 87–112.

[59] Hassler, J., Storesletten, K. and Zilibotti, F. (2007) Democratic public good provision. *Journal of Economic Theory*, 133, pp. 127–151.

[60] Haufler, A. (1996) Tax coordination with different preferences for public goods: conflict or harmony of interest? *International Tax and Public Finance*, 3, pp. 5–28.

[61] Haupt, A. (2005) The evolution of public spending on higher education in a democracy. *CESifo Working Paper* No. 1631.

[62] Haupt, A. and Uebelmesser, S. (2009) Voting on labour-market integration and education policy when citizens differ in mobility and ability, *CESifo Working Paper* No. 2588.

[63] Hockley, G.C. and Harbour, G. (1983) Revealed preferences between public expenditures and taxation cuts: public sector choice. *Journal of Public Economics*, 22, pp. 387–399.

[64] Hindriks, J. and Myles, G. (2006) *Intermediate Public Economics*. Cambridge MA: MIT Press.

[65] Ingram, B.F., Kocherlakota, N.R. and Savin, N.E. (1994) Explaining business cycles: a multiple-shock approach. *Journal of Monetary Economics*, 34, pp. 415–428.

[66] Irmen, A. and Kuehnel, J. (2009) Productive government expenditure and economic growth. *Journal of Economic Surveys*, 23, pp. 692–733.

[67] Koulovatianos, C. and Mirman, L.J. (2005) Endogenous public policy and long-run growth: some simple analytics. *University of Vienna Department of Economics Working Paper* No. 0502.

[68] Krusell, P. and Rios-Rull, J.-V. (1999) On the size of US government: political economy in the neoclassical growth model. *American Economic Review*, 89, pp. 1156–1181.

[69] Lambert, P., Millimet, D.L. and Slottje, D. (2003) Inequality aversion and the natural rate of subjective inequality. *Journal of Public Economics*, 87, pp. 1061–1090.

[70] Lee, J. (1992) Optimal size and composition of government spending. *Journal of the Japanese and International Economies*, 6, pp. 423–439.

[71] Lind, J.T. (2005) Why is there so little redistribution? *Nordic Journal of Political Economy*, 31, pp. 111–125.

[72] Lindbeck, A. and Weibull, J. (1987) Balanced-budget redistribution as the outcome of political competition. *Public Choice*, 52, pp. 273–297.

[73] Lorz, O. (2004) Time consistent optimal redistribution policy in an overlapping generations model. *Journal of Public Economic Theory*, 6, pp. 25–41.

[74] McCaleb, T.S. (1985) Public choice perspectives on the flat tax follies. *Cato Journal*, 5, 613–624.

[75] Madden, D. (1992) Can we infer external effects from a study of the Irish indirect tax system? *The Economic and Social Review*, 24, pp. 63–74.

[76] Madden, D. (1995) An analysis of indirect tax reform in Ireland in the 1980s. *Fiscal Studies*, 16, pp. 18–37.

[77] Meltzer, A.H. and Richard, S.F. (1981) A rational theory of the size of government. *Journal of Political Economy*, 89, pp. 914–927.

[78] Meltzer, A.H. and Richard, S.F. (1983) Tests of a rational theory of the size of government. *Public Choice*, 41, pp. 403–418.

[79] Mera, K. (1969) Experimental determination of relative marginal utilities. *Quarterly Journal of Economics*, 83, pp. 464–477.

[80] Moene, K.O. and Wallerstein, M. (2001) Inequality, social insurance, and redistribution. *American Political Science Review*, 95, pp. 859–874.

[81] Moreh, J. (1981) Income inequality and the social welfare function. *Journal of Economic Studies*, 8, pp. 25–37.

[82] Mueller, D.C. (2003) *Public Choice III*. New York: Cambridge University Press.

[83] OECD Stat. Extracts. Available at: http://stats.oecd.org/Index.aspx.

[84] Oliver, X. and Spadaro, A. (2004) Are Spanish governments really averse to inequality: a normative analysis using the 1999 Spanish tax reform. *Investigaciones Económicas*, 28, pp. 551–556.

[85] Perotti, R. (1996) Growth, income distribution, and democracy: what the data say. *Journal of Economic Growth*, 1, pp. 149–187.

[86] Persson, T. and Tabellini, G. (1992) Growth, distribution and politics. *European Economic Review*, 36, pp. 593–602.

[87] Persson, T. and Tabellini, G. (1994) Is inequality harmful for growth? *American Economic Review*, 84, pp. 600–621.

[88] Persson, T. and Tabellini, G. (2000) *Political Economics*: *Explaining Economic Policy*. New York: MIT Press.

[89] Piras, R. (2001) Government spending composition in an endogenous growth model with congestion. *Metroeconomica*, 52, pp. 121–136.

[90] Polity IV (2007) University of Maryland, Center for International Development and Conflict Management. Available at: http://www.cidcm.umd.edu/polity/data/.

[91] Ravallion, M. (1988) Inpres and inequality: a distributional perspective on the Centre's regional disbursements. *Bulletin of Indonesian Economic Studies*, 24, pp. 53–71.

[92] Renström, T.I. (1996) Endogenous taxation: an overlapping generations approach. *The Economic Journal*, 106, pp. 471–482.

[93] Roberts, K.W.S. (1977) Voting over income tax schedules. *Journal of Public Economics*, 8, pp. 329–340.

[94] Romer, T. (1975) Individual welfare, majority voting and the properties of a linear income tax. *Journal of Public Economics*, 4, pp. 163–185.

[95] Samuelson, P.A. (1958) An exact consumption-loan model of interest with or without the social contrivance of money. *Journal of Political Economy*, 66, pp. 467–482.

[96] Schram, A. and Winden, F.V. (1989) Revealed preferences for public goods: applying a model of voter behaviour. *Public Choice*, 60, pp. 259–282.

[97] Schwarze, J. and Härpfer, M. (2007) Are people inequality averse, and do they prefer redistribution by the state? Evidence from German longitudinal data on life satisfaction. *The Journal of Socio-economics*, 36, pp. 233–239.

[98] Shelton, C.A. (2007) The size and composition of government expenditure. *Journal of Public Economics*, 91, pp. 2230–2260.

[99] Soares, J. (2006) A dynamic general equilibrium analysis of the political economy of public education. *Journal of Population Economics*, 19, pp. 367–389.

[100] Spadaro, A. (2007) Implicit social preferences and fiscal reforms: a microsimulation analysis for Spain. *Research in Labour Economics*, 25, pp. 199–212.

[101] Stern, N. (1977) Welfare weights and the elasticity of the marginal valuation of income. In *Studies in Modern Economic Analysis* (ed. by M. Artis and R. Nobay, R.). Oxford: Basil Blackwell.

[102] Tabellini, G. and Alesina, A., (1990). Voting on the budget deficit. *American Economic Review*, 80, pp. 37–49.

[103] Tanzi, V. (2000) *Public Spending in the 20th Century: A Global Perspective.* Cambridge: Cambridge University Press.

[104] Tridimas, G. (2001) The economics and politics of the structure of public expenditure. *Public Choice*, 106, pp. 299–316.

[105] Tridimas, G. and Winer, S.L. (2005) The political economy of government size. *European Journal of Political Economy*, 21, pp. 643–666.

[106] Tuomala, M. (1985) Simplified formula for optimal linear income tax. *Scandinavian Journal of Economics*, 87, pp. 668–672.

[107] Tyran, J.-R. and Sausgruber, R. (2006). A little fairness may induce a lot of redistribution in democracy. *European Economic Review*, 50, pp. 469–485.

[108] van de Ven, J. and Creedy, J. (2005) Taxation, reranking and equivalence scales. *Bulletin of Economic Research*, 57, pp. 13–36.

[109] Walque, G.D. (2005) Voting on pensions: a survey. *Journal of Economic Surveys*, 19, pp. 181–209.

[110] World Development Indicator (WDI) (2007) Washington: World Bank. Available at: http://go.worldbank.org/B53SONGPA0.

[111] World Income Inequality Database (WIID) V 2.0b (2007) World Insti-
      tution for Development and Economic Research (WIDER). Available
      at: http://www.wider.unu.edu/wiid/wiid.htm.

Index

Aaron, H. 10, 100, 108
ability 166, 169, 171, 201
Acemoglu, D. 36
Agénor, P.R. 127
agent monotonicity 53
Aitchison, J.A. 137, 142, 160, 182, 188
Alesina, A. 20, 22, 52, 99, 101, 120, 174, 175, 198
Allen, R.G.D. 17
Amiel, Y. 137
Angelopoulos, K. 152
arithmetic mean human capital accumulation 151
arithmetic mean income/welfare weighted mean income 174, 180–181, 194
Atkinson, A.B. 27–28, 138, 160
augmented utility function 92
Azzimonti, M. 52, 102

basic inequality 19
Bearse, P. 7, 13, 15, 38, 102
Benabou, R. 198
benchmark parameter values 61, 212–213
Bernasconi, M. 14
Beta coefficient 87–91
Blankenau, W.F. 151
Boldrin, M. 199
Borck, R. 6, 13, 15, 39, 50, 75, 79, 102
Borge, L.E. 54
Bowley, A. 17
Brent, R.J. 175
Brown, J.A.C. 137, 142, 160, 182, 188
budget constraint
    government 17–18, 26, 55–56, 92, 93, 129, 130–131, 133–134, 149, 153–155, 157, 183, 202–204, 217

government budget constraint model 203
    individual 16, 92, 132, 149, 178, 202, 216
    and optimal composition 134–136
business fluctuations 118

Calvo, G. 179
capital
    depreciation 204
    output 205–206
    per unit of labour model 205–206
    rental 204
    tax 212–213, 216
capital accumulation 205–206
    and labour output 210
    and redistributive expenditure 205
capital accumulation model 205, 217
Capolupo, R. 151
Chen, B.L. 127
classical utilitarian welfare function 181
Cobb–Douglas functions 17, 39, 53, 54, 60, 81–82, 92, 93, 95, 98, 106, 109, 128, 131, 132, 149, 150, 151, 177, 178, 181, 204
composition of expenditure 15, 29–30, 128, 129
Conde-Ruiz, J.I. 100
consumption/investment expenditure in growth framework 127
Cooley, T.F. 199
Corneo, G. 174
Coughlin, P. 14
Cragg, M. 175
Creedy, J. 121, 137, 152, 176
culture
    and expenditure 118, 174

233